THE SCOTT COLLECTION

Minnesota's Black Community in the '50s, '60s, and '70s

Walter R. Scott Sr.

Foreword by William D. Green
Preface by Chaunda L. Scott
Introduction by Anthony R. Scott
With Mary McCormack-Scott
Walter R. Scott Jr. and George J. Scott, Executive Editors

MINNESOTA HISTORICAL SOCIETY

www.mnhspress.org

The Minnesota Historical Society Press is a member
of the Association of American University Presses.

Manufactured in the United States of America

10 9 8 7 6 5 4 3 2 1

♾ The paper used in this publication meets the
minimum requirements of the American National
Standard for Information Sciences—Permanence for
Printed Library Materials, ANSI Z39.48-1984.

International Standard Book Number
ISBN: 978-1-68134-060-9 (paper)

Library of Congress Cataloging-in-Publication Data
available upon request.

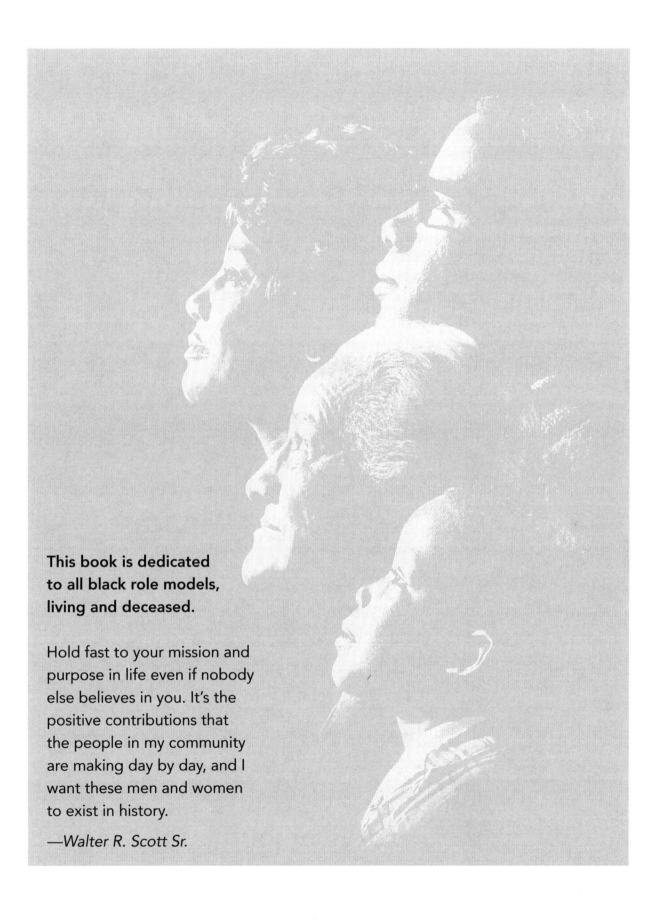

This book is dedicated to all black role models, living and deceased.

Hold fast to your mission and purpose in life even if nobody else believes in you. It's the positive contributions that the people in my community are making day by day, and I want these men and women to exist in history.

—*Walter R. Scott Sr.*

Contents

Foreword

Years ago, when I was superintendent of Minneapolis Public Schools, I was invited to go on a call-in radio program whose listening audience was predominately African American. It was during a time of high drama, when parents and community leaders were speaking out against the persistence of the academic achievement gap and how schools were not addressing the educational needs of African American children; and as the school district's head, I was the target of their anger. For ninety minutes, I received questions that variously accused me of destroying the future of the black community, and many questioned how I could possibly sleep at night knowing what I know about the failure of our system. It was a rough ninety minutes, to say the least. So, when the host invited me back for the following month, I, of course, after girding my loins, agreed.

I was profoundly surprised by how different the next appearance was. First, it was the month of February—Black History Month—and second, the host wanted me, in addition to being available to answer questions about education, to talk about my book on the mid-nineteenth-century African American experience in Minnesota. As I shared the microphone with my friend Professor Mahmoud El-Kati, we collaborated in talking fully about our racial history. Then it was time for call-in, and I braced myself, for I, after all, was still "the superintendent of schools." For much of the remaining program, callers (some of whom I thought I recognized from the previous month) enthusiastically asked questions about our history. And

what impressed me more, albeit in a bitter-sweet way, was how so many callers prefaced their questions and comments with, "I never even knew we had a history." Some had been long-term residents of the state. A few were life-long Minnesotans. But they all said that none of their teachers had mentioned that our state had a rich African American experience. Putting it crassly, we'd been inadvertently led to believe that black Minnesotans have no legacy to learn from and hand down to our children.

It is for this reason that I am excited about *The Scott Collection*. Walter R. Scott described the work as "a bird's eye view at some of the Black people in Minnesota." I think it does much more. This collection, originally published in three separate volumes over the course of three decades, sheds light on a vibrant community that existed in the middle of the twentieth century but was little known to those who were not a part of it.

The period in our history that this collection covers coincided with a time of great tumult. To the casual observer who was buffeted nightly by images of civil rights activists viciously assaulted and murdered by white supremacists and of anti-war demonstrators battling police and hard-hat reactionaries, it seemed that the nation was falling apart. Indeed, the prevailing sense for many was that hope, as it began at the dawn of the 1960s and in large part inspired by the involvement of young people of many races engaged in civic affairs, had died along with the mounting numbers of martyred men and women who fought for social and racial justice. Indeed, it seemed to many that black America as a whole was no longer inspired to "overcome." Through the fog of our domestic war, it quite simply was hard to see the many black men and women who conducted productive lives while daily providing ballast for their children, their families, and their community.

Too often, the most glorious legacy was that which was so easily overlooked, but *The Scott* *Collection* sets it right. The richness of the pictorial record that Mr. Scott compiled, and that his children have reissued here, is found in the many faces and accomplishments mentioned on each page of this work, and it is to the Scott family that we owe much gratitude.

William D. Green
Professor of History, Augsburg College

Preface

As the proud daughter of the late Walter R. Scott, I am ecstatic about the release of *The Scott Collection*!

The Scott Collection is a prominent body of research that celebrates the achievements and contributions of African American men and women in Minnesota during the pre– and post–civil rights eras, from the 1950s to the 1970s. At the time of publication, my father's renowned works celebrated the accomplishments of African Americans in the state during this critical period of our history. Moreover, his books have served as a primary reference for scholars, researchers, and students looking to examine and explore the history of African Americans in Minnesota.

The Scott Collection comprises the following three publications: *Centennial Edition of the Minneapolis Beacon* (1956), *Minneapolis Negro Profile* (1968), and *Minnesota's Black Community* (1976). Each volume utilized pictorial resumes—photographs and brief biographical summaries—to highlight successful African Americans employed in various professions: the arts, authors, beauty and fashion, business, community service, education, entertainment, government, labor and industry, law enforcement, media and communications, medicine, religion, and sports. Each volume also shares a thought-provoking editorial summary written by my father, Walter R. Scott.

My father's objectives for publishing these three volumes were: 1) to applaud and raise awareness of the contributions of African American men and women in Minnesota during these periods of racial unrest and social change; 2) to encourage higher education and career development among African American children, youth, and adults so their footprints, accomplishments, and contributions could be chronicled as a part of the ongoing, rich history of Minnesota's African Americans; and 3) to share these stories of unknown and untold achievements with all Minnesotans and with the broader global community.

Over the past several years, my brothers, Anthony, Walter Jr., and George, along with my nephews, Anthony II and Bryson, and I discussed how we wanted to make our father's research available again. We wanted to ensure that current and future generations of African Americans in Minnesota, as well as individuals everywhere, are made aware of the notable achievements of and contributions by African American men and women in Minnesota and are encouraged to follow in the footsteps of these trailblazers. We further wanted our father's body of work to be made more accessible so that individuals can own copies of this historical research and reflect on it in their own homes and with family members and friends, just as my brothers, nephews, and I have done over the past decades.

In addition, my siblings and I hope to continue our father's legacy of recognizing and honoring the contributions of Minnesota's African American community by producing a new publication that highlights the accomplishments of the state's African Americans in the twenty-first century. The future publication is being developed by Minnesota's Black Community Project, a nonprofit organization. For more information about this project, visit www .MinnesotasBlackCommunityProject.org.

It is our hope that readers of *The Scott Collection* will cherish the book for its historical value and appreciate it as an authentic and vital piece of Minnesota's African American history. We also hope that this book will be shared with children, especially African American children, so they can learn about and be inspired by the achievements and contributions of African American men and women highlighted in these pages—just as I have been throughout my childhood and adulthood.

Lastly, on behalf of the Scott family, I want to sincerely thank Josh Leventhal, director and acquisitions editor for the Minnesota Historical Society Press, along with the Minnesota Historical Society for making the release of *The Scott Collection* a reality.

Chaunda L. Scott
Daughter of Walter R. Scott Sr.

Introduction

Over the years, I have often been asked, "Why did your father create those books?"

"Those books" are the three volumes published by my father, Walter R. Scott Sr., during the middle decades of the twentieth century: *Centennial Edition of the Minneapolis Beacon* (1956), *Minneapolis Negro Profile* (1968), and *Minnesota's Black Community* (1976). A simple answer to the question of why he wrote these books is that they were a part of his life's work and journey.

My father was born in Greenville, Mississippi, on June 4, 1929. His mother, Cozy, was from Mississippi, and she and other family members relocated to Chicago before my father was born, but she traveled back to Mississippi to give birth and then returned to Chicago shortly afterward. I assume that Cozy felt more comfortable giving birth with the help of a midwife in her home state of Mississippi. During the 1920s, and up through the '50s, African Americans had limited access to hospitals, in Chicago as well as other major cities in both the North and the South.

My father came of age in Chicago, and he loved that city. Although he was an only child and raised by his mother, he grew up with several cousins who became like his siblings. They lived in the Bronzeville neighborhood on the South Side of Chicago. It should be noted that several other cities, such as Milwaukee and Detroit, also had African American neighborhoods called Bronzeville. However, Chicago's Bronzeville neighborhood was one of the most prosperous communities for African Americans

Photo courtesy of Mary McCormack-Scott

in the 1930s and '40s, and my father was immersed in it.

During the time that he lived there, the South Side of Chicago was known as the "Black Metropolis" for being one of the largest thriving centers of African American business and culture. It was also a time when African Americans came to northern cities by the thousands to escape the oppression of the South, although they faced many challenges and injustices in the North as well. This was a time when segregation and separate but supposedly equal were the law of the land, and when schools for African American children were funded at less than 80 percent of the schools for white children. Nevertheless, my father was fortunate to have had the opportunity to grow up in the cultural mecca of Chicago, where he saw and got to know African Americans contributing and succeeding in a variety of professions and endeavors. I believe that growing up in this kind of positive environment gave my dad the inspiration and drive to create his publications later in life.

My father graduated from DuSable High School on Chicago's South Side and was elected the 1947 homecoming king. He was also the first African American teen male model in Chicago to work for Louis "Scotty" Piper, a renowned tailor and fashion designer in Bronzeville. Mr. Piper designed clothing for such clients as Nat King Cole, Lena Horne, Lou Rawls, and heavyweight boxing champions Jack Johnson and Joe Louis, to name a few.

Shortly after my father graduated from high school, his mother, Cozy, passed away. In 1948, Cozy's brother, the Reverend William Grossley, brought my dad with him to the Twin Cities, where Reverend Grossley became the pastor at St. James A.M.E. Church on Snelling Avenue in Minneapolis.

After settling in the Twin Cities, my father met Margaret Smith. They married in 1950 and went on to have four children: Anthony, Walter Jr., Chaunda, and George. My father worked at Northwestern Bell, where he would become the first African American to hold a position in personnel management. Our mother, Margaret, passed away in 1980. In 1986, my father married Mary McCormack. He retired from his job at the Metropolitan Airport Commission in 1995. On June 14, 2001, Walter R. Scott Sr. passed away.

In addition to holding a full-time job and raising a family, my father worked passionately on his book projects, beginning in the late '40s, to raise awareness of African Americans and present the community in a positive light. In 1956, he completed his first books profiling African Americans and their contributions, focused on the two cities he knew best: the *Chicago Beacon* and the *Centennial Edition of the Minneapolis Beacon*. I remember him traveling back and forth to Chicago often, sometimes taking the whole family with him. My father not only published his books while working and raising a family, but he

also was self-training to be a writer and author. I remember him working meticulously for hours in our basement, handwriting the text and then editing it by hand, as well as cutting and pasting photographs of successful African Americans, along with their bios, on paper to visualize what the material would look like in published book form. During the years that he worked on these books, my father succeeded in securing the support of Minnesota mayors, governors, and the business community, from whom he received the letters included in each of the publications.

The three books reflect the progress of African Americans in Minnesota over the decades, as evidenced by the increased number of individuals featured in various professional fields—such as doctors, nurses, educators, businesspeople, entertainers, lawyers, and service providers—in the subsequent volumes from 1968 and 1976. Moreover, my father was able to publish his three books under his own publishing company, the Scott Publishing Company, over a thirty-year span.

My father's work is an exemplary product of his desire to highlight the positive side of African American life. He did this to inform and inspire future generations to believe that they could accomplish their goals, regardless of the obstacles. His publications also serve as critical historical records that document African American life in Minnesota in the '50s through the '70s. As Dr. Charles E. Crutchfield III, a close family friend, has said to me, "Every time I go through these books, I see something or someone I hadn't seen previously."

By making these books available again, we hope to celebrate this period of African American history in Minnesota and expose new generations to the achievements of their forebears in a wide range of professions.

Anthony R. Scott
Eldest Son of Walter R. Scott Sr.

THE SCOTT COLLECTION

Centennial Edition of the
MINNEAPOLIS BEACON

A SCOTT PUBLICATION 1956

FEATURING THE NEGROES IN MINNEAPOLIS

ERIC G. HOYER

MAYOR

City of Minneapolis

OFFICE OF THE MAYOR

127 CITY HALL · FEDERAL 2-1116

June 15, 1956

Mr. Walter R. Scott
Editor-Publisher
Minneapolis Beacon
1309 E. 23rd Street
Minneapolis 4, Minnesota

Dear Mr. Scott:

It is my privilege and honor to join with the Minneapolis Beacon, its sponsors and its subscribers in publishing this Centennial issue devoted to an editorial and pictorial history of negro life in Minneapolis. It is a splendid achievement and a real addition to our Centennial activities in the City of Lakes.

As Mayor of Minneapolis, it has been my privilege to participate with the negro organizations of our city, dedicated toward making Minneapolis a better place in which to live. I have always considered it a pleasure to do my small part in helping to make their every endeavor a success.

Through the many programs sponsored by our negro citizenry, the community has become better informed as to the great part you are playing in the progress of this area. It is pleasing to report the achievements you have made and the progressive aims which you are carrying out through activities such as this very informative publication.

May I extend my very best wishes to all of your subscribers and the sincere hope that we may continue to move forward in the best spirit of our American way of life.

Sincerely,

Eric G. Hoyer
M A Y O R

CECIL EARL NEWMAN

He is the first Negro in Minnesota to be listed in "Who's Who;" first Negro publisher elected to the professional journalism fraternity, Sigma Delta Chi, first Negro president of the Minneapolis Urban League.

Newman was also selected as one of Minnesota's "100 Living Great" on the occasion of the celebration of the state Centennial in 1949. Recently he was a member of the Committee for Minneapolis' Future who in cooperation with TIME and LIFE magazines selected Minneapolis' Outstanding 100 Young Men.

MISS D. P. BLACK
Responsible for most all of the top entertainment attractions for dances in this area.

CHARLES JACKSON
Owner of Jackson trucking service.

ARCHIE OWENS
Owner of Owens trucking service.

T. B. BURT

After 37 years as a Postman in the Minneapolis Post Office, Mr. Burt is still active in Social and Civic activities. Past Commander of Johnnie Baker Post of the American Legion, Junior Warden of St. Thomas Episcopal Church. Completing a course in real estate law at Minneapolis Business College several years ago, Mr. Burt finds time to do a lucrative business in real estate.

JOE'S BAR-B-Q — MR. JOSEPH JENNINGS — Proprietor

HOBART T. MITCHELL
President of Hobart T. Mitchell and Son Realty Company.

MR. ANTHONY B. CASSIUS

Mr. Anthony B. Cassius, Minneapolis businessman for the past seventeen years was born in Guthrie, Oklahoma. He came to St. Paul in 1922 and attended Mechanic Arts High School, Macalester College in St. Paul and has taken numerous extension courses at the University of Minnesota where he recently finished the General Real Estate and Appraising course. He is active in union work, having organized Waiters Local 614 and was a former president of the Local Joint Executive Board.

Mr. Cassius went into business for himself in 1938 and is now operator of Cassius Cafe and Bamboo Lounge. He is also associated with the Cassius Realty Company at 412 E. 38th Street and offers investment consuling service to the public.

He is married and has one son and one daughter and three grandchildren. He is a member of St. Peters A.M.E. Church and for the past thirty years has been an active member of the Mechanics Arts "M" Club.

Mr. Cassius has been a member of the Urban League for the pa.. twenty-two years and is currently an active member of the executive board of the N.A.A.C.P. He is a member of the Palestine Lodge No. 7 F. & A.M., a member of the North Star Consistory and Fezzan Temple and of the Elks Lodge No. 106. He is Chairman of the Credit Committee of the Associated Negro Credit Union, a member of the Acrimea Club, the Forty Club and Treasurer of the newly organized Campaign for Courage organization.

8

A. B. Cassius with bartender George Clark.

HARRY JONES — Plymouth Renovators co-owner.
Mr. Jones has his own plant and also makes suits, shirts and guarantees all of his work.
Mr. Jones' partner is Worthy Turner.

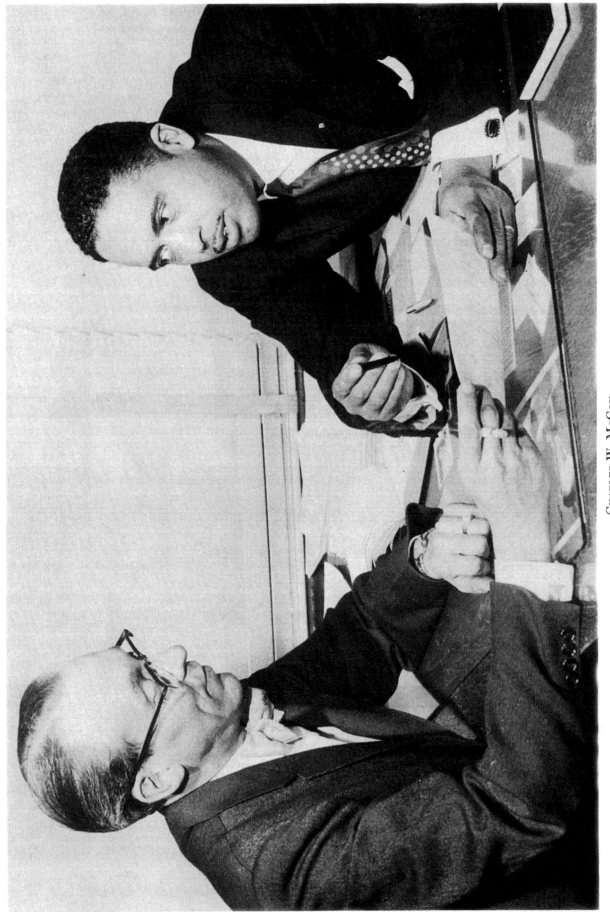

CHARLES W. McCoy

Established the Downtown Employment Agency in 1948. For the last seven years his office has been located at 520-22 Palace Building, Minneapolis. The services of the Downtown Employment Agency is most noted for its policy of NOT being confined to any segment of population. Mr. McCoy is worshipful master of King David No. 2 Lodge; past J.C. member; president of Kato Temple Marching patrol. Mr. McCoy is of the Baptist faith. Mr. McCoy is married and is the father of two children, Charles, Jr., and Janice Sandra.

O'DELL LIVINGSTON

Young businessman, Mr. Livingston is the proprietor of Del's Orchid Club, fountain and variety store and a record shop that carries a complete line of records.

MRS. LOUISE WHITE

Proprietor of Nifty Beauty Nook located at 240 Third Ave. So.

MR. CLYDE W. WILLIAMS

Educated: Lincoln U. and University of Minnesota. Accounting and Business Adm. Age: 36 years. Real Estate Broker: President and General Manager of Williams Realty Co., a Minnesota Corporation. Assets over quarter million dollars. Active in many social and civic organizations. President of Twin City Golf Association. Enthusiastic golfer, Hi-Fi-Jazz recording fan. Married: Marion L. Williams, wife. Father — 4 sons, 4 daughters.

Offices of Williams Realty Company.

MR. JAMES MIREE

Proprietor of Jim's Bar-B-Q, 801 Cedar Avenue South. Employs six persons. Entered business in 1926. Married to Mrs. Mary Miree.

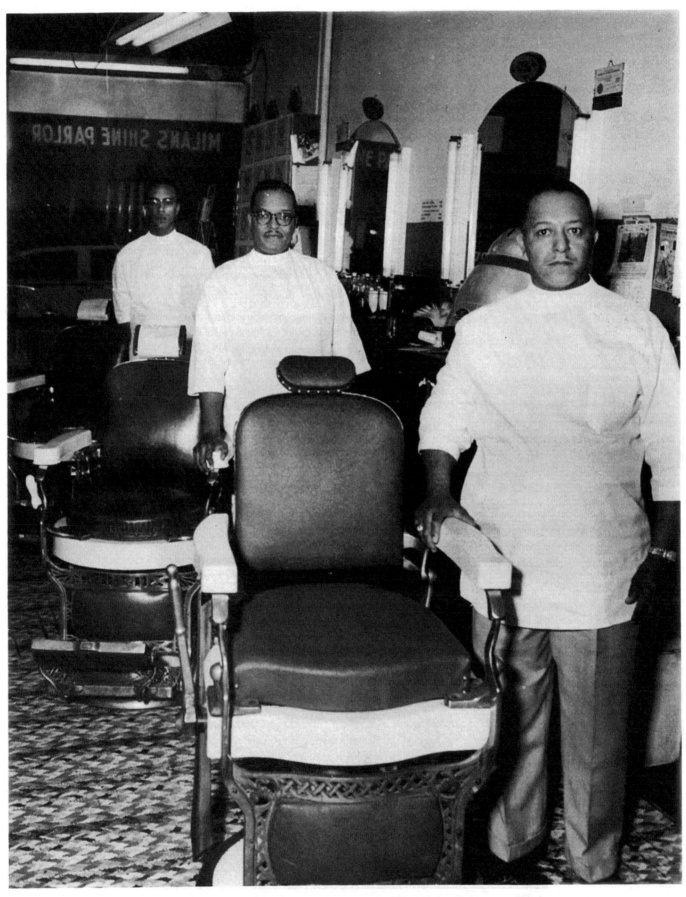

Young's Brothers Barber Shop—Johnny (Chubby), Sylvester, Fred.
The shop will relocate soon. They have a shop at 38th and Fourth Avenue.

Bea Hall and operators.

YVONNE JONES
Proprietor of Chez Paree Beauty Shop.

15

CURTIS C. CHIVERS
Vice President and Advertising Manager of
SPOKESMAN-RECORDER Publishing Co.

Community Activities

1. President of "Old" Minneapolis Sunday Forum 1931-33.
2. Member of Board of Trustees St. Peter's A.M.E. Church for past 20 years.
3. Member of Minneapolis Citizen's League.
4. Vice President Minneapolis Branch NAACP.
5. Past Vice President State FEPC — 1947.
6. Member Men's Club, Phyllis Wheatley Settlement House.
7. In 1947 became the first Negro in the United States to secure membership in Junior Chamber of Commerce Chapter, Minneapolis Branch. Served as Secretary of International Relations Committee Minneapolis Branch.
8. Represented Jaycees on Mayor Humphrey's "Self-Survey" in area of civic clubs.
9. Member of Minneapolis Advertising Club.
10. Ran for Alderman of the 11th Ward in 1953.
11. (Recently Political Activities in Newspapers)
12. Member of Public Relations Committee Minneapolis Urban League.
    (Graduated from high school and attended the University of Minnesota.)

OFFICERS

President .... Rev. Denzil Carty
Vice-President .... C. E. Newman
Secretary and Treasurer .... Talmage B. Carey
Assistant-Secretary .... Ashby Gaskins

DIRECTORS

Rev. Denzil Carty
W. A. Young
Theo. Woodard
James O. Mann
Ashby Gaskins
Talmage B. Carey
C. E. Newman
Archie Givens
Alice Onque

CREDIT COMMITTEE

A. B. Cassius, *Chairman*

J. C. Anderson

Clifford Smith

SUPERVISORY COMMITTEE

Jas. C. Crowder, *Chairman*

William Warricks

A. W. Jordan

TALMAGE B. CAREY
Organizer of Associated Negro Credit Unions in 1937.

Milton G. Williams, center, pictured with Winthrop Rockefeller and Attorney-General Miles Lord.
Mr. Williams is publisher of *Twin City Observer* and *St. Paul Sun.*

MRS. G. H. BUCKNER
The only Negro lady barber in Minneapolis at present.

THEODORE WOODARD

Proprietor of Woodard Funeral Home, located at 1103 Lyndale Avenue North, and established since 1933.

The Woodard Funeral Home is a holder of a Minnesota License, and takes great pride in owning their own rolling stock, casket display room and being the only Negro funeral home in Minneapolis complete with Chapel air conditioning.

Mr. Woodard is active in fraternal work. He is a member of the Trustee Board of the Zion Baptist Church, Exalted Ruler of the Elks, Deputy of the Grand United Order of Lodge Fellows, past president of the Associated Negro Credit Union and Corresponding-Secretary of the Phyllis Wheatley Board.

WALTER R. SCOTT, SR.

Mr. Scott, editor-publisher of the *Minneapolis Beacon*, was born in Greenville, Miss., on June 4, 1929, and was taken to Chicago, Ill., at the age of nine months where he lived until he came to Minneapolis in the latter part of 1949. He attended grade and high school in Chicago, Ill., and also Herzel Junior College and Roosevelt University which are also located in Chicago. He waited tables at the leading hotels in Chicago, and during the summer months he worked for the New York Central Railroad. In Minneapolis, Mr. Scott worked for the Twin City Arsenal as a production clerk until August of 1954, when he was confined to to Glen Lake Sanatorium for a period of nineteen months. It was there that he had time to plan to produce a magazine about the Negroes in Minneapolis.

Mr. Scott is a former member of St. James A.M.E. Church, but now is a member of Bethesda Baptist Church. He is also a member of the 15 Social Club. He is married to the former Margaret Smith and the father of two sons, Anthony and Walter, Jr.

WILLIE H. RASBERRY

He is district manager of the Minneapolis *Beacon*. Mr. Rasberry was born and attended school in Houston, Texas. He is the husband of the former Doris Watkins of Denver, Colo. He is also the father of two children, George Vernon and Deborah Lee.

The Rasberry's have resided in Minneapolis since 1951. Mr. Rasberry is Building Supervisor at the Twin City Arsenal. He is a Master Mason of the Palestine Lodge No. 7. His hobbies vary. He is a collector of records, in which he has a number of collector's items. He likes most outdoor sports. He is a Methodist by faith.

EDUCATION

Due to the fact that vacation time was the same time as the time the Beacon was being compiled and as a result the Editor could not make arrangements to have photos of all teachers in the Minneapolis public schools, we, the staff, would like to commend the Minneapolis Board of Education for its fine work in placing our Negro teachers in schools where it needs teachers. We, at the Beacon, understand that there are approximately forty Negro teachers in Minneapolis.

JIMMY JACKSON
Outstanding amateur boxer is attending the University of Minnesota.
Jimmy recently won a very fine scholarship.

EMPLOYMENT

The employment situation in Minneapolis for Negroes is much better today than it was ten years ago, and it is getting to the point where the Employer is accepting men and women on their ability, rather than their race. In compiling the Beacon, the staff went through the various business concerns, and saw the Negro really climbing the occupational staircase.

TYLER J. HOWELL, JR.
ROBERT E. WALLACE

These two young men are pictured here with a two-fold purpose. First to point up the fact that the career they have chosen to follow lies in a field where there is as little taint of prejudice, racial or religious, as is possible to expect. When inquiry was made as to the number of our race employed in the Post Office, we found that absolutely no record is kept of what a man is, neither the color of his skin, his religious affiliation, nor his national origin.

The other point is merely to bring attention to the parallel in the lives of these two men. It started at South High in the early thirties when they made names for themselves as athletes, reaching a climax in 1936 when they were both honored as All-City football players, after leading South to the City Championship. After graduation they continued to compete side by side as players on the crack Mitby-Sather team in the Twin City Football League.

And now we find them settling on the same career, that of dedicating their lives to the service of their country in the proud ranks of the Letter Carriers of Uncle Sam.

Both are members of the local branch of the National Association of Letter Carriers and as such will be helping to entertain their National Convention in Minneapolis in August of this year.

Jones Press Inc.

FIFTH AND FIFTH SOUTH MINNEAPOLIS 15, MINN

Lincoln 8866

August 9, 1956

Mr. Walter Scott
"The Minneapolis Beacon"
1309 E. 23rd Street
Minneapolis 4, Minnesota

Dear Walter:

It is our sincere wish that your publication "The Minneapolis Beacon" will achieve its purpose and will ultimately serve as a "Beacon" toward the betterment of local Negroes.

We acknowledge with pride our having been chosen as printer to produce the initial issue of this truly great as well as informative pictorial publication.

Very truly yours,

Lowell F. Jones
President

LFJ/aao

LITHOGRAPHERS · PRINTERS

WILLIAM LOUIS DYE

Born in Talladega, Alabama, July 4, 1913; married Gladys L. Lender May 11, 1937; has 6 children; has been employed at D. W. Onan & Sons since November 10, 1946; presently employed as a Finish Spray Painter. He finish paints various Engine and Generator parts. From our point of view, Bill has been a good reliable employee in all respects.

LYLE LASELY

He started with Twin City Transit Co. on September 11, 1947. He has been at the Nicollet Garage through all of his service. He has compiled an outstanding public relations and safety record and is well liked and respected by his fellow employees. He is 35 years of age, is married and has five children: Lyle Jr., age 13; Quentin, 11; Michael, 9; Vivian, 7 and Ray, 6. The Lasley family reside at 3954 3rd Avenue South in Minneapolis. He was recently commended with a feature story by the Twin City Observer, in conjunction with his driving record. He also received a nice write-up in the company publication, "The Windshield."

MR. HAROLD W. WRIGHT

Mr. Harold W. Wright, 3909 Portland Avenue South, is employed in the Mechanical Section of the Plant Engineering Department, Twin Cities Arsenal, Federal Cartridge Corporation.

He has been an employee of the Arsenal since the fall of 1942. His present duties consist of inspection of all steam, water and gas installations and constructions.

AARON ARRADONDO
Tax Examiner, United States Internal Revenue Bureau

Mr. Woodfin Lewis

A physicist in the Honeywell Research Center at Hopkins.

DORIS JONES BAILEY
Employed: First National Bank of Minneapolis. Date Employed: January 29, 1951. Resigned: December 30, 1952. Date Re-Employed: February 9, 1955. Age: 22. Born: Wagoner, Oklahoma. Marital Status: Married. Present Job Title: Cash Collections Clerk, Central Proof Division. Doris is doing a fine job.

MRS. RUTH McQUERRY — Minneapolis Modisté

Mrs. Ruth McQuerry is the leading dress designer for the well dressed women of Minneapolis. She has studied men's tailoring for the past five years at Vocational High School and makes many of her husband's clothes. She has also had courses in pattern drafting for men as well as women's clothes. She is now studying Millinery and her very first hat won the third prize at the Sportsmen's Show this past Easter at the Minneapolis Auditorium. She has her very picturesque studio in her home. She is Minneapolis' leading model, also models her own creations at large social clubs in Chicago, when they give their annual fashion shows. Her attire always advertises her very beautiful work, as she is one of Minneapolis' best dressed women.

MRS. CHRISTINE JOHNSON

Mrs. Christine Johnson of 3835 Fifth Avenue South is a housewife. She designs her own clothes. In this photo she is wearing a creation from the Persian Mode. The hat is turquoise blue, covered entirely with rhinestones and pearls. The dress is turquoise blue slipper satin sheath with panel in the back; also wearing turquoise satin blue pumps with rhinestone heels. This is what Minneapolis wears for the cocktail hour.

ENTERTAINMENT

The local entertainment scene is filled with some of the finest talent in America. It was Minneapolis that produced such outstanding personalities as Oscar Pettiford, Hilda Simms, Lester Young and others. For the Beacon, we wished we could have had pictures of the following local names to appear on our pages: Judy Perkins — Dick Mayes — Walter Daniels — Oscar Frazier — Bill Boone — Ira Pettiford — Maurice Talley and a number of others.

LEON LEWIS
Mr. Lewis has played music for a number of years and was considered one of the country's finest drummers.

HANK HAZLETT TRIO

Percy Hughes

WORTHY TURNER

Mr. Turner was born February 3, 1909, in Gilmer, Texas. After graduation from college he traveled for five years with a name band and came to Minneapolis in 1939. He is a concert favorite throughout the country.

Mr. Ralph Primm, extreme right, one of the top people in local music circles, at the airport with Mrs. Emma Simms, meeting concert singers William Warfield and his wife, Leoynette Price, and their accompanist, Dr. Hess.

TEDDY QUALLS

PERCY HUGHES Band

Incidentally, we would like to state here that Percy is also the director of service at the Neal's Funeral Home, the oldest Negro funeral home in Minneapolis.

Home of Mr. and Mrs. Frank Connors of 3939 Fifth Avenue South.

Home of Mr. and Mrs. Harold W. Wright of 3909 Portland Avenue South.

Home of Rev. and Mrs. W. L. Battles, corner of 42nd St. and Third Ave. South.

Home of Mr. and Mrs. Clyde Williams of 3351 Portland Avenue South.

Home of Mr. and Mrs. Wilbur Henderson of 4036 Fifth Avenue South.
Mr. Henderson was the first to move into these new homes. He is married and has a wonderful family. He is employed at the Waldorf Paper Company and he and his family are members of the Pilgrim Baptist Church in St. Paul.

ALBERT L. ALLEN, JR., President of Northwest Orient Airlines Clerical Unions, Local 3015.

The entry of Negroes into unsegregated unions began in 1935 with the chartering of Local 665, Hotel and Restaurant Workers, A.F.L. This local whose membership approximated 1400 miscellaneous workers in the hotel and restaurant industry was the first to accept Negroes as a group on a non-segregated basis.

During the next years, due to a strong non-discriminatory organizational drive by the C.I.O., the bars were let down in the A.F.L., to pave the way for Negro membership in the manufacturing industries. As a result of the conversion of a number of these plants into defense factories a rapid increase in the number of Negro union members occurred—notably at Minneapolis-Moline, International Harvester and Minneapolis Honeywell.

Today with the wide diversification of Negroes in the field of employment, the race is widely represented both in the C.I.O. and the A.F.L.

Some of those who have and are serving in an official capacity within their respective unions are:

Mrs. Nellie Stone Johnson— Aldrich 4835—Vice president, Local 665, Hotel and Restaurant Workers.

Mrs. Maxine Jones—Colfax 8590—Secretary-treasurer, Local 418, Textile Workers of America.

Rev. Wm. B. Williams—Federal 5-4090.

Mr. Wendell Jones—Colfax 1489.

Mr. William Cratic—Colfax 3765.

EDWARD L. BOYD

District Deputy G.E.R. I.B.P.O.E. of W. Mr. Boyd is one of the officers of St. Peter's A.M.E. Church.

Grand United Order of Lodge Fellows: Leon T. Lewis, Noble Grand; C. R. Mendosa,* Noble Father; T. E. Woodard, Deputy; Willard J. Merrill, Secretary.

* Deceased.

S.M.T., Gertrude Mitchell, W.P.; Hilda Parker, W.S.; Lucille Woodard, W.T.; T. E. Woodard, Deputy Grand Master; W. White, W.R.S.

The Ames Lodge Drum and Bugle Corps originated January 16, 1940, under the then Exalted Ruler, Major M. O. Culbertson, with Theodore Nixon as director and Leon T. Lewis as assistant director.

For the past 8 years they have been under the leadership of Colonel Leon T. Lewis, Minnesota State Director of Junior Elks. Present Captain, Presiding Officer, Harry Dillon. Drum Major, Wayne Cockrell.

During the past 15 years, the drum corps has traveled throughout the United States playing civic parades and public exhibition demonstrations. During the time hundreds of children have had the privilege of making trips to various states they would not have been able to make had it not been for this great organization.

In the year 1952, upon request of Senator Hubert Humphrey, the Ames Drum Corps was asked to make a public appearance to lead the Motor Cavalcade of then President Harry Truman, who was touring the country making public addresses at that time.

In 1954, at the request of the Menelik Lodge, Winnipeg, Canada, the corps took part in the Red River Valley Exhibition Parade in Canada. This is the first time a unit of this type has been out of the country. They are again appearing in Winnipeg this year, June 22, for the same event.

The Ames Corps has been parade award winners in the Aquatennial Parade for the past six years in succession.

Their list of achievements include 12 trophies and 30 plaques and they are constantly adding to their collection.

Minnehaha Temple No. 129, Daughter of Elks Purple Cross Nurses was organized in May of 1948 by Lola Mae Gattling. It's officers are as follows:

President ....Lucille Woodard
Vice-President ....Minnie Hudley
Secretary ....Miss Dorothy Jones
Treasurer ....Ernestine Wright

WILLIAM D. McADAMS
Worshipful Master of Palestine Lodge No. 7, F&AM (PHA), member of North Star Consistory No. 14 of 32°. Recorder of Fezzan Temple No. 26, Shrine. Member of St. Peter's A.M.E. Church.

JOHN L. McHIE, JR.
Potentate of Shrine, Fezzan Temple No. 26, North Star Consistory
Past Master of Palestine Lodge No. 7

LAMAR ROBERTS
Worshipful Master of Anchor Hilliard Masonic Lodge

Annual Oriental Tea of Fezzan Court No. 7. Pictured from left to right: Daughters Ivy Massengale, Viola Madden, Gertrude Greene, Cornelia Gresham, Lela Mae Stewart, Theresa Banks, III, Commandress, Bessie Ratliffe, Dts. Zella Dearing, Irene Braton, Alma Jefferson, Beulah Mitchell, Helen Lawrence, and Margaret Wright. Seated in the same order Daughters Mamie Uptegrove and Ursula Hines Botts, Past Imperial Commandress and Imperial Deputy.

MRS. DORTHY J. HINES

Mrs. Dorthy J. Hines graduated from South School in Minneapolis, June 7, 1941; attended U. of M. School of Practical Nursing, was graduated and awarded a certificate on June 12, 1948. After taking her state board examination, she received her licenses to practice on Nov. 20, 1948. She was employed at the U. of M. hospital for six years. During that time she became the first Negro president of the Minnesota Licensed Practical Nursing Association. Mrs. Hines is the mother of three children, and the wife of Mr. Dennis Hines. She has recently become a member of the nursing staff at Fairview Hospital in Minneapolis. She is a member of St. Peter's A.M.E. Church where she serves as co-directress of the Adult Choral Choir.

HARRY L. SCOTT
Attorney at Law

Harry L. Scott, with offices at 205 Times Annex, was graduated from college at Howard University, Washington, D. C.; and graduated from the Law School of the University of Buffalo, N. Y. Mr. Scott has been active in civic affairs here in this city; he was president of the Minneapolis Sunday Forum and head of the Phyllis Wheatley Auxiliary; was nominated by direct vote of the people for state representative, twice, in the 35th Legislative district and once for the state senate. He is a general practitioner, specializing more or less in the criminal law, domestic relations and negligence law.

LENA O. SMITH, Attorney

DR. WILBERT H. WRIGHT, Dentist

Dr. W. D. Brown, Physician and Surgeon

DR. JAMES ROBINSON

Graduate of Summer High School, Kansas City, Kansas; Chicago College of Optometry, now Illinois College of Optometry. Member of St. Thomas Episcopal Church, Masons Lodge, Mu Sigma Pi, Professional Fraternity; Past member of N.A.A.C.P. Board of Minneapolis.

DR. THOMAS H. JOHNSON, Physician and Surgeon

L. HOWARD BENNETT

Mr. Bennett was graduated (Cum Laude Honors) from Fisk University, Nashville, Tenn. He received his Doctor of Law degree at the University of Chicago, June, 1950. Mr. Bennett was consultant to agencies in Human Relations in nine key cities. He assisted in establishing Minneapolis, Minn., Council on Human Relations. He is president of the Minneapolis Branch of the NAACP. Mr. Bennett is a member of the law firm of Hall, Smith and Hedlund since November, 1950, and of Hall, Smith, Hedlund, Bennett, Juster and Forsberg since September, 1955. He is a member and class leader of St. Peter's A.M.E. Church.

RAYMOND W. CANNON

Mr. Cannon was born in Northfield, Minn., and went through public grade and high schools in Minneapolis. He attended the University of Minnesota where he received a Bachelor of Pharmacy degree. He also attended the College of St. Thomas Law School and Minnesota College of Law. He has a Bachelor of Law degree. He is a practicing attorney with offices at 727 Palace Building for the past 25 years. He is a member of the Hennepin County Bar Association, Minnesota State Bar Association, American Bar Association. He was admitted to practice before the United States Supreme Court. He is a member of the Minneapolis FEPC, veteran of World War I, with service overseas, past national president of Alpha Phi Alpha fraternity for four consecutive terms. This is the oldest and largest organization of Negro men of college grade in the world. He was chairman of the Interim Committee which brought the Minneapolis Urban League into existence and served six years on its board of directors. He is a member of the Budget and Distribution and also Board of Directors of the Community Chest and Council. He is a trustee of St. Peter's A.M.E. Church and served as attorney and legal counsel during the construction of the new church building. He is General Counsel for Most Worshipful Prince Hall Grand Lodge of Minnesota F. and A. M., a 33° member of Masonic Fraternity. Before practicing law Attorney Cannon was a partner in Cannon Bros. Pharmacy in Minneapolis. Mr. Cannon serves as attorney for the Associated Negro Credit Union.

Mrs. Laura G. Gaskins is a Kentuckian by birth. She is a graduate of Kentucky State College and received her graduate training at the Atlanta University School of Social Work. Prior to coming to Minneapolis in 1943, she had been employed as a caseworker with the Jefferson County Welfare Department, Louisville, Ky., and earlier as a social worker with the Municipal Housing Authority of Louisville. While working in Louisville she served as secretary-treasurer of the Fall City Social Worker's Club.

Mrs. Gaskins' present employment is with the Hennepin County Welfare Board, as Supervisor in the Child Service Division, which position she has held for the past nine years.

She is a member of the following professional and civic organizations: National Association of Social Workers; Minnesota Welfare Conference; Minnesota Adoption Council; Urban League Guild; National Association for the Advancement of Colored People; League of Women Voters; Alpha Kappa Alpha Sorority.

In addition to keeping busy with job responsibilities, she is a busy homemaker. She is an avid reader and likes symphony music and the theatre. The Gaskins' 14-year-old niece, Alice Oliver, lives with them at 4409 Third Avenue South. She will enter the 10th grade next fall at Washburn High School.

Mrs. Gaskins is the wife of Mr. Ashby U. Gaskins.

RELIGION

Rev. Mrs. C. E. Parker
Pastor of Rehoboth Church of God

Rehoboth Church of God

Junior Choir of Bethesda Baptist Church

Senior Choir of Bethesda Baptist Church

REV. WILLIAM B. WILLIAMS
Pastor of Fourth Street Church of God In Christ for eight years. Executive secretary for the Board of Elders, Minnesota Church of God In Christ. Member of NAACP, Citizens League, Y.M.C.A., Greater Minneapolis Ministerial Association. He attended Albion College, University of Minnesota and graduated from Northwestern Bible College.

MRS. ROSIE LEE WILLIAMS
Wife of Rev. William B. Williams. Attended Northwestern Bible College. District Missionary (Minneapolis district) for the Church of God In Christ. Employed by L. S. Donaldson for the last eleven years.

MRS. DESSIE MAE GRESHAM
2717 Clinton Avenue South

Mrs. Gresham is directress of Bethesda Baptist Church's Senior Choir, president of the Minneapolis Choral Union, supervisor of the Minneapolis Soloist Bureau and corresponding and recording secretary of the National Soloist Bureau of the National Gospel Choirs and Choruses Convention, Inc. A resident of Minneapolis since 1929, Mrs. Gresham was born in Dallas, Texas, and is a member of various organizations.

Friendship Baptist Church — Rev. L. C. Harris, Pastor

Friendly Five Gospel Singers — WALTER GROSS, Manager

REV. AND MRS. H. W. BOTTS, SR.

Rev. Botts is pastor of Zion Baptist Church and the pastor with the longest point of service in Minneapolis.

REV. WORTH LITTLEJOHN BARBOUR — Pastor of Bethesda Baptist Church

Bethesda Baptist Church, 1118 Eighth Street South, Minneapolis

REV. J. C. WIGGINS — Pastor of St. Paul's Church of God in Christ

St. Paul's Church of God In Christ, 4001 Fourth Avenue South, Minneapolis

REV. M. L. SIMMONS

Rev. M. L. Simmons is a native of Georgia, son of an A.M.E. preacher, one of eleven children. He was appointed to St. Peter's in 1949, is a member of Mayor's Council on Human Relations, and takes active part in other Civic, Religious and Fraternal interests. Rev. Simmons is married to the former Wynona B. Wing, and they are the parents of two children, Martin Luther, Jr., and Phyllis Marie.

St. Peter's African Methodist Episcopal Church has stood for more than Seventy-five (75) years as a haven of hope for the Negro people and people in general in the city of Minneapolis. Throngs come each Sunday to share the blessings of a church dedicated to the high purpose of helping people live full and rich lives. The life of St. Peter's Church is truly indigenous with the life of this city.

She has made, through the years, a definite contribution to the political, social, economic and spiritual life of this and surrounding cities. It is the desire of this church to continue this grand and important task of helpfulness.

The present structure was built from the ground up at a cost of $185,000.00. The present membership is 526.

Graham's Temple Church of God In Christ

WILLARD J. MERRILL, SR.

Willard J. Merrill, Sr., Chairman of the Deacon Board of the Bethesda Baptist Church since 1940. He is married to the former Hazel Russell. He is the father of ten children, 8 girls and 2 boys. Mr. Merrill has been employed by the Soo Line Railroad company for the past thirty-five years as private car chef.

Federated Religious Play — Featuring Mr. Julius Ceaser

REVEREND E. Z. BIRD
Associated Minister of
Bethesda Baptist Church

We wish we could have included pictorially the following pastors and church activities: Rev. J. J. Jackson, Pastor of Pilgrim Rest Baptist Church; Rev. Charles M. Sexton, Pastor of Border Methodist Church; Father Louis Johnson, Rector of St. Thomas Episcopal Church; Pastor of Holsey C.M.E. Church; Pastor of St. James A.M.E. Church; Pastor of Wayman A.M.E. Church; Pastor of St. Phillips Lutheran Church; Pastor of the 7th Day Adventist Church.

CLUB 15

OFFICERS

President .... Lucius Jemison
Vice-President .... Robert Bannon
Financial Secretary .... William Orr
Treasurer .... James Lawler
Secretary .... Wallace Hicks, Jr.
Chaplain .... George Smith

MEMBERS

John H. Vincent	James Washington
Paul Smith	Lester Whittker
George Boatman	Roy Royster (asst. sec.)
Kenneth Wilson	William Dye

James Bedell (Sgt.-at-arms)

Walter Scott (Editor and publisher, *Beacon*)

ACIREMA CLUB — 3949 Fourth Avenue South

Reading right to left: Anthony B. Cassius, member; Howard G. Brown, *Secretary*; Aaron Arradondo, member; Thomas Johnson, *Treasurer*; John L. McHie, Jr., *President*; Claud W. Mason, member.

PROFESSIONAL SINGERS GUILD

THIRTEEN DUCHESSES

MRS. MARION L. WILLIAMS

Married: Clyde W. Williams, Real Estate Broker. Mother of 4 daughters, 4 sons. Active interests: Formerly Supt. of Nurses, Glenwood Hills Hospital, Minneapolis, Minnesota; formerly teacher of Ballet and Acrobatic Dancing; active in Community Chest, Mothers Club of Academy of Holy Angels; active in Church of Holy Name; member of Garden Lovers club; in charge of Public Relations for Williams Realty Co. Cited by the State of Minnesota for her work with mentally retarded children on the State Mental Health program. Hostess: well known for her graciousness as hostess in her beautifully appointed home, personally supervised and created complete interior and exterior decorative scheme. Hobby: Gardening, presently authors the column, "Garden Talk" in the Minneapolis Observer Newspaper.

Mrs. Harold W. Wright

Personable and vivacious Minneapolitan, Mrs. Harold W. Wright lives at 3909 Portland Avenue South. Mrs. Wright, a former Kansas Citian, is a member of St. Peter's A.M.E. Church and the Minneapolis Urban League.

She attended Fisk University, Nashville, Tenn., and Washburn College, Topeka, Kans. Mrs. Wright is the wife of Harold W. Wright.

Mrs. Theodore Woodard

TOYSE ANN WILLIAMS

Age 17 years. Attends Academy of Holy Angels exclusive girls finishing school. Senior year. Active in school dramatic club; student librarian. Models in Downtown Deb Shops; Excellent ballet, acrobatic and tap dancer; Attends Holy Name Church and sings in choir as soloist.

Dances for benefits and charitable organizations. Enjoys: Golfing, swiming, picnics with family.

MRS. FLORENCE CASSIUS

Mrs. Florence Cassius, wife of businessman A. B. Cassius, was born in Minnesota and reared and educated in Minneapolis. She comes from one of the oldest families in the Twin Cities. She is the daughter of the late John Allison, who served with the Sheriff's department for forty years.

Mrs. Cassius has been socially prominent for the past twenty years in the Twin City area. She is currently president of the Twin City Garden Club and a member of the Twin City Book Club. She is also a member of the Forty Club.

She is active in civic affairs and has worked with the Red Cross Canvass groups. She is the mother of Donald and the former Alvedia Cassius and grandmother of Lloyd and Sandra Smith and Lawrence Cassius.

The editor regrets the inability to obtain photographs of the
following socially prominent women.

SOCIETY OMISSIONS

Mrs. Matthew Evans
Ceramics — 3740 Fifth Avenue

Mrs. Robert Murray
President Urban League Guild — Minneapolis
4035 Third Avenue

Mrs. Barbara Cyrus
Librarian — 4053 Clinton

Mrs. Paul Curry
Relief Worker — 3115 Columbus

Mrs. Maxine Jones
First Negro employed by Knickernick Lingerie Company
Also acclaimed best dressed in the city
3622 Third Avenue

Mrs. W. D. Brown
Civic and Social — 608 E. Fourteenth

Mrs. Talmage B. Carey
Mrs. Shelton B. Granger
Mrs. Carl T. Rowan
Mrs. Oscar H. Newman
Mrs. Burrie Carmichale
Mrs. L. Howard Bennett
Attorney Lena O. Smith

URBAN LEAGUE

Ashby U. Gaskins (left) — Shelton B. Granger (right)

ASHBY U. GASKINS
Field Secretary, Minneapolis Urban League

A native of Monessen, Pa., Mr. Gaskins has been a resident of Minneapolis since 1942. He is a graduate of the University of Minnesota and has been on the Minneapolis Urban League staff since October of 1950.

Mr. Gaskins' organizational affiliations include: Secretary-Treasurer Elect, Twin City Vocational Guidance Association; Careers and Intergroup Relations Committee of Third District Nurses Association; National Vocational Guidance Association; Minnesota Welfare Conference; National Association of Social Workers; Minneapolis Branch, NAACP; Minnesota State Conference, NAACP; Chairman, Advisory Board on Minimum Wages for Women and Minors in the Retail Merchandising Industry; Citizens League of Greater Minneapolis; Board member, Associated Negro Credit Union; Past President, Industrial Secretaries Council of the National Urban League; member of Alpha Phi Alpha fraternity; Past president Minnesota State Conference NAACP.

SHELTON B. GRANGER
Executive Secretary, Minneapolis Urban League

Mr. Granger came to Minneapolis in October of 1951 from the Cleveland Urban League where he was Director of the Department of Industrial Relations. Before going to Cleveland, he was a Field Worker with the Urban League of Greater New York.

A native of Harrisburg, Pa., Mr. Granger was graduated from William Penn High School in that city, received his A.B. from Howard University, Washington, D. C., and his M.S. from the New York School of Social Work, Columbia University, New York City.

He has served as Vice President of the Industrial Secretaries Council and the Executive Secretaries Council of the National Urban League.

While in Cleveland, Mr. Granger was chairman of the local chapter of the American Association of Social Workers, and after coming to Minneapolis was elected Chairman of the Twin City Chapter of that organization in 1954. He is currently serving as President of the Southern Minnesota Chapter of the National Association of Social Workers, a newly created organization combining seven social work groups with a local membership of over 400.

Mr. Granger is a member of the Minneapolis Branch NAACP Board of Directors and a member of the Legal Redress Committee. He is State Chairman on International Affairs of the Minnesota Junior Chamber of Commerce. He is a member of the Omega Psi Phi fraternity.

He also serves on the Mayor's Advisory Committee on Housing, Mayor's Committee on Juvenile Delinquency, Citizens Committee on Public Education and the Relocation Advisory Council of the Minneapolis Housing and Redevelopment Authority.

The Minneapolis Urban League sponsors an interracial social work program designed to improve the living and working conditions of Negroes and related minorities, to the end that relationships are bettered between Negro and white citizens of the community.

The Minneapolis League is one of 62 affiliates of the National Urban League and a member agency of the Community Chest and Council of Hennepin County.

The National Urban League was founded in 1910, and the local League is observing its 30th year of operation.

The local program is centered primarily around six major areas which are:

Industrial Relations: Vocational Counseling, selective job placement, management and labor contacts, occupational information.

Community Services: Advisory, informational and consultative services to public, social and civic organizations.

Community Education: Interpretation of problems of adjustment, feelings of prejudice and acts of discrimination between racial groups.

Community Planning: Cooperative interracial planning for community improvement.

Housing: Implementation and support of programs for public and private housing on a non-segregated basis.

Research: Research as it relates to other aspects of the Urban League program.

Membership in the League is open to individuals and groups interested in helping to promote a better community through better race relations.

CARL T. ROWAN
Minneapolis Tribune Staff Writer

Rowan was born August 11, 1925, in Ravenscroft, Tenn., as a son of Mr. and Mrs. Thomas D. Rowan.

He grew up—with a brother and three sisters—in McMinnville, Tenn., where he attended Bernard elementary and high school. He served as president of his senior class in high school.

He attended Tennessee State college in Nashville as a freshman, ranking among the top 10 students and serving as vice-president of the class.

After taking a nationally-competitive examination, Rowan volunteered to enter the United States Navy in May 1943 and was assigned to a V-12 unit at Washburn Municipal university, Topeka, Kansas. After V-12 training at Washburn and at Oberlin college, Oberlin, Ohio, he underwent midshipman training at Fort Schuyler naval reserve midshipman school.

In March of 1945, at the age of 19, he was commissioned as an ensign in the United States Naval Reserve, becoming one of the first 15 Negroes to attain commissioned rank in the navy. He later served in "operation integration" as a communications officer aboard two fleet tankers with racially-integrated crews in the Atlantic fleet.

Upon release to inactive duty, Rowan returned to Oberlin college where he received an A.B. degree in mathematics in June 1947. He received an M.A. degree in journalism from the University of Minnesota in August 1948. While at the University, he worked for the Minneapolis Spokesman and St. Paul Recorder.

After handling a brief special project for the Baltimore Afro-American during the 1948 presidential campaign, he went to work on the copydesk of the Minneapolis Tribune. He soon transferred to his present position of Tribune staff writer.

He is the winner of three "Page One" awards from the Newspaper Guild of the Twin Cities for (1) headline writing, (2) articles on vocational guidance and (3) a series of articles on race relations in the south called "How Far From Slavery?"

He was cited for "service to humanity" in 1951 by the Minneapolis Junior Chamber of Commerce for articles on race relations, cited for the "best newspaper reporting in the nation" in 1951 by the Sidney Hillman foundation for articles on the south, designated as Minneapolis' "outstanding young man of 1951" by judges for the Minneapolis Junior Chamber of Commerce, and cited by the curators of Lincoln university, Jefferson City, Mo., for "high achievement, high purpose and exemplary practice" in the field of journalism in 1951.

Rowan is the author of the book, "South of Freedom" based on a 6,000-mile tour of his native southland, published in August, 1952, by Alfred A. Knopf. His book was selected by the American Library association as one of the "53 best books" of 1952. His book was named by the India Journalists' association as the "best negro literature of 1953."

He was selected by judges representing the United States Junior Chamber of Commerce as "one of America's 10 outstanding Young Men of 1953" and was honored at a banquet for the 10 men at Seattle, Wash., in January 1954.

Rowan is the holder of two awards from Sigma Delta Chi, national professional journalism fraternity for "distinguished service to journalism."

He received the organization's 1953 general reporting award for his series in the Tribune entitled "Jim Crow's Last Stand?" It was the first award given to a negro newspaperman by the fraternity. Rowan went to the sources for these articles which reported the background of the school segregation cases then pending before the United States supreme court.

Rowan was given Sigma Delta Chi's 1954 foreign correspondence award for his Tribune series "This Is India." He wrote the series after serving during the summer and fall of 1954 as a specialist in the international educational exchange program for the United States state department. He traveled throughout India lecturing on American newspapers and their role in social change. His lectures took him to places not usually visited by the few American newsmen there, which enabled him to write with special insight about the problems and progress of India and its people.

Upon completion of his assignment with the state department, the Tribune sent him from India to Pakistan, Burma, Thailand, Indochina, Indonesia, Malaya, Hong Kong and the Philippines, covering close to 52,000 miles by air. A result of this trip was his Tribune series "Asia: Terror and Turmoil."

He currently is on the board of directors of the Minneapolis Urban league, Elliot Park Neighborhood house and the Minneapolis chapter of the National Foundation of Infantile Paralysis and is a member of the National Association for the Advancement of Colored People.

From 1951 to 1953 he was president of the Minneapolis Urban league and the youngest man in the nation ever to hold such a post. He has served as a director of the Citizens League of Greater Minneapolis, Travelers Aid Society, National Association for the Advancement of Colored People and the child and family welfare division of the Hennepin county Community Chest and council and president of the Frontiers of America.

Married to the former Vivien L. Murphy of Buffalo, N.Y., they have three children, a girl and two boys.

BEAUTY

Antoinette Hughes, better known to most people as Toni, is a graduate of Minneapolis Central High School. Toni was an honor student, in National Honor Society, President of the Drama Club, Vice-President of the Spanish Club, Vice-President of All City Y-Teens, Representative to Girls State, Representative Centralite, Student Council, G.A.A., Representative to the Student Council Convention held in Albert Lea in 1955, and many other activities.

Toni was graduated from the Helen Stefan Modeling School and is now a professional model.

This fall Toni plans to enroll at the University of Minnesota and will major in Fashion or Psychology. At present she is employed by Red Owl as a cashier.

Her hobby is Fashion Designing and doing modern interpretive dancing. Antoinette is the daughter of Mr. and Mrs. Solomon Hughes of 3716 Fourth Avenue South.

MISS JUANITA NEVELLS

Mrs. Lucille McAdams—wife of William D. McAdams
Member of St. Peter's A.M.E. Church. President of Jolly 16 Club of St. Peter's A.M.E. Church. Supervisor of the Junior Ushers of St. Peter's Church. Member of Pride of West No. 9, Order of Eastern Stars (P.H.A.)

MRS. VIOLA MADDEN

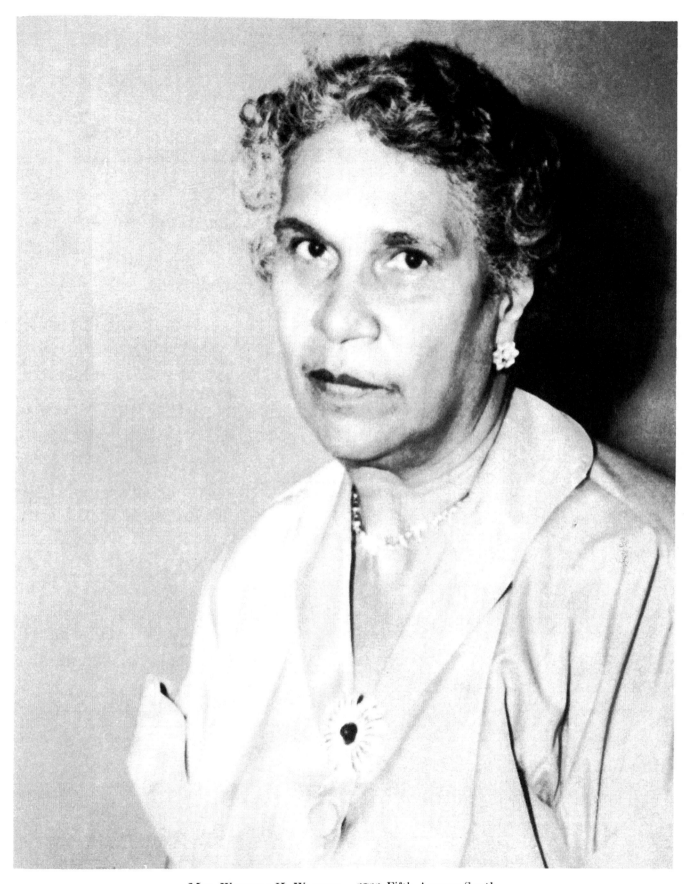

MRS. WILLIAM H. WALKER — 3733 Fifth Avenue South
Housewife, charter member of Minnehaha Temple No. 129. Vice President of the Helpers Club of St. Peter's
A. M. E. Church. She is the mother of Mrs. Ruth Pierre.

Minneapolis Star & Tribune Photo

DANNY DAVIS
Minnesota State Lightweight Champion

Minneapolis Star & Tribune Photo

PLUMMER WILLIS
Lightweight Professional Boxer

Minneapolis Star & Tribune Photo

MONROE GAGE
Light Heavyweight Professional Boxer

Minneapolis Star & Tribune Photo

WILLIE JEMISON
Middleweight Amateur Boxer

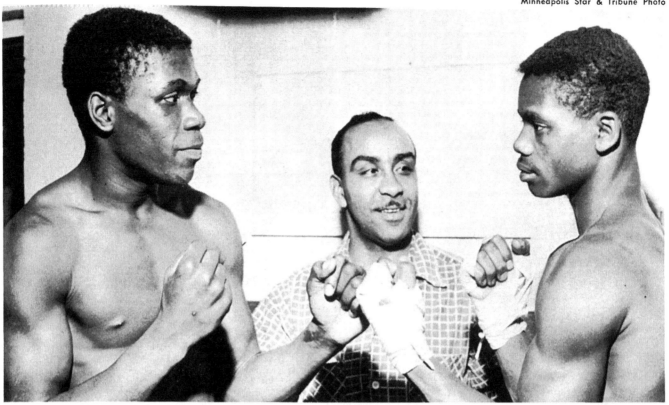

HARRY DAVIS (One of Northwest's Outstanding Boxing Coaches) with LEROY BOGAR and JIMMY SHAW

Golfers — Right to Left — JACK HOWARD, CLEO JOHNSON, ERNIE HARRIS, WILBUR DUGAS

—Photo from Jimmie Slemmons tournament.

BOB WILLIAMS
First Negro to play with the Minneapolis "Lakers"

WILLIE KIRKLAND
One of the mainstays of the Minneapolis "Millers"

BILL WHITE
Now with New York Giants

We wished we could have included pictorially the following people in the Golf world: John Williams, Clyde Williams, Ernest Anthony, Clyde Johnson, Solomon Hughes (professional), Dick Charum, Bert Davidson, Fern Hughes, and a number of others.

It is the sincere hope of the "Beacon" staff that the reading of the Centennial Edition has been most enjoyable as well as informative. The assistance rendered by Mr. Newman, Mr. Cassius, Rev. Williams, D. W. Onan & Sons, First National Bank, Jones Press and others too numerous to mention here has been deeply appreciated, and we, the "Beacon" staff extend our most sincere thanks to all of you.

WALTER R. SCOTT
WILLIE H. RASBERRY
JAMES WASHINGTON
MRS. MERCEDES DAVIS

WATCH
YOUR LOCAL
NEWSPAPERS
FOR
PUBLICATION DATE
OF THE
ST. PAUL
"BEACON"

FOR INFORMATION CALL

PA. 1-2873   **PA. 1-1984**

Dear Reader:

This is the newest local publication by Negroes, which after being in eclipse for many months, is offered to you in the hope that you will give some study to its aim, without which, we, the staff wouldn't have any real reason to begin this venture.

Our aim here at the "Beacon", is to publish the achievements made by Negroes locally.

Negroes, like other races can turn back to some badly smeared pages in the history of our country, where even today we contribute our share to the chaotic condition in the world. However, through our actions, guarded by our faith, continued efforts will bring better results.

The results I am referring to are the things we have here in Minnesota, and they are, admission to any school at the State University, buying the home we can pay for, that is for sale in the open market, getting more jobs that we are qualified to do, and the joy from the assurance that we too can go to the top in the local industry, only to be conspicuous by Gods' action and not by the pigmentation of our skin.

We here at the "Beacon" have been inspired by the tireless efforts of: Cecil Newman, Talmage Carey, the local branches of the N. A. A. C. P., the Urban League, Carl Rowan, Raymond W. Cannon, Reverend Simmons, Dr. W. D. Brown, as well as the people and firms of other races, that are helping us to gain equality, and first class citizenship—Thank you.

To all of you (local) old soldiers, that are on the way to new battlegrounds, nationally, as well as locally, to brighten up the future pages of history, we would like to apply as a recruit to bolster your efforts. We are certain that we can make you happy that we of the "Beacon" come to join you.

Since space was not available for the "Beacon" to include each and every individual that represents the sections of activity that we covered, it is here that we—the staff—state that no club, business or Church, or any section was omitted willfully.

Sincerely yours,
WALTER R. SCOTT
Editor and Publisher

MINNEAPOLIS NEGRO PROFILE

A Pictorial Resume of the Black Community, its achievements, and its immediate goals.

"We Shall Overcome"

"Lift every voice and sing" . . .
are the first five words of the
Negro National Anthem,
and Black Americans
throughout this nation have
lifted their heads, their hearts,
their voices, and their dreams
to the promise of full partnership,
and full citizenship in this land.
They have lived for generations
in the shadow of injustice,
without just recognition,
without fair reward for their
countless contributions.
They now demand to be heard,
to be identified, to be respected.
They challenge the false traditions,
the old taboos, the historical
distortions of the past.
To them, "We shall overcome"
is not just a phrase, not just a song
but a declaration of intent,
a dedication of firm resolve.
And on this cover, the young and
the old, face the future fearlessly.
And in this book we offer but
a fraction of proof.

Dedication

Dedicated to my father and step-mother,
Mr. and Mrs. George Scott, of Detroit, Michigan.
And also my father and mother-in-law,
Mr. and Mrs. George Smith, Minneapolis,
Minnesota.

Contents

The Staff

Walter R. Scott, Sr. .... Editor and Publisher
Cecil Dewey Nelson, Jr. .... Art Director Designer
                             and Editorial Assistant
Eugene McMiller .... Photographer
John M. Warder .... Advisor
Earl Glomsrud .... Advisor
Ruth Jackson .... Artist
Dave Brandon .... Production
The Colwell Press .... Printers and Production
Leo Browne .... Sales

CREDITS — Ashby Gaskins, Mgmt. Consultant, The Minneapolis
Star and Tribune, The Minneapolis Board of Education,
The Twin City Observer, The Minneapolis Spokesman,
The Minneapolis Chamber of Commerce, The New York Times
Service.

From the Governor

Greetings!

I would like to take this opportunity to express my sincere appreciation to the Negro community of Minneapolis for the excellent record of achievement made in the past year.

I recognize the path to attainment and community improvement is often strewn with obstacles. Fortunately, we have learned in Minnesota that these obstructions are not insurmountable.

We have discovered a key ingredient — cooperation. Minneapolitans can be proud of the cooperation displayed in the past year toward providing equal opportunities for all. They can also point with pride to the leadership in community projects given by Negroes.

I look forward to a continual advancement and pledge every resource of this Administration to that end.

Sincerely,

Harold LeVander
GOVERNOR

From the Mayor

Dear Mr. Scott:

I am pleased to learn about your new publication, *Minneapolis*.
It will help give our city a fuller appreciation of the Negro community and an understanding of the new leadership and the new opportunities that are being developed. It is further evidence that the barriers of discrimination and prejudice continue to come down.
We have yet a long way to go and we need every constructive assistance.
Best wishes for every success.

Sincerely yours,

Arthur Naftalin

Minnesota and the Negro

The date of the earliest migrations of Negroes to Minnesota is unknown, but Minnesota history records their active presence as early as 1782. Several names like George Bonga, James Thompson and Harriet Robinson appear in the records of Fort Snelling in 1836. Also, history shows that Negroes, known to the Indians as "Black Frenchmen" settled in the area around Fort Snelling and hired out on boats from St. Louis and other points south on the Mississippi.

By far the most famous of all Negroes in Minnesota, the state which today is known for its many contributions to liberalism in leadership, was Dred Scott, whose impact on the history of the United States is well known. The entry of the state of Minnesota into statehood itself was related to the question of free versus slave states and of Negro suffrage. The issue to give the Negro his vote was finally carried affirmatively in 1868 and preceded by two years the adoption of the Fifteenth Amendment to the U.S. Constitution. However, the Negro population of Minnesota was then and has been since, far below that of the other Northern states thus pointing up the fact that the state has not been in the main stream of Negro migration. Whereas this smaller population by comparison with other states has tended to favor more liberal thinking on the part of his white neighbors, it also has tended to reduce the impact and voice of the Black Community in affairs of this state.

Minnesota has been a part of a national trend in minority group employment. From 1940 to 1960, the number of Negroes, both male and female that attained the various white-collar jobs increased. Nevertheless, the Negro's chances of getting skilled jobs are, even at present, subject in large part to his chances of being accepted by organized labor Unions, still dragging their feet with "father and son" traditions.

From the Chamber of Commerce

Mr. Walter Scott
Scott Publishing Company
c/o Colwell Press, Inc.
Minneapolis, Minnesota

Dear Mr. Scott:

The Executive Committee, and subsequently the Board of Directors of the Minneapolis Chamber of Commerce are pleased to endorse your new publication, "Minneapolis Negro Profile".
The Board feels that this book, properly placed, would have a very good effect on young Negro people moving into the business and community life of Minneapolis.

Sincerely,

Gerald L. Moore
Executive Vice President

From the Publisher

The American Negroes' future is bright with promise as we enter the "next one hundred years". Progress during the past 100 years gives us reason to believe that we can achieve the great potential that is inherent in that promise — and we can achieve it in the year just ahead — if we continue to hold fast to our goals, to plan wisely, cooperate effectively and to work hard.

But the years ahead offer more than great promise. They present us with the challenge of demonstrating, to ourselves and to others, that Negroes can in a spirit of cooperation and through the machinery of democratic government — peacefully achieve the potential for abundance that scientific progress has now made possible for the first time in history. Events of the 1960's may well determine the future of the American Negro, and the future of the rest of the world.

In this turbulent period, we must affirm our goals and evaluate our progress toward these goals. The United States, as a leader of the free world, must develop strength for defense and a positive program that will advance democracy throughout the world. Negroes in the past had no function with regard to national defense or the conduct of foreign policy. But we will play an important role in the building and maintenance of the foundation on which all future policy must rest.

This foundation must include a strengthened program emphasizing that Negroes be seated in state houses in each section of this country. It must include economic growth and expansion, it must include progress toward greater efficiency and integrity in our local, state, and national governments.

The people you will see on the following pages, to some degree in our opinion, are succeeding in helping to build this foundation for American strength as we help build a Greater Minneapolis, and we hope a Greater America.

The Negro

The following is part of an address by Theodore Roosevelt, then the President of the United States to the Congress. We think its historical importance is significant especially as it was concerned then with the identical national problem of today, 64 years later, namely, the wall between the races. Men, black and white should have heeded then and must heed now the words of this great leader of his day.

It is a good thing that the guard around the tomb of Lincoln should be composed of Colored soldiers. It was my own good fortune at Santiago to serve beside Colored troops. A man who is good enough to shed his blood for the country is good enough to be given a square deal afterward. More than that no man is entitled to, and less than that no man should have. (1903)

I have not been able to think out any solution to the terrible problem offered by the presence of the Negro on this continent, but of one thing I am sure, and that is that * * * * the only wise and honorable and Christian thing to do is to treat each Black Man, and each White Man strictly on his merits as a man, giving him no more and no less than he shows himself worthy to have. I say I am "sure" that this is the right solution. Of course I know that we see through a glass dimly, and, after all, it may be that I am wrong; but if I am, then all my thoughts and beliefs are wrong, and my whole way of looking at life is wrong. At any rate, while I am in public life, however short a time that may be, I am in honor bound to act up to my beliefs and convictions. I do not intend to offend the prejudices of anyone else, but neither do I allow their prejudices to make me false to my principles. (1901)

To me, the question of doing away with all race and religious bigotry in this country is the most important of all. (1904)

— Theodore Roosevelt

Opportunity? You Bet!
Meet some of the "Doers"

In the Black Community things are really moving, sometimes quietly, sometimes dramatically, but moving! And the Black Citizens of Minneapolis are "Doers." The vitality and imagination of youth, the gentle but firmly determined set of the educated, and the wonderful charm beauty are capsulized here. We know you will enjoy meeting a few of them.

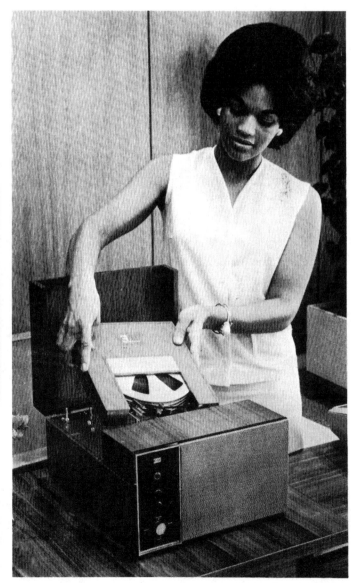

"Are Negro Publications Necessary?"

In 1827 John B. Russwurm became the first Negro editor when he published the first Negro newspaper, *Freedom's Journal.*

Since then the number of Negro publications has risen to 179, with a combined circulation of nearly three million.

These facts seem to indicate that Negro publications have had a measure of success. Nevertheless, critics of the Negro press continually ask the question, "Are Negro Publications Really Necessary?"

The critics contend that newspapers and magazines published by and for Negroes are nothing more than scandal sheets that give too much publicity to crime, sex, violence and other news which tends to depict an undesirable image of the Negro. Furthermore, the critics say, the news in Negro publications is usually that which has already appeared in other newspapers and magazines.

Granted, some Negro publications do seem to depend heavily upon material which tends to be defamatory to the Negro. It is also conceded that many times articles printed in Negro publications have already been published in other publications.

Nevertheless, the way we see it, the critics seem to be overlooking some of the beneficial functions which the Negro press performs.

First of all, in the fight for equality and justice, the Negro press has been the voice of the Negro. Not only have Negro publications continually pointed out the injustices practiced, but they have been the ones to sound the rallying call by which the Negro and his sympathizers have banned themselves together.

Secondly, the Negro press has filled the vacuum created by other publications by giving analysis and emphasis to news of particular interest to Negroes.

Thirdly, through the efforts of the Negro press, merchants have been made aware of the giant Negro market and thus have helped to open up many avenues heretofore closed to the Negro.

Fourthly, most Negro publications have helped to replace the false and undesirable image of the Negro with a more true and reasonable one by publishing articles on the good and worthwhile endeavors in which Negroes are involved.

This last role is justification in itself for Negro publications. If the war was over and peace prevailed, there would be no need for a magazine such as TOPIC — one which mirrors the good things Negroes are doing.

Therefore, when the question is asked, "Are Negro Publications Really Necessary?" THE PROFILE answers with an emphatic, "Yes!"

In grateful memory of
JOHN B. RUSSWURM
first Negro in the United States to receive a college degree, and whose pioneering spirit and clear vision motivated him to establish, in Manhattan in 1827,
FREEDOM'S JOURNAL
the first Negro newspaper and the forerunner of the Negro Press in America, which has conscientiously striven to meet the challenge he initiated.

FREEDOM'S JOURNAL.

NATIONAL NEWSPAPER PUBLISHERS ASSOCIATION
FREEDOM'S JOURNAL — John B. Russwurm
March 17, 1827   March 12, 1965

INDUSTRY

In Minneapolis Industry Today

In constant search of opportunity for the gainful employment of his ever increasing skills, the Black citizens of Minneapolis have contributed greatly to the production and services of this highly industrial community.

They have jobs in sales, as secretaries, as engineers, as factory workers and as managers. Some work with familiar products like telephones, automobiles and insurance policies. Others work in strange new fields like nuclear electronics, outer space projects and data processing.

Some have worked in local industry for many years. Some are just starting their careers in industry.

Some are high school graduates. Some are graduates of top-flight colleges and universities. Some dropped out of school too soon, and have had a hard time overcoming their lack of formal education.

All have one thing in common. They are Negroes.

We will tell you about their jobs and their backgrounds to show you the kinds of jobs that capable Negro men and women can hold in the City of Minneapolis. We are talking about *TODAY*. As these words are written, each of these men and women is at work — designing, typing, drafting, repairing, managing, planning, selling, working standard machinery, or operating some of the most complex equipment the world has ever known.

In the words of Mr. W. E. Hollinger, personnel supervisor, Northwestern Bell, Minnesota area, "We think the equal opportunity theme accomplished a lot if it replaced some frustrations with motivations; that is one of the big things we're trying to do. It's not an overnight project."

We aren't inferring that the employment arena in Minneapolis is perfect. Even today we sometimes find the laurels of old worn-out antagonisms. What we feel

here at SPC is that the local industry has been trying for a good many years to live up to high standards of fairness in hiring and in employee progress, but don't think for a second that it is lowering its requirements for new applicants. We know the local industry is not perfect — we also know the local industry is not complacent. It's still trying to make progress — and complacency is the enemy of progress.

That's the main reason for our effort. Many white and Negro business men have told us that years of hopelessness about the future have produced a "don't care" attitude toward good grades among many Negro young people. "It isn't enough for us to tell them about good job opportunities", we've been told, "You have to show them". Maybe this pictorial resume will help.

The Progress Road will be rocky for the boy or girl who drops out of school too soon — and because jobs are getting more complicated all the time, the way is getting rougher for any school drop-out — white or Negro, or any other race. To the drop-out we can only say:

Try to go back, or try for night school. The sooner the better. And how about the Negro youth who does care, who does well in high school and earns his diploma? The Negro men and women who have made the greatest progress in the local industry are those who have looked on graduation from high school as a milestone in education — but not the end. They have gone on to Secretarial Schools, to Trade Schools and Business Schools.

And of course, some have gone on to college; however, college deans tell us that many outstanding Negro students shy away from courses which would lead to careers in industry. "They are uncertain about their chances in industry, so they tend to move into

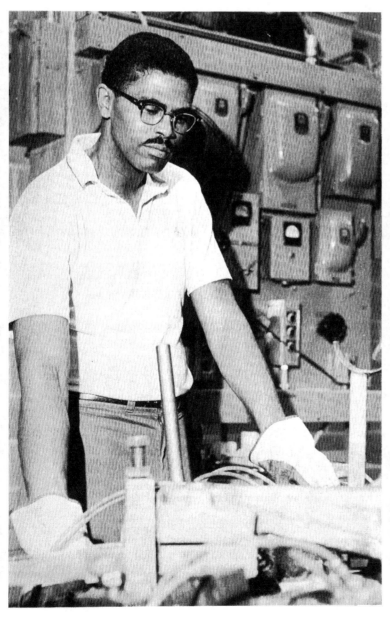

such fields as medicine, law, the Ministry, dentistry and teaching" we're told. Minneapolis needs outstanding doctors, lawyers, clergymen, dentists and teachers of course. But this industrial city also needs young people — of every race, creed and color — who can become outstanding economists, factory supervisors, scientists, advertising writers, product designers, sales representatives, auditors and electrical engineers. Maybe our bird's-eye view presentation will help here too.

To the young Negro, we can say this: Can you find your own "Success Image"? Do you have the desire? The willingness to bring out the best in yourself? The determination to get the essential education and training? Yes? Then we at Scott Publishing Company believe that you can look forward to a career in industry — in the All-American City of Minneapolis — a career in which success is not based on race, but on your own ability, education and ambition.

One of the most rewarding projects to grow from the tireless efforts of the National Urban League was the formation of an honorary award to business organizations and companies for meritorious service to the full employment equally of minority group workers. It is a designation highly honored by these companies. And we are proud that all the companies and businesses included here deserve this designation, "An Equal Opportunity Employer".

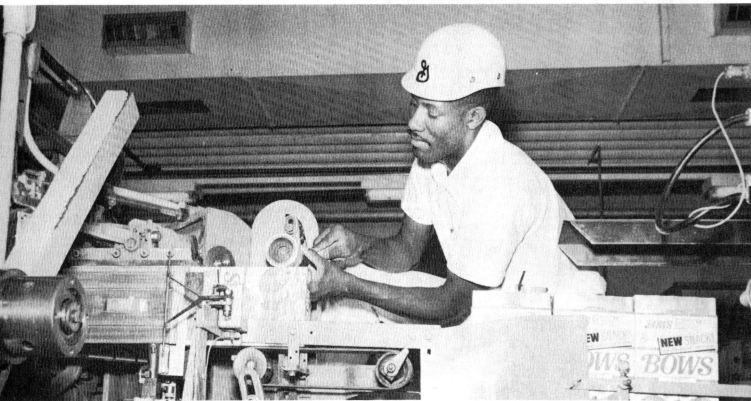

GENERAL MILLS

Frank Wyche
30, is a staff assistant to the Director of
Corporate Personnel at General Mills. Beginning
in the statistics section of the corporate
Computer group in July 1965, Wyche became
Personnel Assistant at the General Mills Research
Center in September, 1966.

Herbert D. Grevious
30, Supv. Transportation Dept. Began as a Mgt.
Trainee — August 1965. Promoted to Supervisor —
July 1966. Graduated from Morgan State
College — June 1962 — B.S. Bus. Adm. At time of
publication, has been on temporary leave

of absence from General Mills, Inc. on loan to
the Mayor's Office as Youth Coordinator,
Mayor's Council on Youth Opportunity. Will
return to General Mills, Inc. in a new position
as a New Ventures Analyst.

Eddie L. Battier
25, is a Process Technician in the cereal/snack
pilot plant at the General Mills James Ford
Bell Technical Center. Currently, he is taking
advantage of the company's Educational
Assistance Plan by working toward an Associate
of Arts degree in Basic Engineering at the
University of Minnesota.

Joyce M. Hillman
came to Electric Machinery Mfg. Company recommended by the T.C.O.I.C. As the first colored female office worker, she has made the transition well. Joyce has fitted into "a man's world" as a Maintenance Clerk having actually replaced a male secretary. "It's fun," says Joyce.

George M. Thompson
started with Electric Machinery Mfg. Company as a Janitor on March 14, 1946. He was promoted to Millwright and then to Maintenance Mechanic "A". George has progressed well in his chosen field and was promoted to a working foreman status on April 2, 1962. He is responsible for a group of Maintenance people on the third shift.

INTERNATIONAL MILLING

Oceanna Holley
key punch operator in International Milling's data processing department in Minneapolis, is a native of Albany, N.Y., and a graduate of the business college there. She has also taken advanced training in machine automation at the Minneapolis Business College, and has worked for IM since April, 1967.

Robert L. Hughes
laboratory technician at International Milling's Central Laboratories in New Hope, Minn., records data from a maze of instrumentation which measures the performance characteristics of industrial flours. Bob, a graduate of Albion College, Albion, Mich., started working for International in May, 1967.

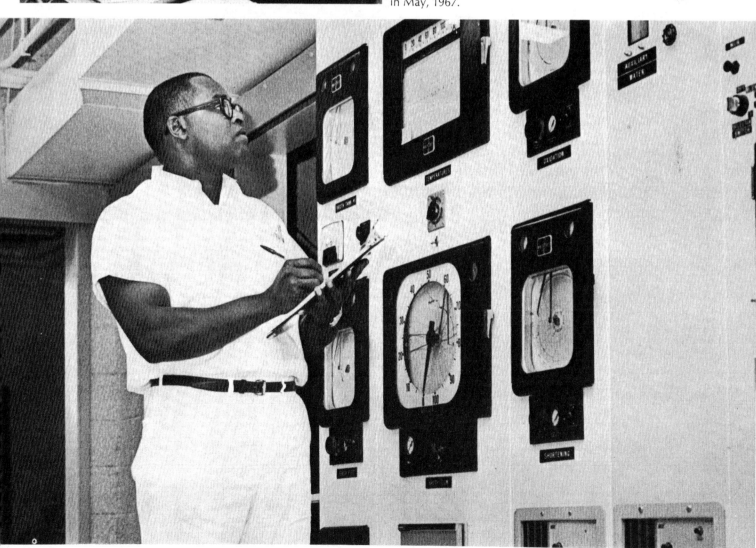

Northwestern Bell Telephone Company

Jeannette Lightfoot Sutton
After graduating from North High School in 1964, became an Information Operator with Northwestern Bell. In the fall of 1967, she was appointed senior clerk in the Force Adjustment group in the Traffic Department's District Office. Here she helps compute the detailed information needed for the complicated task of predicting the number of operators required to be on duty each day based both on past experience and current facts.

Dorothy Butler
one of six children, received her first taste of business experience through the "work program" at Central High School. As part of that course, in her senior year, she worked part time as a long distance operator at Northwestern Bell. When she graduated in June, 1965, she started on a full-time basis. She helps callers place telephone calls throughout the nation and even to other countries.

Thaddeus W. James
started his telephone career with Northwestern Bell in 1946 as a house serviceman, progressing through several other jobs before being named to his present position in the company's central office located at 816 - 21st Avenue N., which houses the equipment serving telephone customers in the northwest Minneapolis area. As a "frameman," he connects the customers' telephone lines to the dial switching equipment. This includes coordinating the work of the central office equipment men with the telephone man installing the phone in the customer's home or place of business and testing the newly installed service to insure accuracy.

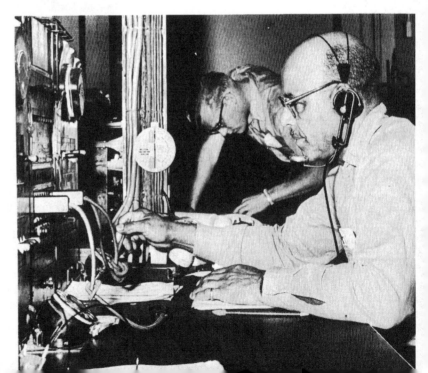

Jane Bogen
went to work for Northwestern Bell as soon as she
graduated from South High School in June, 1963.
As a Service Representative, she is the primary contact
customers have with the telephone company, handling
customers' orders for service, payment of bills
and other business transactions. After two and one-half
years of experience of dealing with residential
customers, she was assigned to a group handling
business accounts exclusively.

American Telephone & Telegraph Company
Parent Company of the Bell System

Pat Fraction
American Telephone and Telegraph Company's
Long Lines Department is responsible for telephone
circuits which link various operating companies of
the Bell System such as Northwestern Bell. As a Facility
Clerk for AT&T, Pat Fraction uses her training she
received in North High School's business course in
her work of collecting data used in determining
adequacy of these circuits and long distance routing
equipment. Special jobs also arise such as investigating
the extent of restoral of service needed when
tornadoes, hurricanes, floods and other disasters
affect telephone communications. She started with
Northwestern Bell in October, 1962, and transferred
to AT&T in 1965.

Western Electric
Manufacturing and Supply Unit
of the Bell System

Danny Sheffield
Keeping track of between 35 and 40 thousand
telephone sets each month is a very responsible job —
one that Danny Sheffield has proved capable
of doing since going to work for Western Electric
Company in August, 1965. In his work, he classifies
each phone that is returned by Northwestern Bell to be
reconditioned by Western Electric, the manufacturing
and supply unit of the Bell System. Western Electric
employs about 400 men and women in its
Minneapolis House.

Robert A. Murray is assistant vice president - investments, for Gamble Alden Life Insurance Company. Bob resides at 2164 North Rosewood Lane in Roseville and he is chairman of the Roseville Human Relations Commission. The Murrays have three children, R. Arnold, Neal and Jeffery.

PROFILES in MINNEAPOLIS...

William Quinn is a pharmacist in the Snyders Drug Store in Fridley's Holly Shopping Center. Bill resides at 3852 Florida Avenue North in Crystal and he is a member, appointed by the village council, of the Crystal Human Relations Council. The Quinns have two children, Quentin and Krystal.

LeRoy King, who was recently promoted to the position of candy and bakery merchandiser for Red Owl, has been manager of the Red Owl food store in Glenwood Shopping Center. LeRoy resides at 622 Thomas Avenue North and he is a deacon and Sunday school superintendent at Zion Baptist Church. The Kings have three children, LeRoy, Jr., Kenneth, and Sonita Michael.

The three Minneapolis-based companies mentioned above are subsidiaries of  **GAMBLES**

ROGER DAY

is 25 years old and a programmer
in Apache's Electronic Data Processing
Department. He worked hard to get there.
After graduation from St. Paul Central
High School, Roger attended the University
of Minnesota, then specialized in a data
processing course at Minnesota
School of Business.
Roger's future is bright. His initiative
and tenacity are paying off.

1800 Foshay Tower, Minneapolis, Minn. 55402

Sherrie Mazingo

suburban reporter for The Minneapolis Star, is a graduate of Central High School, St. Paul, and Howard University, Washington, D.C.

Miss Mazingo joined The Star staff in 1965. She is a member of the Minnesota Press Women and Gamma Sigma Sigma.

Among her major articles was a series written in 1967 about Negro families in Minneapolis-St. Paul area suburbs.

Miss Mazingo, who has traveled extensively throughout North America and Europe, is single and lives in St. Paul.

Patricia McKinnie

a copy editor for The Minneapolis Tribune, graduated from Englewood High School, Chicago, Ill., in 1951. She attended Wilson Junior College for one year and obtained a B.S. degree from the University of Illinois in 1955.

Before joining the staff of The Tribune as a copy editor in October, 1966, Patricia McKinnie held several writing positions including editor of the employee publication at Univac.

Patricia McKinnie is married and has one child. She and her family live in Golden Valley, Minn.

Floyd Clark

a native of Joliet, Illinois, was recently promoted to Building Security Supervisor for the Minneapolis Star and Tribune Company. He also recently was elected vice-president of the company Men's Club, and he serves as liaison man between the Personnel Department and various employee organizations and their activities.

Clark joined the Minneapolis Star and Tribune Company in 1949 in the maintenance department.

Carl T. Rowan

a roving editor of Reader's Digest magazine and a nationally syndicated columnist, was on the staff of The Minneapolis Tribune from 1948 to 1961. He first worked as a copy editor and, in 1950, was named a general assignment reporter.

Rowan wrote a number of prize-winning series as a reporter for The Tribune, including "How Far From Slavery?" which later was published in book form entitled "South of Freedom," and he extensively toured India and Asia during the 1950s.

In 1961, Rowan was appointed a deputy assistant secretary of state by President John F. Kennedy. Later he was named ambassador to Finland and, until 1965, was head of the United States Information Agency.

Mrs. Sandra Kelly

a 1959 graduate of Central High School, Minneapolis, has been a receptionist at the Minneapolis Star and Tribune Company since 1963, with time out to have a baby in 1966. She attended the University of Minnesota and worked part-time at the University of Minnesota hospital. Later she worked full time there until she joined the Star and Tribune Company.
Mrs. Kelly is a receptionist for the executive offices and news departments.

Carter Ellis

a classified advertising salesman for The Minneapolis Star and Tribune Company, was graduated from Central High School in Minneapolis in 1965, and attended West Virginia State University for two years.

Before joining the staff of the classified advertising department in March of 1968, Carter Ellis held several summer jobs while attending school.

He is 21 years old, is married and has one child. Mr. Ellis and his family live in Minneapolis.

IBM

Rita Dickson

is a Customer Service Dispatcher in Minneapolis for the Field Engineering Division of IBM. Her job involves receiving customers' phone calls, selecting the proper Customer Engineer based on the requirements of the job, and dispatching him to the customer's office by radio. Rita is a native of this area, attended college in Virginia, is married, and has one child.

Claude Thomas

is a Systems Engineer in the Data Processing Division of IBM in Minneapolis. His responsibility involves guiding his customer, a large bank, in making effective use of their IBM computers. Helping the customer decide what should be done and how to do it are important parts of his job. Claude has a BSEE and a Masters Degree in Physics, is married, and has two children.

Alta Jackson

is in the Accounts Receivables Section of the Minneapolis Office Products Division. Her work involves control of invoices, processing of employee records, collections, tax reports, and customer records. Alta's preparation for her position includes on-the-job training with IBM, preceded by attendance at the University of Minnesota and a special secretarial course co-sponsored by the Urban League.

114

Jim Betts
is a Systems Engineer in one of three Twin Cities Data Processing Branch Offices of IBM. He works with his customers in educating and assisting them in the use of computers. He previously held several other positions with IBM since his attendance at the University of Pittsburgh. Jim is active in community affairs, is married and has two children.

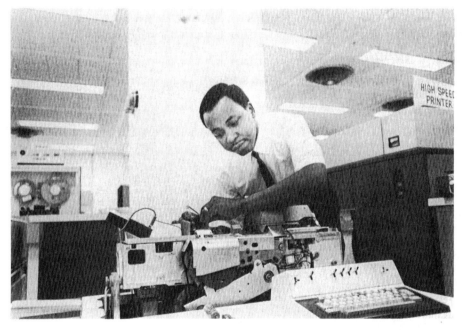

Mel Lawrence
is a Customer Engineer in the Minneapolis Field Engineering Branch. His duties involve the installation, improvement, preventive maintenance and emergency service of IBM machines. He was hired after attending a TCOIC Basic Electronics Class in Minneapolis. He recently completed an IBM training class in San Jose, California. Mel is married and has two children.

Phil Kemp
is Administration Manager in IBM's Minneapolis Branch of the Office Products Division. His responsibility is the effective management of the fifteen people on the local Office Products administrative staff. He received a B.A. degree from Lincoln University in Pennsylvania. Phil is married, has two children, and is very active in a variety of community affairs.

115

Julius Lee
Chef and Assistant Manager, Northstar Cafeteria. Responsible for all food preparation and serving. Supervises 15 people.

Lee Britton
Supervisor, Maintenance, Baker Block (4 buildings) Division. Supervises 14 people.

V.I.P.

Very Important People to Baker Properties Management Company

In the day-to-day management of top-flight buildings and customer services, Baker Properties must be staffed with capable people who maintain the highest possible standards. Mr. Britton, Mr. Jones and Mr. Lee are key men among Baker executives.

Harry Jones II
Supervisor of Night Maintenance, Marquette (4 buildings) Division. Supervises 35 people.

Mrs. Nelda Beasley
who is employed in our Central Records Department,
is one of the many capable people who make Twin City
Federal an efficient financial institution — an institution that
regards community growth and development as important
as its own growth and development.

AT NORTHWESTERN BANK, THE PHRASE

"Equal Opportunity Employer"

IS A MEANINGFUL ONE

Lower left:
Adrienne Ratliff, teller, checking over her cash supply with supervisor Harold Kennedy at the beginning of her day.

Lower right:
Rita Lyell, a computer section supervisor, counsels keypunch operator Carole Robertshaw in this highly technical area of the bank's operation.

Pictured upper right:
In the bank building law library is assistant vice president in Northwestern's legal division, Cornell Moore, a young attorney whose background includes experience with the U.S. Treasury Department.

KEN WALLACE
(left) is a Territory Technical Representative
covering the New England states for PAKO
CORPORATION and is currently stationed in
Wakefield, Massachusetts. PAKO markets
processing systems for the photographic,
motion picture, graphic arts and medical and
industrial x-ray industries.

Meet the Manager of our Payroll Department

This is Mrs. Joseph McFarland of 3838 Portland Avenue in Minneapolis. She's in charge of our payroll office, and it's up to her to keep things running smoothly and efficiently. She's just the one who can do it, too, because in addition to her thorough knowledge of payroll accounting operations at Dain, Kalman & Quail, Inc. (she started here in 1961), Mrs. McFarland also gained much valuable experience in this work in her previous position at the National Cash Register Company in Chicago.

Knowledgeable, experienced people are our most important assets at Dain, Kalman & Quail. *We provide these services: Investment Banking / Investment Management / Municipal Bonds / Mutual Funds / Listed and Unlisted Securities.*

DAIN, KALMAN & QUAIL
INCORPORATED
Investment Research With a Regional Accent
Member New York Stock Exchange
Minneapolis / St. Paul / Brookdale / Southdale / Rosedale

Lonnie Morgan, 720 Sixth Avenue S.E., Minneapolis, Public Relations Representative in F & M's Public Relations and Advertising Department working primarily in the area of community relations with emphasis on minority considerations, talks with his supervisor Robert E. Harris, Assistant Secretary and Director of Advertising

Carolyn Brewer of 1100 Oliver Avenue North, Minneapolis, a Senior Clerk in the Mortgage Servicing Division of F & M, is shown receiving information from Roger Larson, Mortgage Account, and her supervisor, Kenneth Kirchoff, Assistant Treasurer and Manager of the Mortgage Servicing Division.

Burie Carmichael, 4537 Portland Avenue S., Minneapolis, shown assisting an F & M depositor, works in the Administrative Services Department as a floorman with responsibilities of customer relations, information and general supervision of the main banking lobby.

Joyce Webb of 3244 Clinton Avenue S., Minneapolis, is a Stenographer in F & M's New Accounts Department. Vida Johnston, Secretary to the manager of the New Accounts Department, is shown working with her on the processing of an account while her supervisor Ronald Booth, Administrative Assistant, checks information.

Meet Jess Bell . . . Our Employment Counselor

One of Jess Bell's primary duties at Super Valu includes working
with the disadvantaged. Super Valu, through Jess, maintains
close working relationships with the Twin Cities Opportunity
Industrialization Center, The Minneapolis Urban League, and
The Concentrated Employment Service. We are a member of the
National Alliance of Businessmen and the local "Plans for Progress"
program. Jess is a graduate of the University of Pittsburgh.
He and his wife, Nancy, have two children and reside at
5011 Third Avenue South, Minneapolis.

Fariest Brown

Mr. Brown has been working as maintenance
engineer in Super Valu's manufacturing subsidiary,
Preferred Products, Inc., since 1962. He is
married, has two children and resides at
715 Queen Avenue North, Minneapolis.

SERVING MID-AMERICA'S
MOST SUCCESSFUL
INDEPENDENT RETAILERS

122

James R. Lawrence, 25, knows what it means to work under pressure. In the trading department of Piper, Jaffray & Hopwood, Incorporated, Minneapolis investment firm, his job requires split-second decisions often involving thousands of dollars.

Mr. Lawrence majored in English at the University of Minnesota and was a member of the Union Board of Governors. He recently married the former Margaret Brewin, a stewardess with Northwest Airlines.

He is continuing his training and education, both off and on the job, in order to advance his career in the field of finance.

Robert J. Adams
began work at Sears on March 26, 1962. For the past five and
one-half years he has been a salesman in the retail paint
department. In this photo Mr. Adams discussed the most
desirable selection of paint for a customer's needs.

124

Bill Johnson
joined Northern States Power Company's personnel
department in 1966. A wage and administration specialist,
Bill shares responsibility for efficient administration of NSP's
equitable pay policy.

Phyllis Hudson
is a key puncher in NSP's computer department. Assuring
correct customer billing is the task of Phyllis and
her associates.

Marv Crawford
supplementary electric heating and air conditioning
specialist, has been in sales at NSP since 1965. Marv began as
an appliance salesman and later moved up to specialize in
selling electric heat and cooling.

Minnegasco
MINNEAPOLIS GAS CO.

Sylvia Farmer
A graduate of St. Paul Central High School, Mrs. Farmer works in Minnegasco's Credit Department. Sylvia and her husband live at 1308 N. 69th Ave. She joined the company in 1967.

Ronald Wilson
A Minnegasco employee since 1963, Mr. Wilson handles Meter Reading assignments for the company. He has also worked in the company's gas distribution department. Ron and his family live at 1108 W. 90th St.

Gerald L. Bailey
a factory placement interviewer in Honeywell Inc.'s Minneapolis
personnel department, is shown discussing employment
possibilities at the firm's 15 Twin City plant locations. Bailey joined
Honeywell in 1952 as a materials handler, and has worked in
various capacities for the State's largest private employer
since then.

Donaldson's Discovered
Joseph Ferguson 22 years ago

Stationed in England and on the continent during World War II, Joseph won four campaign stars and participated in the Battle of the Bulge. After the war, instead of returning to his home state of Florida, he turned to Minneapolis (in his own words) "for employment opportunities."

On June 7, 1946, Mr. Ferguson joined Donaldson's as package collector, quickly moved to packer and supervisor in shipping, then to receiving and marketing. Because of his keen interest and his quick and dependable response to every challenge, he soon became assistant to the traffic manager, the assistant manager of the Distribution Center, . . . a complex assignment.

In April 1968, Mr. Ferguson became employment manager of Donaldson's . . . and a valuable and respected member of the management team of this 87 year old firm.

His activities in the community are many. Not only is he a member of the Research and Social Action Commission of the American Lutheran Church, an initiator of Project Summer Hope and a popular guest speaker . . . but he also serves as co-ordinator of the National Alliance of Business men and Plans for Progress in the hiring of disadvantaged persons.

Mr. Ferguson is now enrolled in the Minneapolis School of Business, continuing his education in general business law. His beautiful wife and six wonderful children join us at Donaldson's as proud, appreciative admirers of a man who has inspired many of us in the Twin Cities Community.

PROFESSIONS

Thirty years ago in Minneapolis, there was only one Negro professional person employed in the field of intergroup relations in Minneapolis. In recent years, especially after the Northside "incidents", more agencies have come into being and more people were added to existing agencies (but not necessarily as a result of the incidents).

Before the demonstrations of 1966 there was increasing concern on the part of government, church groups, schools and social agencies. The concern was to be translated to today's action programs which call for more staff, more money, and more active interest on the part of the white community. It is estimated that there are 4 Negroes employed in Minneapolis whose responsibilities are primarily those in Intergroup Relations. They are employed in the School System, church groups, group work at community organization agencies, government, and serve the Mayor in the areas needed.

Negro professionals whose job duties have no relationship to intergroup Relations, per se, are called on to serve on panels, present talks on the subject, and give direction to civil rights, oriented community groups. Locally, Negro leaders have been quite active in this second approach to the problem.

Syl Davis

Mr. Davis is the Director of The Way Opportunities Unlimited, Inc., a store front community center formed in 1966 after the outbreak of somewhat aggravated incidents involving Negro youths in the Northside Plymouth Avenue area. Located at 1913 Plymouth Avenue, it proposes to act in response to the desires of the Black Community in areas of youth recreation, employment, Afro-American history and other community action programs for improved housing and school problems. It is funded primarily by private donations.

Harry Davis

Mr. Harry Davis has long been active in inter-group relations in the Minneapolis community. He is currently the Director of the Urban Coalition, a group of outstanding community leaders of bi-racial makeup, with the aim of enlisting economic aid and direction to the various agencies working in social and economic problem areas of the community. He is also the chairman of MOER, Hennepin County Mobilization of Economic Resources. This latter is the local community-action agency required under the 1964 Economic Opportunity Act (the "War on Poverty" bill), to receive and administer anti-poverty funds from the OEO (Office of Economic Opportunity), and other federal funds. MOER consists of 33 elected residents of poverty areas, 14 public officials, three representatives of private welfare agencies, and 16 members at large, who include Negroes and American Indians.

Mr. Frank Kent and Reverend Battle in a discussion of some of the community's problems.

In 1958, there were 40 Negroes employed in the Minneapolis School System. Today there are about 200, including principals, assistant principals, counsellors, visiting teachers and social workers.

In the health field, Negroes are employed, or are in private practice, as nurses and nurse anesthetists, physical therapists, doctors, dentists, health inspectors, and pharmacists.

In the personnel field there are Negroes who are engaged in recruiting, interviewing, wage and compensation administrators. It is estimated that there are 15 employed in some phase of personnel work here.

L. Howard Bennett

Dr. Bennett, who now resides in Washington, D. C., was named Municipal Judge in Minneapolis, 1957 and 1958, the first Negro judge ever appointed in Minnesota. He was quite active locally in race relations and in politics (prior to his appointment). And, following a loss by election to this office he has been very active as a representative of this area's views, nationally, in the political scene.

This former Minneapolis jurist is now with the Defense Department in Washington, D. C. Mr. Bennett was graduated (cum laude honors) from Fisk University. He received his Doctor of Law degree at the University of Chicago, June, 1950. Mr. Bennett was consultant to agencies in Human Relations in nine key cities. He assisted in establishing Minneapolis Council on Human Relations.

Cecil Newman

Mr. Newman is a Twin City newspaper editor and civic leader who came to Minnesota in 1922. He rose from a bellhop and porter to being named as one of Minnesota's 100 "living great citizens" in 1949, and became the first Minnesota Negro to appear in Who's Who in America. He is the editor, publisher of Twin City Spokesman and in 1957 received the Annual Citation of Merit for his outstanding contributions in the field of journalism. He currently serves on several boards of first-line community service agencies including T.C.O.I.C., of which he is chairman, and is a member of the Board of Directors of Midwest Federal Savings and Loan here in Minneapolis. He has served on many advisory committees and has been very active with the Urban League and the N.A.A.C.P.

In the area of skilled labor, mechanical, electrical, and electronic engineers, computer programmers, servo-mechanism engineers, technical writers are some of the technical positions held by Negroes in Minneapolis.

A position as a management trainee can be the beginning of something worthwhile. Several local companies have employed Negro college graduates who were not business administration majors in college. Upon successful completion of the training program the trainees can aim to become managers of one of the companies in this area.

If Negroes were represented in management rolls in the same proportion they are found in the management age (35 to 54) labor force, there could be 500,000 extra managers by 1975, according to Labor Department national statistics. Only 2% (90,000) of the 4.4 million salaried male supervisors in the U.S. work force are Negroes: and it is predicted that the number of management age Negroes will rise 26% by 1975.

This does not necessarily mean that there will be 500,000 additional Negro supervisors by 1975 as more than half of them will not have completed high school. The Negro graduates tend to shy away from industry because until very recently, industry showed no interest in them. Some of the interested and qualified Negroes are going to experience rebuffs when they apply. But this is gradually changing.

Clyde Hatcher

Mr. Hatcher, President and Mr. Ronald Judy, Vice President (standing) are shown here discussing the national recruiting program of Balance Incorporated. The business was one of the first in the area here of enlistment and employment of minority group workers. Mr. Hatcher has been very active in local minority group affairs.

Mr. Theartrice Williams

Mr. Williams was appointed Executive Director of Phyllis Wheatley Community Center, October 1, 1965. The Phyllis Wheatley Community Center is located in a multi-racial, multi-religious urban renewal area with a public housing project representing the only housing now standing. The agency is active with a resident group that proposes to redevelop the area. Under Mr. Williams' leadership, the agency has undertaken a building program that will culminate in a School-Park-Community Center Complex partly financed from a neighborhood facilities grant from HUD. Mr. Williams, a graduate of the University of Minnesota, is married and has two children.

It is changing because of the growing shortage of qualified people, (there are laws and government contracts, and "the streets", not necessarily in that order), nor are they all applicable to each company undergoing a change.

What's being done to close the managerial gap? Negro executives, under a program sponsored by Plans for Progress, visit predominately Negro schools and universities to demonstrate to the students that there are opportunities in the industries.

Negro educators and administrators are less knowledgeable than their white counterparts about the exact nature of careers in industry. They are provided summer employment by companies so that because of this exposure, they can better counsel their students, and in some cases, revamp their curriculum. This is a summer program of the National Urban League.

Many companies employ Negro college students during the summer months preceding their last school year. In addition to an income, the student, not necessarily a business administration major, gets very beneficial experience. Should the company and student enjoy the engagement, "marriage" is the name of the game after graduation.

Every major corporation offers scholarships in some form. Virtually all predominately white colleges are actively recruiting Negroes and other minority groups; many offer full scholarships.

Ashby Gaskins

Ashby Gaskins hails from Moresson, Pennsylvania, a small steel and coal mining town southwest of Pittsburgh. He is a veteran of World War II, serving in a navy band which was stationed for some time at Wold-Chamberlain Field. After the war, Gaskins decided that Minnesota was for him.

He is a graduate of the University of Minnesota with a B.A. degree in Sociology and Psychology. After graduating, he joined the Minneapolis Urban League, first as a volunteer while in graduate school, then was appointed Industrial Secretary, acting Executive Director, and his latest post as Vocational Services Director.

Mr. Gaskins' major service to clients is local and national recruitment of minority-group professional people in small towns such as Sparta, Wisconsin; Bismarck, North Dakota, and Lincoln, Nebraska, to major cities — Chicago, Milwaukee, Detroit, St. Louis, New Orleans.

Skills acquired in years of experience in vocational counseling negotiation with business, industry and labor unions as a member of an Urban League staff are now being used to good advantage in private business by Ashby U. Gaskins, former Minneapolis Urban League staff member.

He is a member of the American Personnel and Guidance Association. He has served as president of the Twin City Vocational Guidance Association, president of Southside Social Workers; president, Industrial Secretaries Council, National Urban League; chairman of the Social Action Committee of the Minnesota Welfare Association and other professional groups in the area of counseling and career selection. He was the founder of the State Conference of Branches of NAACP. He is a member of the Society for the Advancement of Management and the Boule, a national fraternal organization. He is listed in Who's Who in the Upper Midwest and is affiliated with 12 civic groups both local and national. As a member of the Minnesota Committee for the Study of the Negro he assisted in the research and development of the book "The Negro in Minnesota" by Earl Spangler.

Business and Professions

Are the requirements realistic? Is a college degree truly necessary, or is industry caught up in hide-bound tradition? It is not suggested that standards be lowered, but rather that they be reevaluated. Unrealistic standards, including heavy reliance on test results, reduce the number of potential Negro managers, supervisors, etc. Do white people suffer the same fate? We are talking about the Managerial Gap. We recognize the cause — years of discrimination.

It is not suggested that standards should be lowered so that companies can be coerced into hiring incompetents. It is urged that a job be re-evaluated to determine whether a person who is highly specialized could be more productive if he is relieved of routine activity that could properly be performed by an intelligent, business-oriented Negro who shows good potential. This in effect is changing the standards, not lowering them.

Josie Johnson

One of the recognized leaders and voices of the Black Community, Mrs. Johnson has been and currently is a personification of the phrase, "Woman-on-the-Go." She is a housewife, mother, community leader, career woman, and socialite and has managed to do them all with equal fervor and accomplishment. She and her husband Charles Johnson arrived in Minneapolis from Houston, Texas in 1956. She had attended Fish University and received a B.A. in 1951. She had also done graduate work at Texas Southern U. She immediately began making her presence felt in this community, becoming the First President of the local Chapter of the National Council of Negro Women. She was also active in the Fair Housing Legislation Lobby in 1961 and contributed greatly to the passage of the present statute. She was named a member of Who's Who in Minnesota in 1964. She became a member of the Board of Directors of the League of Women Voters of the U. S. 1968, was named special assistant to the Mayor in Community Affairs (1967-68) and is currently Community Services Director for the Minneapolis Urban League.
Also as a volunteer she has been the director of the WTCN hour long program each week devoted to the Black Community (public affairs) in the area of Afro-American history, the program called "New Schools of Afro-American Thought." With all this she has three children, girls, ages 14, 12, and 10 and has a lovely home in Bloomington, Minnesota.

Frank C. Kent

Mr. Kent is a native of Los Angeles, California. He attended Los Angeles City College and later Los Angeles State College. In 1957 Mr. Kent spent two years in the United States Army serving as a lecturer for the United States information agency in Munich, Germany, and traveling behind the Iron Curtain into Czechoslovakia.
He is married to Carol J. Ervin of St. Paul, Minnesota. They have one daughter, Angela, age 6. Mr. Kent has an extensive background in service. He is Commissioner, State of Minnesota Department of Human Rights; member, Youthpower of Minnesota, Inc.; Trustee, Minneapolis Library Board; Chairman, Fifth Ward Republicans; board member of Minneapolis branch of N.A.A.C.P.; member, Public Relations Committee of the Minneapolis YMCA. He is also President of the Minnesota Sentinel Publishing Co., which publishes the Twin City Courier. He also is a member of the Alpha Phi Alpha Fraternity, Inc. He has been one of the outstanding spokesmen for the Negro community in its struggle for complete equality.

There will be continued "pressure" on all segments of our economic community to assure equal opportunity to all people. It is hoped that the same kind of "pressure" is applied to encourage Negroes and other minorities locally to prepare themselves for the opportunities of tomorrow, both here, and in the Nation.

Two of the oldest organizations in Minneapolis concerned about equality of opportunity are the Urban League and the National Association for the Advancement of Colored People.

The Urban League was formally established in the summer of 1925. Its function was to fight discrimination in industry, job development, research and public education. Its scope is much larger today and includes a housing program, youth incentives, and on-the-job training programs.

The Urban League is quite properly in the field of human rights, with social work (community organization) as its basic tool.

The Minneapolis NAACP Chapter was formed in .... (formed nationally in 1910). The NAACP approach to problem solving is legalistic in nature, raising the counts to change conditions: it proposes legislation to correct inequalities — to change legislation considered to be inadequate or unjust. The local branch is run by a board of directors and has no paid staff.

Another important agency is the Minneapolis Human Rights Department. Formed last year by combining the Fair Employment Practices commission, it uses the legal approach as well as the human rights through education the community by using mass media and city government directives.

Lillian Anthony

Miss Anthony is Director of the Minneapolis Department of Civil Rights, a department charged with the job of public education and community mobilization on civil rights matters. Her job is to enforce the city's new civil rights ordinance which bars discrimination in housing, employment, education, public accommodations, and public services. She and her department perform administrative functions for the 21-member Minneapolis Commission on Human Relations. This department replaced the Fair Employment Practices Commission and the Mayor's Human Relations Commission. Miss Anthony has been a militant in the open confrontation with the bigoted, planned status quo, stay in your place, members of the city's reactionary element. She is regarded as one of its most able spokesmen by the Black Community. The ordinance which she and her department enforces was voted upon and passed August 27, 1967. The Commission which she serves was sworn in April, 1968. Since then many complaints have been processed and investigated by Miss Anthony.

Professions, Legal

Minneapolis' many contributions to the legal world are well known, particularly those dealing with minority group problems. One of Minnesota's most important post war accomplishments which served as a model to the rest of the nation was the passage of the Fair Employment Practices Act (FEPA) and the setting up of the Fair Employment Practices Commission (FEPC). This law and the Councils of Human Relations were tremendously helpful in the whole area of race relations and economic gains made here by Negroes since 1945.

Gains have also been made which have indicated a growing faith in the appreciation of the Negro as a citizen. Some of these have been through appointments to various high positions, including L. Howard Bennett to the position of municipal judge in Minneapolis in 1957, and Hobart T. Mitchell to the Minneapolis Board of Realtors (1958). Recently

Stephen Lloyd Maxwell

Judge Maxwell was born January 12, 1921, St. Paul, Minnesota.

He is married to the former Betty V-M Rodney of Duluth, Minnesota. They have two children.

He is a veteran of World War 2, U. S. Coast Guard. Presently active as LCDR, U. S. Naval Reserve.

He attended St. Paul College of Law, BSL 1951, LLB 1953; University of Minnesota, post grad. 1946-47; Morehouse College, BA 1942 in accounting.

His legal career is as follows: Judge, Municipal Court, St. Paul, Minnesota, July 1, 1967 to present. Assistant Ramsey County Attorney, St. Paul, Minnesota, January 3 to July 1, 1967. Republican U. S. Congressional Candidate, August to November, 1967. Corporation Counsel, City of St. Paul, Minnesota, 1964 to August 9, 1966. Assistant Ramsey County Attorney, St. Paul, Minnesota, 1959 to 1964. Attorney in Private Practice of Law, 1953 to 1959. Special Agent Investigator, Office of Price Stabilization, 1951 to 1953. Accountant, St. Paul Municipal Auditorium, 1948 to 1951. Auditor, Bureau of Internal Revenue, 1948. Zone Deputy Collector, Bureau of Internal Revenue, 1945 to 1946.

He has been admitted to the bar of: State of Minnesota, 1953; State of Illinois, 1955. Federal District Court, Minnesota Division; Practice before U. S. Treasury Department; U. S. Armed Forces Certified Trial/Defense Counsel; Ramsey County Bar Association; Minnesota State Bar Association; Illinois State Bar Association.

Judge L. Howard Bennett

Shown at the brightest hour of his career, sworn in as Judge of the Municipal Court, Minneapolis, Minnesota.

there have been several such appointments. Still it must be concluded there is much to be done legally about segregation. It does continue not because of official intent necessarily but because of geographical and economical patterns. Thus most of the legal confrontation now is with housing bias and "closed door" realtors.

Earl Lewis

A former bookkeeper for one of the leading law firms in Minneapolis. He assumed that position upon graduation from the Minnesota School of Business. Earl is a native Minneapolitan and is married and the father of one child.

Joyce Hughes Smith

Joyce received the B.A. degree, magna cum laude, from Carleton College, Northfield, Minnesota, where she was elected to membership in Phi Beta Kappa. Recipient of a Fulbright Scholarship, she studied at the University of Madrid, Spain. The first Negro woman to be graduated from the University of Minnesota Law School, Mrs. Smith was awarded a John Hay Whitney Opportunity Fellowship. She received the J.D. degree, cum laude, and was elected to Order of the Coif. She was a member of the Editorial Board of the Minnesota Law Review and is currently listed in Outstanding Young Women of America. She is a member of the Board of Directors of the Minneapolis Urban League and the Board of Directors of the Twin City Institute for Talented Youth. Mrs. Smith served as law clerk to Federal District Judge Earl R. Larson and is now associated in the practice of law with the Minneapolis law firm of Howard, LeFevere, Lefler, Hamilton and Pearson, 2200 First National Bank Building.

Leroy Jackson

Mr. Jackson is presently a Minneapolis Assistant City Attorney performing legal work in the Civil Law area. He has been a life-long resident of the city, having attended Central H.S. and the University of Minnesota Law School. He is a Korean war veteran. He was quite active in sports, lettering in football, basketball and baseball, and as a sophomore he was the state novice flyweight Golden Gloves champion. He is married to Glenda Payne of Minneapolis and has one child, Terry.

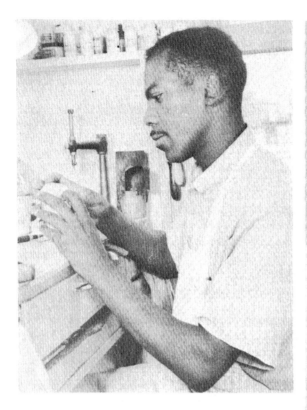

James Bryan

Mr. Bryan, a dental technician, native of Boston, Mass., has been acclaimed one of the top men in his field. Presently employed by the Brekhus Dental Laboratory. His main hobby is collecting jazz records, new and old, and he always in the summertime wants to know "What did the Red Sox (Boston) do?", while he is attending a (Twins) game. Jimmy and his two brothers Fred P. ? and Charles (Chick) are three of the most popular guys in Minneapolis — and they're from (Boston).

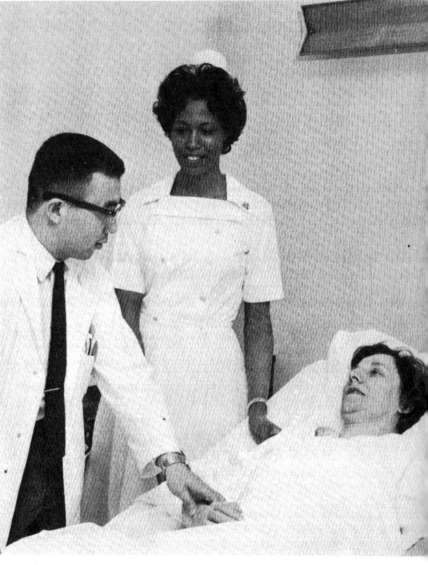

Beulah Jackson

Born in Gainesville, Florida, is a graduate of Columbus City Medical Center School of Nursing at Columbus, Georgia. After finishing her training, she worked as a staff nurse for the U. S. Army. She then came to Minneapolis and became an employee of St. Mary's Hospital before coming to Mount Sinai Hospital, where she now works as an R.N. in the Intensive Care Unit. When she's not busy nursing, Beulah likes to read and swim.

Antoinette Hughes Allen

Better known to her friends as Toni, is a Registered Nurse, presently engaged in public health nursing through her employment as an Epidemiological Research Fellow. Her work involves compiling of medical histories through patient interviews and record investigations the results of which are to be used for a health study.

Toni attended the University of Minnesota and then matriculated at St. Mary's School of Nursing, where she was elected President of the Junior Class and received the Outstanding Student Award. Toni transferred to the College of St. Catherine where she completed her nurses training and received the B.S. degree on May 27, 1967. A professional model, Toni's hobbies include ballet, modern dance, and sewing. She is married to Robert F. Allen and is the mother of Roxanne and Byran Allen. She is the daughter of Mrs. Bessie Hughes and Solomon Hughes, Minneapolis.

The medical professions have been traditionally in most Negro communities one of the principal economic areas of individual gain. Until recent times, the Negro doctors or dentists are usually included in the leadership list of any given community. However, as is in the case of Minneapolis, the size of the minority group does determine the number of individual practitioners in the community. It is true that the Negro doctor here does include among his patients many Whites, but it also is true that his success still depends, now as in the past, on his reputation in the Negro community.

Minnesota is famous, nationally as a great medical center, in medical schools, hospitals, research centers, and laboratory technical schools. And the Negro has for years been a participant in this greatness. However, most of the Negro graduates of this area go elsewhere to establish their practices. Medical treatment and care of the Negro patient here has usually been without racial barriers or incidents.

In addition to the M.D. and the Specialist, the Medical Technical field has become an ever-increasing opportunity for young Negro high school graduates. Many are being encouraged by their job counselors to enter these training schools. The jobs are there. It is a matter of training and being prepared.

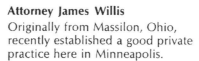

Attorney James Willis
Originally from Massilon, Ohio, recently established a good private practice here in Minneapolis.

Dr. B. Robert Lewis, Veterinarian
Dr. Lewis is a graduate of Kansas State University. He has a doctorate in veterinary medicine. Dr. Lewis practiced in Omaha, Neb., before coming to Minneapolis, Minnesota. He has an out-patient clinic located on Minnetonka Blvd., and a pet hospital in St. Louis Park.

He feels that pets should have check-ups just as people do. "This office is just like a doctor's office for people," he said. "If you need surgery or hospitalization for some other reason you go to a hospital."

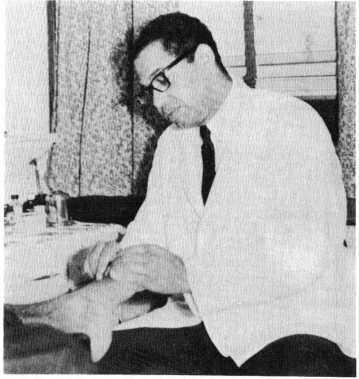

Dr. John Warren
This very busy doctor is shown with one of his many patients. He has been located in the same vicinity for a number of years. This popular medic is active in many social activities, as well as his professional area.

Bank the American Way

Pictured with fellow employees in the Instalment Loan Division of the American National Bank & Trust is Robert F. Allen, who is employed by the St. Paul bank as an Instalment Loan Interviewer. In our modern economic system, credit plays a very vital role, and it is the duty of Instalment Lending Personnel to make an extensive investigation and complete a discerning analysis of the willingness and the ability of a debtor to repay a proposed loan in accordance with its terms. Bob, who was born and raised in the Twin Cities, is a graduate of Minneapolis Central High School, the Minnesota School of Business and has an Associate of Arts Degree from the University of Minnesota. He is married to the former Toni Hughes, and they are the parents of two children.

Mrs. Louise Gooden is pictured, here, receiving a deposit from one of the many customers she greets and helps each day as a teller at the American. Teller work is a demanding and exacting job involving great detail and accuracy. Mrs. Gooden, a widow, was born and raised in Chicago and graduated from Du Sable High School. She moved to Minnesota in 1951. She lives in St. Paul with her three children Janeane, Debra and Royal, Jr.

The American
National Bank and Trust Company
7th & Robert   228-2345   Member FDIC

140

Clayton Hughes

Clayton Hughes received his education at the
University of Minnesota. After serving an apprenticeship
and six years' experience with Herbert B. Crommett,
Architect, St. Paul, Minnesota, he joined the firm of
Armstrong, Schlichting, Torseth and Skold, Inc.

He is chief draftsman, supervising the architectural
drafting section of a firm engaged in performing
all phases of architectural services for educational,
religious, commercial, recreational, industrial and
residential buildings. Recent projects include the
Minneapolis Southwest High School Addition, John F.
Kennedy High School located in Bloomington,
Minnesota and Hubert Olson Elementary and Junior
High School also in Bloomington, Minnesota.
He has designed several contemporary homes in
Wisconsin. He also designed the building that houses
the office of The Minneapolis Spokesman newspaper.

Gleason Glover

Mr. Glover resides at 902 Thomas Avenue. North,
Minneapolis, Minn. He is the Executive Director of
The Minneapolis Urban League. Mr. Glover is a
native of Newport News, Virginia. He is a graduate
of Huntington High School in Newport News, Virginia.
He attended Virginia State College for two years
before he enlisted for four and a half years in the
service. The majority of his service was spent in
Japan as a member of The United States Military
Advisory Group.

After receiving an honorable discharge from the
United States Air Force, Mr. Glover returned to college

later and received his B.A. Degree in Sociology in
June of 1961. He also attended graduate school at
Western Reserve University in Cleveland, Ohio.
He received a Masters Degree in Social Service
Administration in June of 1963 from Western Reserve
University.

He also held numerous state and local offices in
various college organizations and he was one of the
Student Leaders who played a prominent role in the
sit-in movements in Norfolk, Virginia, and he was
president of his college graduating class. Mr. Glover
is active in many organizations at the present.

Professions

The Negro Press has since its early beginning continued to be the chief agitator for Negro rights and dispenser of news concerning the Black Community. Early publications such as *The Appeal*, and the *Northwest Bulletin* did their part in the early 1900's. In 1924 they were supplanted by the *Twin City Star* (Minneapolis), the *Twin City Herald* (Minneapolis) and the *Minneapolis Spokesman*, still edited and published by Cecil Newman. Since then two others have emerged, the *T.C. Observer*, and the *Twin City Courier*. Outstanding service to the Negro news media has been given by journalists and writers, Mary Kyle, Jeannie Cooper, J. Q. Adams,

Charles S. Smith, Owen Howell, Cecil Newman, Curtis Chivers, Lillian Warren, and others.

Recently there have been several Negro authors locally who have written important books in the area of race relations for school study. One of these is Mrs. Sandrah Grevious, a school teacher, whose subject is teaching minority groups in schools. Several nationally known writers, columnists and lecturers in the area of civil rights have won their spurs in this community. Three bright names of which Minneapolis is justly proud are Sheldon B. Granger, Whitney Young, and Carl T. Rowan, all recognized leaders in the affairs of minority groups.

Jeanie Cooper

Mrs. Cooper is Editor-Publisher of the Twin City Observer and the St. Paul Sun Newspapers. The papers were started by her uncle, the late Milton Williams, in May of 1941. Since taking over the publishing company her duties and assignments are quite varied. She has made quite an impression on the merchants in the area and many are quite impressed with her business acumen. In addition to keeping busy with business responsibilities she is a busy homemaker. She is an avid reader and likes music and the theatre.

Carl Rowan

A truly outstanding author, and journalist, Mr. Rowan is the holder of two awards from Sigma Delta Chi, National Professional Journalism Fraternity, for distinguished service to Journalism.

Minneapolis Negro Profile Directors, Walter R. Scott, Sr., and Cecil Nelson, Jr., Publisher and Art Director, are shown in this photo going over the final phase of publication. We both feel that this venture has been a marvelous experience, because of the sincere efforts being put forward by the city's entire citizenry in bridging this vast social gap.

Mary J. Kyle (Mrs. Earle F. Kyle, Sr.)

Professional status: Managing editor-Associate publisher, TWIN CITIES COURIER (January 1967 to present); Business manager, staff writer, editorialist with another local Negro weekly from 1947 until December 1966; Free-lance writer prior to and during early part of journalism career (short stories, articles, verse published in national magazines).

Education: Elementary (parochial and public), secondary schools in Minneapolis; attended University of Minnesota; advanced writing through U of M Extension Division; Correspondence courses in writing at Croydon Institute, Illinois, Palmer Institute, California.

Civic Affiliations: Governor's Human Rights Commission (1962 until merger); Minneapolis Urban League, board member, former vice president; Minneapolis Branch NAACP, board member; Phyllis Wheatley Community Center, board member; Catholic Interracial Council, former board member; Children's Home Society of Minnesota, former board member; Service League of Hennepin County General Hospital, 1964-65 member; Mayor's Commission on Juvenile Delinquency, 1958-60; Minneapolis delegation, March on Washington, 1963; National "Women's Wednesdays in Mississippi" affiliate, 1965.

Curtis Chivers

Shown with Congressman Clark MacGregor (R. Minn.) is vice-president and advertising manager of the Spokesman-Recorder Publishing Company. He is a member of the Board of Trustees of the St. Peters A.M.E. Church, a post he held for more than 30 years.

Don Pryor

Mr. Pryor, very active in new challenging concepts in the solution of minority group problems, was the recent director of New Careers, a program to employ 207 low-income adults as aides to professionals in any one of nine social service agencies and to provide them education leading to an associate of arts degree from the University of Minnesota. Funded for $1,241,000 in 1967 by the Labor Department.

William E. English

joined 3M Company in July, 1963, as a sales correspondent in the 3M Company's Printing Products division. He became a sales trainee for that division in 1966 and was promoted to salesman in February, 1967.

Prior to joining 3M, English was a probation officer in Michigan, and from 1948 to 1963 worked for Group Health Mutual Company as a home office risk appraiser. He joined the Sabathani Community Center, Inc., 3805 3rd Av. S., incorporated in 1966 as an outgrowth of a Sabathani Baptist Church program started in 1964. Operates recreation, teen center, cultural enrichment, Afro-American heritage and educational assistance programs. Planning a day-care center, and senior citizen and street academy programs. Mr. English has a B.A. degree from Lincoln University, Jefferson City, Mo., and served in the U.S. Army two years.

Robert Watson,

general aviation operation inspector. Among his various duties are giving all types of flight tests for pilot certifications and ratings, investigating accidents and many other duties too numerous to mention.

Mr. Joseph O'Neal

Property Disposal Assistant in the Minneapolis Area Office of the Federal Aviation Administration. Mr. O'Neal is responsible for the disposal of excess personal and real property generated by Federal Aviation Administration Offices and facilities in the states of Minnesota, Montana, North Dakota, South Dakota, and Wisconsin. In performing his responsibilities to the FAA, Mr. O'Neal has contact and liaison with higher level management within the FAA and other governmental agencies.

Charles E. Mays

is Youth Field Director for the Great Plains Area (Region IV) of the NAACP.

Formerly a volunteer worker in the NAACP, Mr. Mays joined the staff in 1966 after having served as an executive committee member of the Minneapolis Branch, vice president of the Minnesota State Conference NAACP and chairman of the Youth Committee. He served as a Branch Field Director on the West Coast until joining the Youth and College Division staff in June, 1967.

Mr. Mays' community activities include service on the Board of Directors of the Minnesota Council for Civil and Human Rights, chairman of their Anti-Poverty Committee and chairman of the Joint Committee for Equal Opportunity. In addition, he worked with the Milwaukee Mayor's Committee on Human Rights and with the Neighborhood Job Corps.

A social worker by profession, his former employment includes YMCA Group Leader and Supervisor of the Commodity Program in the Minneapolis Relief Department.

Mr. Mays received his B.A. Degree from the University of Minnesota in Sociology and has served in the Armed Forces.

Barbara Sybil Mallory Cyrus

was born in Minneapolis and was graduated from Central High School. She attended Spelman College in Atlanta and the University of Minnesota. She is now employed by Control Data Corporation as a technical editor. Before joining the staff of Control Data, Barbara worked at Honeywell in a similar position. She has been employed by the State of Minnesota Industrial Commission as a labor investigator.

She has worked extensively with books, having been assistant childen's librarian at Sumner Branch Library, librarian at Phyllis Wheatley Settlement House and librarian at the Ordnance Branch of the Seattle Port of Embarkation. At Dayton's she worked in the business office of the book department.

On a part-time basis during school attendance she worked at the Minneapolis School of Art, Walker Art Center, Northrop Collegiate Academy and the University of Minnesota as a fashion and portrait model.

In the community civic life she has served as president of the Minneapolis Urban League Guild, board member of the Urban League, secretary of the State NAACP, chairman of the Twin City Book Club, Great Books Leader and as a member of the Speaker's Bureau of the United Fund. For four years she was secretary and news letter editor of the Society of Technical Writers and Publishers, a national professional society for the advancement of technical writing. Currently she is serving on the planning committee for "Black Voices" on KTCA-TV Educational Television station. Perhaps she is best known recently as the author of "etcetera" by Barbara Sybil, which appeared in the Twin City Observer and Saint Paul Sun. Mrs. Cyrus has contributed much of the information and history of Minneapolis in this publication through reesarch and personal knowledge as a member of the Black Community.

Richard C. Estes

Mortician, Estes Funeral Chapel, Inc., Minneapolis, Minnesota. Son of Mr. and Mrs. Ray Estes. Born February 5, 1929, in Baxter Springs, Kansas. Graduated from Baxter High School in 1948 and attended Kansas State Teachers College, Pittsburg, Kansas, for 3 years, seeking a B.A. degree. He entered the U.S. Marine Corps, serving in the Korean War and was honorably discharged in 1953. Mr. Estes graduated in 1956 from the College of Mortuary Science in Los Angeles, California. He served his apprenticeship under John M. Estes, Estes & Son Funeral Home, in Des Moines, Iowa. Mr. Estes, who comes from a long line of morticians, holds a license to practice mortuary science in the states of Iowa and Minnesota. The Estes Funeral Chapel, 1401 Plymouth Avenue No., was established on April 14, 1963.

Personnel Assistant

Curt Ewing is Personnel Assistant in Manpower Resources in the Regional office of the Postoffice Department. He has held his present position for one year. Mr. Ewing is a graduate of the U. of M. and the father of three children, and resides in North Minneapolis.

Mrs. Laura Grevious Gaskins

A Kentuckian by birth — daughter of a
Baptist Minister.

One of 10 children.

A.B. degree from Kentucky State College,
Frankfort, Kentucky.

Graduate work in Social Work from Atlanta
University School of Social Work.

First Negro student accepted in a private
Social agency for training in Kentucky.

First professionally trained Negro Social Worker
employed by Housing Authority in Kentucky.

First Negro Social Worker to hold office
in Social Workers Association in Kentucky.

First Negro Social Worker to be employed
by Hennepin County Welfare Department.

First Negro Supervisor employed by Hennepin
County Welfare Department.

Mrs. Gaskins has held the position of
Supervisor in the Child Service Division of
Hennepin County Welfare Department since
1947. She has appeared on television and
radio, and spoken to many civic and professional
groups in Minnesota. 1968 Summer school
lecturer at University of Minnesota
in Social Work.

She is a member of the following
organizations: The Academy of Certified Social
Workers • National Association of Social
Workers • Minnesota Adoption Council •
Minnesota Welfare Conference • National
Association for the Advancement of Colored
People • Urban League Guild • Board of
Directors of Planned Parenthood of Minneapolis
• President of Twin City Section of National
Council of Negro Women • Former member of
League of Women Voters of Minneapolis •
On Citizen Alert Advisory Board, Minneapolis
Chamber of Commerce • Member of Executive
Board of Directors of Minneapolis, Urban
Coalition • Alpha Kappa Alpha Sorority •
Women's Association of the
Minneapolis Symphony Orchestra.

Mrs. Gaskins is married to Mr. Ashby U.
Gaskins, Management Consultant,
4409 Third Avenue South, Minneapolis.

William S. Posten

Mr. Posten attended Augustana College, 1949
through 1951; attended the Minneapolis College
of Law, 1951 through 1953. He served in the
United States Army 1953 to 1955.

He attended the William Mitchell College
of Law, 1956 through 1959, and graduated
with an LL.B.

He worked for the United States Government
1960 through 1961, and became employed
with Hennepin County Attorney's office in
September 1961. He is currently in the
Hennepin County Attorney's office.

Professions

One of the strangest and most inexcusable phenomena in America today is the absence of Negro participation in the specific area of media advertising and graphic or visual arts. In an economy which depends, one national magazine recently estimated, upon a Negro purchasing power of almost 30% of the national gross, it is inexcusable that the Negro has had little or no say on how products are advertised or sold. This is true even when they are being advertised and sold to the *Negro community.*

Minneapolis, nationally regarded with identifiable leadership in educational, social, and political breakthroughs is yet just another city with typical failure in the use of or even encouragement of Negroes in advertising or visual communications. Most of the fault can be placed with the advertising agencies, many of them acting as public relations advisors and advertising directors for the major companies who themselves have already begun programs to include Negro professionals and management in their organizations. Unfortunately the ad agency seems to be the last to accept the Negro as a professional. There are approximately 145 ad agencies and counselors listed in Minneapolis. They are of varying sizes and gross billing serving the Upper Midwest. However, four of them are nationally ranked, servicing major companies and selling goods and products in all media to millions of Negroes throughout the country. As of the date of this publication none of them include Negroes as staff members or account directors, and only a few of them have ever employed trained Negro office

CONTINUED ON PAGE 150

A Successful Show of Negro Art and artists was held at the home of Mrs. Marion Williams by the local branch of the N.C.N.W. last year. In addition to local artists the show included several inmates in the state penitentiary who are being rehabilitated through creative workshops and show amazing skills in arts and crafts. Some hopefully forward to careers in the arts upon their release.

Cecil Dewey Nelson, Jr.

Mr. Nelson was born in Champaign, Illinois. He was a member of a pilot experimental intermediate grade school program of the University of Illinois. Received four full years of high school art training as well as two years of drafting in addition to college preparation curriculum. Graduated with National High School honors (Grade Average A—). Member Wig and Paint (Art) and Quill and Scroll (Journalism).

Following High School, worked as a Topographic Draftsman, Civilian Conservation Corps, Cook County (Chicago) Forestry Service (1938-1940), achieved Junior Rating of Topographic Draftsman (Civil Service).

Entered University of Illinois (1940-1942) College Fine and Applied Arts.

Worked with U.S. Coast and Geodetic Survey (Civil Service), Baltimore, Md. (also Office of War Information,

Bronze Tablet Scholastic Honors (1948), upper 2% of graduating class. (Degree B.A.).

Received additional Art training, summer studies with Fredrick Taubes, Dale Nichols, Jerry Farnsworth (Painters) accumulated hours toward M.A. degree — incomplete).

Commissioned by State of Illinois (under the sponsorship of the U.S. State Department) to paint a mural for the Freedom Train (on the history of Liberia) 1948. Received a letter of commendation from President Harry S Truman on this project.

As a painter he has in the past exhibited in many major national shows. His work is owned permanently by several galleries and collectors including the Atlanta University permanent Negro Painters' collection, which he won top honors for several years.

As a designer and illustrator he has worked for two

Washington, D.C.) 1942 as artist and Topographic Draftsman (Senior Rating) (War Department Work—Classified), also artist on National Defense Posters at beginning of the war. Received Cadet (Pilot Training Basic and Advanced U.S. Army Air Corps at Tuskegee, Ala. (1942-43), became an enlisted man (Sgt.) with Public Relations Division of that field. Created cartoon strip ("Private Taafu") for 3 years. Received "Stars and Stripes" award for this strip and letter of commendation for special work from the Air Corps Command, Art Director for G.I. show "Roger" 1945. Honorable discharge 1946.

Following service discharge became Art Director for "The Norfolk Journal and Guide," Negro newspaper, Norfolk, Va. (1946-1947). Did political and editorial cartoons and feature illustrations. Was a member of the Associated Negro Press.

Re-entered school (University of Illinois) and graduated with

newspapers, a nationally syndicated art service, four major art studios, two advertising agencies, and has owned his own studio in the past. He is presently art director with the local Merlin Krupp studios specializing in financial, banking and investment advertising and corporate design for local industries.

Organizations: Illinois Alumni Association, Kappa Alpha Psi Fraternity, Illustrators and Designers of Milwaukee, National Designers Council, Art Directors Club of Milwaukee.

Awards: Painting: Decatur Art Annual (Illinois) — 1940-1943-1946, Audubon — 1946-47, Atlanta Annual Negro Painters — 1943-1944-1948-1949, University of Illinois Contemporary American Painters — 1949-1950.

One Man Shows — 1964-1965 (Milwaukee).

Awards: Commercial: Milwaukee Art Directors Awards — 1957-1958-1960-1961-1963-1964, National Point of Purchase Award — 1963, National Art Directors Awards — 1962-1963.

personnel. The same can be said, with few exceptions, of the Publishing and Printing or Graphics industry. Several well trained and competent Negroes have attempted to cross the advertising color line in Minneapolis with very little success. Negroes trained in Public Relations have encountered the same barriers, with the same result.

In commercial and graphics arts the individual Negro can find some acceptance at a fixed level. But here too he has encountered the wall erected by the ad agency. The excuse offered has been the lack of trained, highly skilled Negro applicants but the same can be said for many white applicants who regularly find employment in advertising without these special skills.

In photography recently there has been a trend toward the use of Negro models. Most of this has been caused by the challenge of Eastern Negro militancy in the specific media of television. With few exceptions however, the Negro commercial photographer himself has been ignored by television and the agencies. The same can be said for the Negro artist, designer,

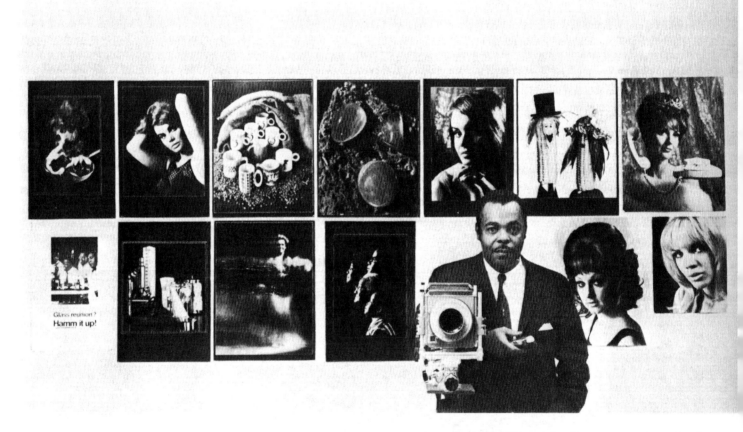

Gene McMiller

Gene McMiller, commercial creative photographer and owner of the McMiller studio located in downtown Minneapolis is an honor graduate of Brooks Institute of Photography, Santa Barbara, California. His career in this field has been varied and thoroughly professional. He served as a photographic supervisor in the military service. He is a former associate of the Merle Morris Photography Studio and the Bill Gale Studio, both outstanding locally owned firms. His work, commercial, fashions, and editorial has appeared in several national magazines.

He is a member of A.P.A. and MICPA professional photographers groups and has served as an advisor for many Black community projects including this book. A list of his clients include BBD & O Advertising Agency, Campbell Mithun Advertising Agency, McManus John and Adams Advertising Agency, First National Bank of Minneapolis, Apache Corporation, 3M Company, and the Dayton Company. His studio is responsible for most of the company endorsed pages in this publication, representing many long hours of painstaking, patient effort on location and in the darkroom.

Mr. McMiller's philosophy in the constant fight for professional recognition is "locate the problem, accept the assignment, pin point the solution and call on your professional training and experience to solve it." Any competitive profession such as advertising photography is fraught with problems, and challenges, for which there are no simple solutions. Each assignment has its own unique solution. To find it takes a sense of dedication which many times cannot be compensated for solely in terms of dollars and cents. Part of the compensation is pride in the finished product. And it is his feeling that this approach can be applied to any profession or job.

Gene is married to the former Constance Goss of St. Paul and they have two children. He is working with several local groups to try to find a solution to the use of the Black model in advertising in this area.

illustrator, commercial or painter. This has resulted in little or no encouragement to the talented young kids in the Black community to further train for a role in this very important industry.

The Negro artist has much to offer to the graphic arts. Given a fair chance to participate, he can do much to aid in understanding the unique problems of his community. To continue to overlook his skills is to ignore a valuable resource of culture in this land.

Below: One of two artists at the Federal Reserve Bank of Minneapolis, Kathleen (Kathy) Gilchrist does illustrations, charts, lettering, etc. Art is both a way of making a living and a hobby with Kathy. In her spare time she free lances in abstracts and portraits, and has modeled for

Pictured is Miss Ruth Jackson, engaged in one of the many complicated art assignments necessary in the preparation of Coast to Coast Stores' promotional material. On Miss Jackson's board is a photograph that must be modified prior to printing. Aside from being artistic and creative, the commercial artist must be well versed in the many production procedures.

Miss Jackson's work has proved to be a valuable contribution to the ever-growing volume of work in the Coast to Coast Stores' Art Department.

art classes. She attended the St. Paul School of Associated Arts, and has gone to night school at the University, St. Paul Vocational, Minneapolis Vocational, and the Minneapolis Institute of Arts.

Kathy lives in St. Paul with her two sons, Shaun and Jeffrey. Recent household additions are "a Doberman Pinscher dog and a Siamese cat that get along surprisingly well."

It is no longer true that insurance and finance are fields of low salaries. Banks and insurance companies are actively recruiting Negroes with or without training or experience, as are stock brokers and investment firms. Negro women are rapidly being accepted in jobs such as tellers, bookkeeping, clerk typists, etc. Recently two major banks plan new branches on the Northside and plan to have them staffed predominantly with Negro personnel, including the offices of President of the bank. Insurance companies also have become aware of the Negro potential, both as agents for the companies, and as hired personnel in the companies. However there *still* remains the use of Negroes in the area of Insurance.

John Warder

First Bank System has received from the Comptroller of the Currency in Washington preliminary approval of its application to establish First Plymouth National Bank, its proposed new affiliate to be located in a predominantly black community in the Plymouth Avenue area in Minneapolis.

Federal Reserve Board action on the application is pending.

John M. Warder has been selected to be president of the new bank. Pending final action by regulatory authorities, he has been elected assistant to the president of First Bank System, with administrative responsibility for organizing and planning the new bank.

A native of Paola, Kansas, Warder is a graduate of the University of Kansas, Lawrence, receiving a bachelor of arts degree in sociology in 1952. Prior to his graduation, he served with the Army and Air Force from 1946 through 1948.

In 1964, he was elected a member of the Minneapolis School Board and appointed Clerk in 1967. His community service includes board membership in the Greater Minneapolis Chamber of Commerce and the United Fund, member of the board of trustees of Children's Hospital of Minneapolis, Inc. He served as director of the Minneapolis Urban League from 1958 through 1962 and was first vice president of the league from 1962 through 1964. He is also an active member of the National Association for the Advancement of Colored People, Urban Coalition and Citizens Committee on Public Education.

In his recent business associations, he has been vice president of Litho Supply Depot, Inc.; active in the work of the Minneapolis Chapter of the Jaycees, serving as director and secretary; delegate to the Jaycee International World Congress in Tokyo, Japan, and secretary of the World Congress Committee.

First Bank System is a Minneapolis-based registered bank holding company which owns approximately 98 percent of the stock of 87 banks with locations in the states of Minnesota, Montana, North Dakota, South Dakota and Wisconsin.

MIDWEST FEDERAL

Believes in people . . . One example
of its practicing what it preaches
is the presence on its policy-making
Board of Directors of Cecil E.
Newman, a distinguished Minnesotan
of Negro ancestry.

"An equal opportunity employer"
it also daily demonstrates its
concern for the welfare and progress
of all segments of the common
population of our great nation.

HAROLD W. GREENWOOD, JR.

President

Cecil E. Newman
Midwest Federal Board Member. Editor and Publisher
Minneapolis Spokesman and St. Paul Recorder.
Mr. Newman's election in December 1967 was the first of its
kind among the 40,200 financial institutions in the U.S.

Interest and Involvement In the Entire Community

Jackie Gillotte
is co-hostess of "Jobs Now," a new concept in television programming aimed primarily at unskilled and unemployed persons. Also a successful model, Miss Gillotte assists in the presentation of actual job openings over the air on Jobs Now.

Dan Pothier
is a field interviewer for Jobs Now. He conducts filmed interviews with minority group employees to learn of their experiences in seeking employment and to examine the conditions under which they work. In addition, Dan is involved in human relations work as a staff member at The Way Community Center in Minneapolis.

Jobs Now has been developed with the assistance of such organizations as the State Department of Employment Security, the National Alliance of Businessmen and the Plans for Progress program. In addition, it enjoys the support of the office of Governor Harold LeVander, right.

"The company believes in the integrity of the individual. In support of this belief we need to find ways to help people to attain economic independence, to assume positions of responsibility and become contributing citizens."

— Judson Bemis, President
Bemis Company, Inc.

"I like a job that gives you an honest day's wages for an honest day's work."

Pat Connors
30, is a member of the Bemis Sales Development Division which has headquarters in Northeast Minneapolis. Working with customers and potential customers, Connors' job involves occasional travel — but whether he's in another city or working out of Minneapolis, he is busy helping to develop new products and new markets. A native of Willmar, Minn., Connors is a former high school teacher and policeman.

"I took the job because it offered exactly the kind of things I like to do."

Nolita Micheau
20, works as a secretary in the Bemis Company Personnel Department located in the Northstar Center in downtown Minneapolis. She also serves as artist for the company's monthly magazine — a job which offers her a chance to create illustrations and cover designs. Miss Micheau grew up in South Minneapolis and is a graduate of Washburn High School, the Minneapolis Business College and of a basic art course conducted through the Art Instruction School.

"I was interested in the summer intern program because eventually I plan to work in marketing auditing."

Clyde Wesley
22, spent summer '68 as an intern in the Bemis Company Intern Auditor Summer Program conducted in Minneapolis. A native of Talladega, Ala., Wesley was graduated from Talladega College in June, 1968. He learned of the Bemis program through his college placement office and will receive college credits for his work.

155

Janette Walker

A recent arrival in Minnesota, Mrs. Walker has been at Dayton's since May of this year. She is now assistant department manager in the Bra and Girdle department. Asked what attracted her to Dayton's, she replied, "Its dominance in the retailing field was important to me. And its fashion leadership. Dayton's also employs so many young people . . . the opportunities seem unlimited!"

Following graduation from Kansas State University, Mrs. Walker was employed by Macy's in Kansas City, Missouri, rising to the position of assistant buyer in the Infants' department.

During her leisure hours, Mrs. Walker also likes to fish; and both she and her husband, who is employed by Honeywell, are looking forward to the many sports activities that Minnesota offers.

Conrad (Connie) Balfour

Mr. Balfour is administrator of Dayton's Employment Opportunity Program which provides employment for members of disadvantaged groups. Previous to this, he was deputy director for Twin Cities Opportunities Industrialization Center, Inc.

Since the program began a little over a year ago, 90 disadvantaged persons have been placed in Dayton's stores. Asked about EOP's future potential, Mr. Balfour replied, "I evaluate the program in direct relationship to how I evaluate Dayton's. Dayton's has a concept that says, 'How do we upgrade ALL employees?' This high priority on human growth plus Dayton's own continuing economic growth should insure continued success for the Employment Opportunity Program."

Ralph Williams

Dayton's new Rosedale store is Ralph Williams' business address. There he holds the responsible position of sales manager for three important departments: Luggage, Cameras and Sporting Goods.

Mr. Williams joined Dayton's in April, 1968, as merchandise trainee in the Sporting Goods department, later becoming assistant buyer in Cameras. Previous to this, he was in sales and service with Prudential Insurance Company and also attended the University of Minnesota.

After working hours, you're likely to find Mr. Williams playing with his two youngsters, a six-year old girl and a two-year old boy. Or perhaps enjoying his favorite sport, fishing.

James D. Tucker

has been promoted to supervisor of recruiting and placement in the personnel and organization planning department of The Pillsbury Company.

Tucker joined Pillsbury in 1964 as a Minneapolis sales

Calvin G. Norris

Scientist, Industrial Research and Development. Mr. Norris received a B.S. in biochemistry (minor — organic chemistry) from the University of Minnesota in 1948; his field of study was science specialization.

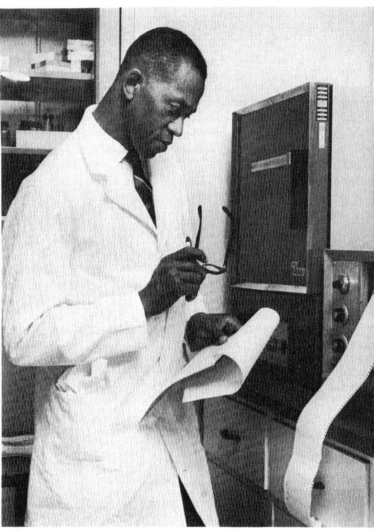

merchandiser for the grocery products division.

A graduate of Duquesne University, Pittsburgh, Pa., Tucker was named an All-American basketball player in 1952-54. He played professional basketball from 1954 to 1959 with Syracuse (now the Philadelphia 76ers) in the National Basketball Association, the Harlem Globetrotters and the Harlem Magicians.

Tucker was a social caseworker for the State of Pennsylvania from 1958 to 1960, and a groupworker at the Hallie Q. Brown Community House in St. Paul from 1960 to 1964.

In his new position he will handle the recruiting and placement of personnel for Pillsbury headquarters and other Minneapolis operations, and be assigned special recruiting efforts for field locations.

Tucker, a native of Rose Hill, Va., attended high school in Paris, Ky. He is the son of Mrs. Edward Fields of Paris.

He and his wife, Lyda Jo, have three children: James D. II, 12; Barbara Jo, 11; and Jon Maurice, 7. They live at 1587 East Grandview Ave., Maplewood.

Mr. Norris joined The Pillsbury Company in 1958 as a Research Baker and was responsible for the evaluation of the development of new milling products and of air classification of flours. He also served as a trouble shooter on flour problems and was directly involved in the solution of problems associated with consumer retailed flours. Mr. Norris was also directly involved in the development of Oriental food products made from cereal by-products and has completed extensive research on problems associated with pastas. His research on pouched breads includes the development of pouched bread and bread type products. Mr. Norris is presently a group leader for the development of a new bread type product. In addition, he is supporting the evaluation of a new milling process.

Publications by Mr. Norris include:

Cuendet, Larson, Norris and Geddes, "The Influence of Moisture Content and Other Factors on the Stability of Wheat Flours at 37.8° C.," *Cereal Chemistry* 31(5):362-389, 1954.

Madelyn Perrigan, Norris, Boyer and Geddes, "The Penetration of Urea and Orthophosphate into the Wheat Kernel," *Cereal Chemistry* 33(4):240-253, 1956.

Rezoe Gracza and Calvin Norris, "Flour Strength and Particle Size," *Baker's Digest* 35(3):56-64, 1961.

— The new home office of NWNL.

Robert C. Burton
top, second from left, an NWNL life insurance salesman
with the company's Minneapolis Agency since 1964, counsels
with one of his many policyowner families in the Twin City
area — the Warren H. Watsons of South Minneapolis.
Mr. Watson owns and operates the Crown Barber Shop at
38th and 4th Avenue South. NWNL Agent Burton wrote nearly
$1,000,000 of life and health insurance protection during 1967.

Barbara Washington
bottom, for four years an Executive Secretary in NWNL's
Advertising and Public Relations Department. Mrs.
Washington became an NWNL employee in 1960 following
her graduation from Minneapolis South High
where she was an outstanding student and member
of the National Honor Society.

Robert A. Murray
bottom, as a Mortgage Analyst for NWNL, studies plans
with Archie Givens, Sr., center, and his son Archie Givens, Jr.
for a $750,000 150-bed nursing home built by the Givens
and financed by NWNL in St. Paul. Negotiated by Mr. Murray,
who started with NWNL in 1950, this was the first loan
commitment by NWNL under its $3.5 million share of the
life insurance industry's $1 billion pledge to improve
city core areas throughout the U.S.

NORTHWESTERN NATIONAL
LIFE INSURANCE COMPANY
HOME OFFICE • MINNEAPOLIS, MINNESOTA

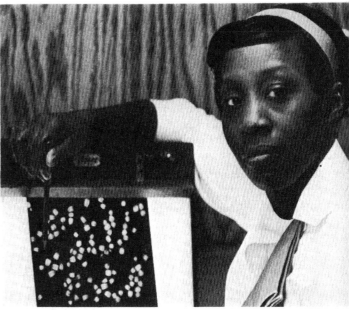

Margaret Sorrell
is a technician in the grain research laboratory of Cargill, Inc., Minneapolis. She is shown with an x-ray of kernels of corn.

Mrs. Sorrell is a native of Indiana and attended West Virginia State College and the University of Minnesota, where she is working toward a bachelor's degree.

Floyd Lee Henderson
is assistant librarian at the general research library of Cargill, Inc., Minneapolis. The photos show him at his job in the Cargill library.

Mr. Henderson is a native of Oklahoma, a graduate of Valparaiso University in Indiana, a two-year Army veteran and holder of a Master's Degree from the University of Minnesota.

Gloria Woods
is secretary to the personnel director of Cargill, Inc., Minneapolis.

Mrs. Woods was born in Kansas City and attended high school and Metropolitan Jr. College there. She is a Sunday school teacher and supporter of little league football, which her son plays.

The House of Craftsmen

Lucy Jenkins and Willie Brown
These ladies represent 43 years of employment at The Colwell Press, Inc. Working with our maintenance department, Mrs. Jenkins joined the firm in 1953 and Mrs. Brown has been with the Colwell organization since 1943.

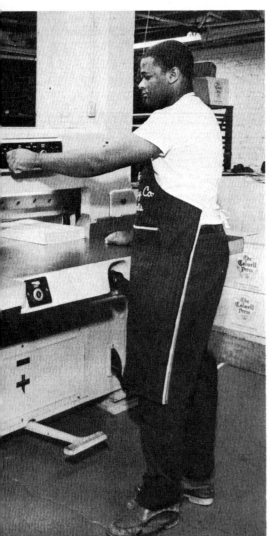

Ronald Hughes
The record for the longest term of service at "The Colwell Press, Inc." belongs to Ronald Hughes. Ronnie began his career with us in 1913 and retired as a driver in 1963 after 50 years. Currently working part time, he has extended his record of consecutive employment with one firm to 56 years.

Prince Tyler
Shown working on a cutter, Prince Tyler is now an apprentice at The Colwell Press, Inc. working toward his journeyman rating. Prince works with Colwell Color Cards, a division of the company which provides merchandising aids for the paint industry.

160

James P. Hughes

Mr. Hughes recently reached a five-year goal providing the saying that "hard work has a way of meeting opportunity."

Hughes received a journeyman-shopman electrical license after 8,000 hours of training and schooling.

He took advantage of Ford's upgrading program for employes. Starting as an electrician's helper in 1962, Hughes has been studying at home and learning on the job.

There are two main approaches to higher pay and skilled trades at Twin Cities. One is the method employed by Hughes. The other method is to apply and be accepted for training under the Twin Cities Apprenticeship Program. This program was started a little more than a year ago.

A Ford employe for more than 18 years, Hughes underscored two types of opportunities. There are opportunities that one watches passing by and opportunities that are grasped as they present themselves.

"Twin Cities has always made it a point to hire personnel on the basis of their qualifications and experience," explained Industrial Relations Manager R. G. Korpi,

"without regard to race, color or national origin."

Ford is a member of the President's Committee on Equal Opportunity and its "Plan for Progress."

Hughes and his family live in a modern rambler in Maplewood, a suburb of St. Paul.

Hughes says getting his electrician's license was a "team effort." He credits wife Myrtle wtih supplying the inspiration and test-cramming assistance.

His 13-year-old son James, Jr. lent encouragement and youthful enthusiasm. Young Hughes is proud of the way his dad showed determination in getting his skilled trades license.

Six-year-old Elizabeth (Lizzy) furnished a cheery smile and was a ready playmate when her dad wanted to take a 15-minute break away from his electrical books.

Hughes said he hopes young men will take advantage of today's opportunities that are being offered at Ford. "It takes many hours of study and hard work to reach a set goal but it is well worth the price one has to pay," Hughes emphasized with a look of intensity and self satisfaction.

Virginia De Bose

Virginia De Bose, passenger service agent, became a North Central employee in May 1968. She had been with the Wisconsin Telephone Company five years as an information operator, prior to joining the airline.

Miss De Bose, 24, is a graduate of West Division High School, Milwaukee, and attended the University of Wisconsin in that city for 1½ years.

As a passenger service agent, Miss De Bose is responsible for telephone sales, flight information and booking of reservations for North Central passengers.

Eugene Lumpkin

A lead cleaner in North Central's Minneapolis/St. Paul maintenance department, Eugene Lumpkin, 33, has been with the company nearly nine years.

He joined the airline in October 1960 as a cleaner at Chicago's O'Hare International Airport. The following year, Lumpkin transferred to Minneapolis/St. Paul and was then named lead cleaner.

His job requires the supervision of a twelve-man maintenance crew, working with cleaning chemicals, replacing seat covers and all interior upkeep of North Central's planes.

Brenda Moon

Stewardess Brenda Moon, 21, joined North Central in January 1969.

A 1966 graduate of Southeastern High School in her home town of Detroit, Miss Moon attended Ferris State College, the University of Michigan and Wayne State University before beginning her North Central stewardess training in Minneapolis/St.Paul. Miss Moon has also been employed as a secretary and with the Detroit Board of Education's Student Aid division.

Fourteen years ago Mr. Harold Stone came to Napco as a laborer. Since that time he has advanced from a class "B" assembler to a class "C" mechanic. From there, through Napco's training program in industrial relations, Mr. Stone became foreman of plant engineering. Supervising eight men, he insures the even flow of machine parts being processed in the machine shop.

Mr. Rodell Murrell came to Napco in November of 1964 as a material handler. Since then he has advanced to assistant foreman for shipping operations. Today he supervises 14 men in the proper packaging and labeling of military shipments.

 NAPCO INDUSTRIES, INC.

Dick Hall

(Above) Meet Richard D. Hall, a member of the management team at Great Northern Railway. A career railroader with 28 years' experience at GN, Mr. Hall is Manager of Dining and Buffet Cars. Active in political and community affairs, Dick, a Minneapolis resident, has served as commissioner of the Minneapolis Park Board for four years.

Great Northern long has been a leader in providing meaningful employment for minority members of the Twin Cities society. This leadership is exemplified today by the railway's commitments to equal employment opportunity action programs and by its involvement in hiring programs sponsored by the National Alliance of Businessmen and the Twin Cities Opportunities Industrialization Center.

A major employer in the Minneapolis-St. Paul area, Great Northern offers job opportunities in a variety of crafts. Non-technical trained Negroes have found gainful employment on the railway as stewards and waiters in dining cars service, and as clerks, shop laborers, freight handlers and messengers. Others with technical backgrounds or special training are computer programmers, secretaries and keypunchers.

GN representatives regularly visit some 35 colleges throughout the nation to interview senior students and interest them in career positions with the railway. Collegians are recruited without regard to color or race. Upon graduating, those hired are enrolled in a corporate management training program. Future company leaders are drawn from the trainee ranks and all advancements are based entirely on personal qualifications and ability.

GREAT NORTHERN

Eugene Moore talks with Mr. and Mrs. Leland R. Schultz about a plan
for their financial future. As an IDS representative of the St. Paul Division,
Mr. Moore helps people set up plans to attain their financial goals.

Martin Lewis is an Associate Counsel of IDS, a member of a legal staff of
15. Mr. Lewis handles a variety of legal matters pertaining to transactions
with customers, direct purchase of securities, and relationships with
the IDS sales organization, among others.

As an important national company based in the Twin Cities, we're
glad to introduce you to these men carrying out vital functions for the
Company.

Mr. Moore's responsible sales position gives us contact with the
public, a function he carries out with great credit both to the Company
and the industry. Mr. Lewis' position in the legal department
also makes him an important representative of IDS in legal contacts
with other organizations and with customers.

With others in the IDS organization, their efforts help conduct the
business of the largest investment company organization of its kind in
the world.

now in our 75th year

INVESTORS DIVERSIFIED SERVICES
733 Marquette, Minneapolis, Minnesota 55402

165

Fredric B. Herndon
24, joined Northwest Airlines as a Transportation Agent in 1965. He is a graduate of Minneapolis Central High School and attended the University of Minnesota.

Boyd M. Francisco
39, has been a mechanic for NWA for more than 10 years. He is a graduate of Nehawka High School, Nehawka, Nebraska, and was in the U.S. Air Force for seven years before joining Northwest.

Mrs. Leslie L. Morrow
has been with NWA as a Reservations Sales Agent since April, 1967. She is a graduate of Minneapolis Central High School and attended Mankato State College.

Irene K. Gardner
St. Paul, Minnesota joined Northwest on August 24, 1966. She completed Northwest's stewardess training and is currently serving the airline on Domestic flights.

Northwest serves 36 U.S. cities, from New York to Seattle, and from Miami to Minneapolis. Miss Gardner has served on flights reaching many of the destinations served by the airline.

EDUCATION

Education

Thomas Jefferson, author of the Declaration of Independence and third president of the United States, said that "Democracy presupposes an educated electorate." Accordingly, we should not be surprised if slum dwellers do not exercise their citizenship responsibly. Nor should we be surprised if our democracy is weakened because some citizens cannot make it work.

The schools are crucial to any positive solution to the problems of the ghetto. A good education is the key to getting a good job, to good citizenship, and to being a generally useful person. Yet the slum schools graduate thousands of functional illiterates each year. Thousands more are expelled from school or drop out, taking their place in the self-perpetuating misery of poverty.

The Minneapolis Public School System as a whole is changing its approach to education of the disadvantaged. The racially imbalanced school, and the

concept of the neighborhood school are targets of a far-reaching program that may eventually see all children gathered in a few central locations.

Minneapolis educators feel that prejudices are established by the time a child completes the eighth grade. The white child who attends an all white grade school comes to a racially mixed high school without any accurate knowledge of Negroes. The same can be said of Negroes who have had little contact with whites. Instead of learning to cooperate, the two groups learn to hate, basing their knowledge of the opposite group on the myths and generalities of the street.

Teachers in ghetto schools are fighting against almost insurmountable odds. They were not prepared in college to teach youngsters with so many problems. Some quit. Their patience runs out. Some become frightened, others dispirited. They become custodians or disciplinarians with no effective ways of disciplining.

Hard at work — These Lincoln Junior High School students are hard at work preparing for a mid-term quiz.

If for some reason they cannot escape, they stay on and on in the ghetto school, developing an ability for self-preservation, but not for teaching.

For these reasons Minneapolis public school officials feel that the traditional concept of the neighborhood school must be altered to erase *de facto* segregation. They urge a policy that no school should have a greater percentage of students of one race than the percentage of that race to the whole population. The balance in Minneapolis is about nine white to one non-white. However, twenty-five of the city's one hundred schools educated ninety-one per cent of the city's non-white population.

Now elementary schools with more than twenty per cent non-white enrollment are classed as imbalanced. School district boundaries are being reviewed each year and changed to include more students from all economic classes and races. Students may transfer to any school in the city at their parents' request.

The goal of centrally located schools that will mix students of all classes is a long way off. The costs will be enormous. In the meantime, Minneapolis educators are trying to get more qualified and sensitive teachers. The teacher's race is not as important as his dedication and understanding of the economic and racial problems to be faced in the inner-city school.

As inducements for teachers assigned to the inner-city school, the school system offers employment on a year round basis and workshops to help them with their problems. A team of experts — sociologists, psychologists, doctors, and administrators — stands ready to help with difficult children.

One of the most important education changes taking place is in the curriculum. Teachers have found that textbooks written for and about middle class children mean very little to disadvantaged children. Dick and Jane, living in the suburbs behind a white picket fence, have little in common with ghetto

Earl W. Bowman, Jr.

Mr. Bowman was born in Minneapolis 41 years ago. He attended Warrington, Bryant Junior High and Central High Schools in Minneapolis. Graduated in January, 1945. He was an outstanding athlete, participating in football, basketball and track. He attended Macalester College in St. Paul. Graduated in 1950. He participated in the same three sports as in high school; played guard in football. He was All-Conference football player for three years. He served in the U. S. Cavalry for 1½ years. His career has been as follows: Played semi-professional football from 1950 to 1953. Worked for the Phyllis Wheatley House from 1952 to 1955. Worked at Central as teacher and coach from 1955 to 1968. Worked at Lincoln Junior High School as Special Assistant to the Principal from January, 1968 to June, 1968. Appointed Coordinating Principal of the Hay-Lincoln Concentrated Education Center, September, 1968. He is married and has two children.

Charles F. Nichols, Sr.

Mr. Nichols is in his third year as principal-director of the Minneapolis Public Schools' Work Opportunity Center, a vocationally-oriented school in the Minneapolis public schools. He came there following two years as assistant principal at North High School in Minneapolis which followed a similar assignment at Bryant Junior High.

Before his secondary experience, he spent three years as an assistant instructor at the University of Minnesota's College of Agricultural Engineering with emphasis on farm school programs and agricultural education.

He received his B.S. (Industrial Arts) in 1948 and his M.A. (Industrial Arts) in 1956 — receiving his administrative certificate in 1957 at the University of Minnesota.

He is currently secretary of the University of Minnesota chapter of Phi Delta Kappa Professional Education Fraternity.

Education

children. So new texts are being written about racially mixed groups living in situations these children can understand. Minneapolis and a number of other cities are starting to use such texts.

To reinforce the Negro's importance to our society, Minneapolis has declared Martin Luther King's birthday a school holiday. Students can also take a day off on May 20, "Black Hero's Day."

Minority groups —notably Negroes and Indians — have largely been ignored by writers of history and social studies texts. Educators feel that this is damaging to the children of these groups. It deprives them of a sense of identity, which is important to mental health. Now Minneapolis schools offer an elective class in minority history.

In Minnesota history, segregation in education has followed much the same pattern as suffrage. Once it was abolished by legal action in 1869, there has been no major effort to change or revise the law. It is true,

however, that Negroes have not always been accepted willingly into all public schools of the state. Recent events and explorations into the solution of the problem of disproportionate enrollment and matriculation of minority students, such as "Busing," a technique of distributing students equally regardless of their residential location, have met with typical reaction and limited success. The use of Negro teachers in predominantly white schools is another. The latter has met with a little more success. In short, however, there still remains *much* to be done in all of these areas before a gold star of complete equality can be placed after the name, Minnesota. Although this book proposes to show the extent of progress made by the Negro in the specific area of Minneapolis, it does not contend that "all is well" as witnessed by the recent incidents arising from long endured racial inequities on the North side of this city.

Thomas L. Jackson

Mr. Jackson is the Administrative Assistant (Assistant Principal) of Marshall-University High School. He has a B.S. Degree, Major in History, Minor in English, from Southern Illinois University, Carbondale, Ill., 1951; M.A. Degree, Educational Psychology (Counseling and Guidance), University of Minnesota, Minneapolis, Minn., 1959; M.A.P.A. (Masters of Arts in Public Administration), University of Minnesota, 1967.

His honors include: V. A. Center Employee of the Year, 1966, Ft. Snelling, St. Paul. Outstanding Air Force Reserve Airman of the Year, 1965, 934 Troop Carrier Wing, Milwaukee, Wis. Reserve Captain Commission. Bush Management Scholar, 1966-67.

Melvin West

Mr. West graduated from the Jefferson City, Mo., Senior High School in 1957. He received a four athletic scholarship (football) to the University of Missouri. The Missouri Tigers were selected for the Orange Bowl two years in a row. He was selected as the outstanding player of the '61 Orange Bowl.

He graduated from the University in June of 1961 with a B.S. in Education. After college he played two years of professional football until a knee injury forced his retirement. He returned to Missouri U to begin work on his master's. In September of 1963 and in the spring of 1964 he traveled to Minnesota and began working with emotionally disturbed children as Head of Recreation for the Minnesota Residential Treatment Center.

In 1967 he joined the Minneapolis Public School System and at present he is an assistant to the Principal of Bryant Junior High School in Minneapolis.

John M. Taborn

Mr. Taborn was born in Carrier Mills, Illinois. He received a B.S. degree from Southern Illinois University and a Master' degree from the University of Illinois. He is currently a Ph.D. candidate in Educational Psychology at the University of Minnesota.

He was recently the project director for the Adult Basic Education Project for Minneapolis Public Schools. Currently he is serving an internship in Community Involvement for the Public School System, concerned with planning the new North Community High School.

Mrs. Joyce T. Jackson

Mrs. Jackson was appointed Assistant Director of Personnel by the Board of Education.

Mrs. Jackson, who has been on study leave from the Schools for the past two years, is completing her requirements for the Ph.D. Degree at the University of Minnesota, with emphases on Counseling and Special Education. She holds the B.A. and M.S. Degrees from Southern Illinois University.

She came to the Minneapolis Schools in September, 1952, to teach classes in Special Education at the Hay Elementary School. Since that time she taught Special Education at Harrison School, taught English and Spanish at Central High, was part-time counselor at Central; and was full-time counselor from 1962 to 1966. She is qualified as a certified psychologist.

Active in community affairs, she is a member of the Golden Valley Human Relations Committee; and Secretary and member of the Board of Directors of the Minneapolis Urban League. In 1966 she was included among the Who's Who of American Women, and in 1967 was included in the National Register of Who's Who.

Mrs. Rozmond Kennon

Mrs. Kennon, the wife of an outstanding Physical Therapist, is shown here going about her daily chores at Breck School. She teaches in a predominantly white school and has found this no handicap, at least as far as her young students are concerned.

Schools

Clifton E. Davis

Mr. Davis received his B.S. degree from Kentucky State College, Frankfort, Kentucky, and his M.A. from Bowling Green State University in Ohio with a major in Speech Pathology. He entered Syracuse University with a three year Vocational Rehabilitation Act Fellowship to study toward his Ph.D. With the course work completed, he accepted the position of Coordinator of Speech Therapy for the Minneapolis Public Schools. He is a member of American Speech and Hearing Association, Minnesota Administrators of Special Education Council for Exceptional Children.

Clarence H. Bledsoe

Mr. Bledsoe was born in Chicago, Illinois. After high school he enrolled at Roosevelt University where he received his undergraduate and graduate degrees.

In 1964 he resigned from the Chicago Public Schools and became a sixth grade teacher at John Hay School.

While on the staff of John Hay, Mr. Bledsoe and other members of the staff developed a supplement to the Minneapolis curriculum on the contribution of Blacks to the American way of life along with a bibliography. This study received state and national recognition.

In August of 1968 he was appointed principal of Emerson Elementary School near downtown Minneapolis.

Anna Lou Blevins

Miss Blevins is the curriculum assistant in the Hay-Lincoln Educational Complex and a curriculum planner for the Minneapolis Public Schools Human Relations Center dedicated to the improvement of communication, understanding and education. The Human Relations Center provides leadership in connection with school and community groups. Twenty-four community advisors have been selected for this purpose. During its second year, work will be concentrated in 25 schools which serve 28% of all students and 85% of all minority group students in the Minneapolis Public Schools.

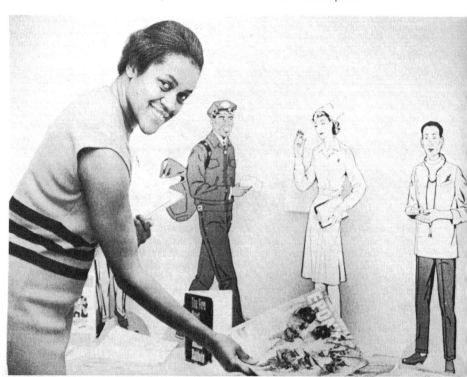

Rufus O. Webster

Mr. Webster is the Assistant Director of Urban Affairs. His education is: Sumner High School, St. Louis, Mo.; University of Minnesota (B.S. degree); University of Minnesota (M.A. degree). He has been a professional musician with many name groups with world travel experience. Social Studies teacher 17 years: C. C. Hubbard High School, Sedalia, Mo., 2 years; St. Francis High School, St. Francis, Minn., 2 years; Jordan Junior High School, Minneapolis, 5 years; Roosevelt High School, Minneapolis, 8 years.

Mrs. Hallie B. Hendrieth

Mrs. Hendrieth is a graduate of Selma University and Alabama State College. She has taught at Selma University and served as Dean of Girls at Southern Normal School at Brewton, Alabama.

Mrs. Hendrieth has studied at the University of Minnesota and is currently enrolled in the graduate program at Mankato State College.

She is very active in religious circles working by the side of her minister husband Rev. Marlin J. Hendrieth who is pastor of Wayman A.M.E. Church, 1221 7th Avenue North, Minneapolis.

Mr. Lowery Johnson

Mr. Johnson was born in Minneapolis and attended Warrington, Bryant and Central High School. He attended Macalester College. Graduated 1950. He served in the Armed Forces 1½ years, and played in semi-pro football from 1950 to 1953.

He worked for Phyllis Wheatley, 1952 to 1955 (teacher and coach); Central High (teacher and coach), 1955 to 1968; Lincoln Junior High (special assistant to principal); and is presently Coordinating Principal (Hay-Lincoln Concentrated Education Center) since September, 1968.

Matsolonia A. Pullens

Mrs. Pullens is a product of the Omaha Public School, Omaha, Nebraska (elementary and high school). She received a B.S. degree from University of Omaha and an M.S. degree from the University of Nebraska at Omaha.

She has gained all of her teaching experience in the Minneapolis Public Schools, was assistant Principal in Minneapolis Public Schools and is principal at Marcy Elementary School.

173

Mr. Harvey Rucker

Mr. Rucker was born in Chillicothe, Mo., and attended Drake University at Des Moines, Iowa. He took a B.A. degree in sociology and worked on an M.A. in Guidance Counseling there and attended the U. of M. graduate school in Ed. Adm. He joined the Minneapolis Schools in 1963 at Lincoln Jr. H. S., teaching civics. He became Asst. Principal at this school after a nine month interim as Neighborhood Youth Corps Coordinator at Central H. S. He is married with two children.

Below — An ever-helpful kindergarten teacher and a future Minnesota Twin.

Marvin Trammel

A native of Kansas City, Kansas, he received both his B.S. and M.S. degrees from Kansas University. His teaching experience includes three years as an English teacher in Kansas City, Kansas, and three years as a teacher and debate coach at Edison High in Minneapolis.

Currently he is an Assistant Principal at North High, chairman of the Minneapolis Public Schools AAAE Steering Committee, and a member of the Superintendent's Forum.

He is married, and has three children.

The Park Avenue School — Students learn in their "Talking Typewriter" class.

Wilbur K. Lewis

Mr. Lewis was born in Oxford, Ohio, and graduated from Miami University in 1951. He was elected to Epsilon Pi Tau and Kappa Phi Kappa. He joined the city system in 1954 at Marshall High. He entered graduate school at Minnesota, completing the specialist program in educational administration. He was appointed assistant principal at Roosevelt High on February 1, 1968. Served in the U. S. Marine Corps during the Second World War (January, 1943-March, 1946). Is a member of Minn. and Amer. Vocational Assoc., Amer. and Minn. Ind. Arts Assoc., Amer. Fed. of Teachers.

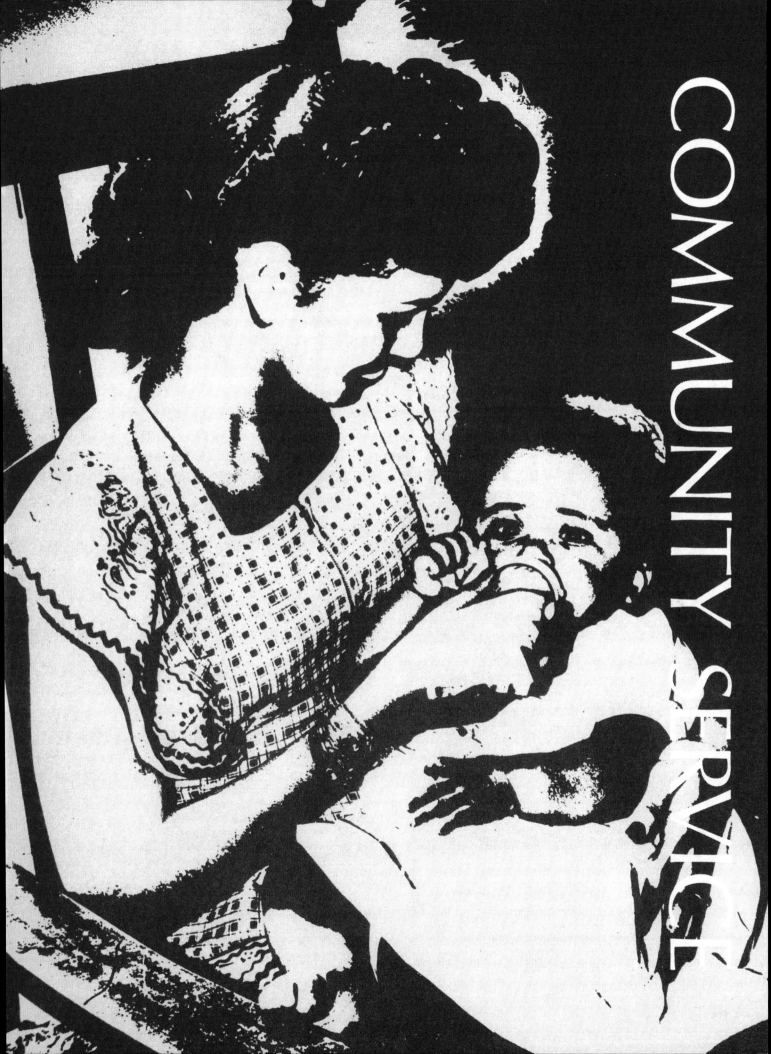

COMMUNITY SERVICE

Community Services

An article in the *Minneapolis Tribune* appeared April 21st of last year under the heading "City's Social Services: Who Does What for Whom?" The article, a full page, begins by noting, "A tangle of agencies and programs concerned with poverty and race confronts Minneapolis area residents. So complex are the government programs alone that Mayor Arthur Naftalin has proposed and the City Council is considering an assistant city coordinator to help synchronize their planning and efforts."

With just a casual look at the partial list of principal public and private agencies now functioning one cannot help but be impressed positively. The city and county has provided us with this partial list:

Public Agencies: Youth Opportunity Center (Funding Federal), Minneapolis Dept. of Civil Rights (Funding City Council) headed by Miss Lillian Anthony, Model Neighborhood Project (Funding, Dept. of Housing and Urban Development).

War on Poverty Programs: Hennepin County M.O.E.R., Mobilization of Economic Resources (Funding O.E.O. and Federal), Office of Economic Opportunities (Funding Federal), Director, Edgar D. Pillow. Citizens Community Centers CCC, four centers with O.E.O. Funding. Legal Aid Program, using five lawyers at Juvenile Court, Pilot City Center (Funding local and Federal). Director is James Mosley. Parent Child Development Center (O.E.O. grant Funding) and T.C.O.I.C., discussed elsewhere in this section.

Private Agencies: Minneapolis Urban Coalition, headed by Black and White leaders of the community funded by individual businesses in the community (some of whom appear as sponsors in this book). National Alliance of Businessmen, Mpls. Chapter with J.O.B.S. as a local and national program (also privately funded), Plans for Progress M.E.V.P. (funded by dues from employer members).

Reggie Commodore
Mr. Commodore is a Hennepin County Deputy Sheriff and has been in law enforcement since 1966.

Kymphus R. Workcuff
Minneapolis police officer since September, 1964; started work as a park policeman. He and his wife Shirley participate in various civic functions. The Minneapolis Police Department feels that Officer Workcuff is a very competent and personable policeman. He has been assigned to the Juvenile division as a liaison man at Central High School.

Mildred Alston
Appointed July 5, 1966; birth date May 25, 1928. Works in Bureau of Records, very congenial and a very good worker

Private Agencies Minority Oriented: Minneapolis Urban League (United Fund), Pres. Luther Prince, Director, Gleason Glover. Phyllis Wheatley House, Recreational and Educational, Director, Theatrice Williams. The Way Opportunities Unlimited Inc., a storefront community center on the Northside, Director is Syl Davis and the N.A.A.C.P., director is Charles Mays. Funded by dues and membership donations, the truly outstanding established and productive agency in the area of legal rights.

There are others too numerous to mention. With such an impressive list of titles, people and funds it is *surprising* that there is a single social problem left to be solved! However the best laid plans of mice or men do go astray. And Minneapolis still has giant problems of intergroup relations with as yet no visible

Walter A. Rhodes
Appointed January 1, 1948; retired August 5, 1968; birth date April 22, 1916. Wife Gloria. Worked in the Bureau of Identification classifying fingerprints, records and taking pictures.

John Hartsfield
Mr. Hartsfield has given sincere devotion to duty in the Sheriff's office. This approach to law enforcement along with his personal concern has won him many friends in the community.

Purcell Jackson
Mr. Jackson, also a deputy sheriff for the county, is the father of three. His daughter, Ruth, is listed as a staff member of this book.

Eugene Robinson
A native Minneapolitan who graduated from Central H. S., Mr. Robinson, a deputy sheriff, is active in St. James AME church work.

William Wade
Bill, a deputy in the County Municipal Court, is quite active in the Masonic order, and has held many high offices.

solution. Whether it is "integration" or "separation," "amalgamation" or "isolation" the respect between men *must prevail* if there is ever to be a solution acceptable to Blacks and whites alike.

The process of "tokenism" or the "instant-Negro" is simply not acceptable to the Black community and does not *really* serve the white community.

A Negro heads the Human Rights Commission of the State, another recently resigned the important position of assistant to the Attorney General to return to private practice, and a Negro judge occupies the Ramsey County District Court Bench. Hennepin County Attorney's office has a Negro assistant. Five Negroes serve as deputy sheriffs, supervisors, and clerks. Negroes and white groups concerned about this "tokenism" have instituted a "Buy Black" campaign, designed to put the Black man in the economic mainstream of the city. The Urban League and the N.A.A.C.P. have worked tirelessly toward this end.

YMCA Registering
Registering for the Wednesday night dance at the West Central Branch YMCA, 3335 Blaisdell Ave. S. (right side, front to rear) are: Mike Brady, 336 E. 39th St.; Ted Hunter, 1342 Xerxes, and Barb Lilleberg, 306 University. Handling the registration table chores are (left side, front to rear) Ronny Thompson, 3038 Harriet; Gary Chin, 3429 Columbus, and Joe Carlson, 3125 First Ave.

Milton Harrison
Mr. Harrison, who at the time of this picture was the Minneapolis YMCA Director, is active in another area.

Wilver A. Lee
Appointed July 24, 1942; birth date January 30, 1913. Wife Geraldine. Has worked on various details including several walking beats and the patrol wagon, and is now in the Pawnbrokers division.

Tony Oliva
Tony, a famous Minnesota Twin, is shown here in a recent "Play It Safe" police campaign with ex-Minneapolis police chief Calvin Hawkinson.

Curtis Chivers
Mr. Chivers is here directing work in the "Freedom Spectacular" event in 1967.

Youth in Business
A part of the program, "Youth in Business," sponsored by the Minneapolis Junior Chamber of Commerce in youth achievement in the Black community. This program encourages the young to make their mark in the business world.

Camp Fire Girls
Here as in most other communities these girls quietly go about the service of the needy and becoming the wonderful women and mothers of the future.

Volunteers Unlimited
This organization was formed to aid in the dispersal of information to the unemployed and the needy. Above is Mrs. Prentiss Gary, herself a volunteer and wife of a local photographer.

Halloween Party
To the right, a happy, wonderful group of youngsters forget their cares and wait for the wicked old witch. Party was in honor of Linda Stewart, daughter of Mr. and Mrs. Warren Stewart.

Under the private *Plans for Progress* (Metropolitan Employers Voluntary Plans for Progress Council) programs last year the following items were headlined: "Northwestern Banks Active in the Inner City," "Minority Sensitivity Training Conferences Held," "Honeywell Recruiting in Area Community Centers," "Control Data Plans Plymouth Ave. Plant," "Migrant Workers Want to Stop," "N.S.P. Supervisors' Program Conducted." This organization of E.O. Employers

has on its impressive list of directors, Donald C. Dayton, Dayton Corp., Earl Ewald, NSP, W. L. Huffman, N.W. Bell, John Morehead, N.W. Natl. Bank, Gerry E. Morse, Honeywell, John S. Pillsbury, N.W. Natl. Life, and Don Peddie of the Mpls. Star and Tribune. It has as its principal objective the hiring of hard core youths, and a stronger program by business and industry to change the lives of the underprivileged minorities.

Something here should also be said about another

CONTINUED ON PAGE 184

Mr. John L. Sims
is the Project Director of the Citizens Community Centers, Inc., an Anti-Poverty Program. He took a leave of absence from the Hennepin County Welfare Department for one year to set up this program in Minneapolis, Minnesota. In his former employment at the Hennepin County Welfare Department, he was a supervisor in the Child Welfare Division of that agency for approximately twelve years. Prior to that he was employed at the Children's Home Society of Minnesota as a Social Worker in the Adoption Agency.

He earned a B.A. Degree in Social Sciences from West Virginia State College in 1947; and a Masters Degree in Social Work from the University of Buffalo, Buffalo, New York, in 1953.

He and his wife Hattie have two children: Harriet, age 14; and John, Jr., age 13.

Edgar Pillow,
director of the Minneapolis Community Action program, spoke at ceremonies which launched three State Employment Service JobMobiles Thursday, March 14. Looking on are Governor Harold LeVander, left, and St. Paul Mayor Thomas Byrne, center.

Mr. Pillow is also the director of the Hennepin County Economic Opportunity Program, OEO, of Minneapolis.

This Little Girl
Her future looks brighter, day by day through the efforts of the Minneapolis area social service agencies. She will be ever grateful for their efforts.

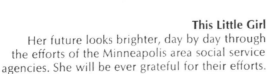

Saundrah Clark Grevious

Mrs. Grevious is a teacher of Afro-American Contributions with the Minneapolis Public Schools. A graduate of Chicago Teachers College, she has also taught in Baltimore, Maryland, Fairbanks, Alaska, and Chicago, Illinois. She is a member of the Human Relations Commission in her community and of the National Council of Negro Women.

The wife of Herbert D. Grevious and the mother of three sons, Mrs. Grevious is the author of *Teaching Children and Adults To Understand Human and Race Relations.* The book, published by T. S. Denison and Company, is a result of her background and experiences and suggests consistent educational methods for combatting racial problems. It is designed for use by teachers, parents and other members of the community.

Jerry Beal

Mr. Beal of St. Paul is in charge of all duplicating and stock control in the Minneapolis Regional Office of the Small Business Administration.

Above, Mrs. Grevious holds a copy of her book. The work has attracted many interested people in Education as related to minority group children.

Charles W. McCoy

Program Assistant Charles W. McCoy is shown conferring with Regional Director Harry A. Sieben (seated), regarding SBA's Economic Opportunity Loan Program.

The State JobMobiles

Governor Harold LeVander, at the podium, dedicated three State Employment Service JobMobiles for neighborhood service at ceremonies in front of the State Capitol Thursday, March 14.

T.C.O.I.C.

The most Dramatic evidence of breakthrough in the area of training and guidance in the Black Community is the Twin Cities Opportunity Industrialization Center (T.C.O.I.C.), a largely Negro staffed and directed agency. Its impact has been uplifting and directional in the community. The following are just a small group of the "Doers" in this very important operation:

REVEREND DR. LEON H. SULLIVAN. Founder of the original Opportunities Industrialization Center in Philadelphia. Dr. Sullivan has had limited contact with the Twin Cities OIC, but it is on his dream, a need and a desire to see black people improve their own opportunities, that OIC philosophies now exist around the country in some 60 cities.

CECIL E. NEWMAN. Chairman of the TCOIC Board of Directors. Mr. Newman is one of the most respected black newspaper men in America. Mr. Newman has served many long laborious hours as Chairman of the TCOIC Board without compensation, yet has served with unswerving fidelity. Voted one of Minnesota's outstanding 100 young men in 1949, Mr. Newman is highly regarded at TCOIC.

REVEREND STANLEY R. KING. A graduate of the University of Minnesota, Rev. King has spent 13 active and productive years in the Twin City area. His long line of accomplishments began with him becoming assistant pastor of the Zion Baptist Church while still a student. After graduation he organized the Sabathani Baptist Church in South Minneapolis. King is responsible for introducing the OIC concept to the Upper Midwest. Serving as Executive Director since its enception, King through his dynamic leadership, has made the Twin Cities OIC the most innovative in the country.

THOMAS H. TIPTON. A graduate of Morgan State College, Mr. Tipton joined the staff at TCOIC in 1968, as the Director of Public Information. Thomas has gained much experience from his previous associations in previous associations in numerous community and professional organizations in Washington, D.C., that will readily apply to his position at OIC. Since Mr. Tipton joined the OIC staff the image of the organization has been greatly improved through exact and stimulating news that originated from the Public Information Department at the Minneapolis OIC.

T.C.O.I.C. MINNEAPOLIS

MR. TIPTON

MRS. PHILLIPS

182

MRS. LILLIAN WARREN. Originally the secretary of the initial Steering Committee responsible for the establishing of the TCOIC program in the Twin Cities. Mrs. Warren was hired by the OIC board as the senior clerical person in September of 1966. Since this date she has continued to serve as secretary to the Board of Directors, Executive Secretary and clerical supervisor for the Minneapolis branch. She is a member of the Minnesota State Human Rights Department, Minnesota Republican Party and the American Lutheran Church. Lillian is a free-lance writer, and is the author of a weekly column in the Twin Cities Courier, "Lillian's Corner."

ANNA MAE PHILLIPS. Began with TCOIC as bookkeeper, she is now Director of Personnel. Because of Mae's broad background in a number of areas, she has been able to assume different areas of responsibility, making her one of OIC's most valued employees. Mrs. Phillips joined the TCOIC staff in October of 1966.

DONALD A. WILLIAMS. A St. Paul native, served as the first branch director of the St. Paul OIC. Donald lent a vast knowledge to the St. Paul operation because of his experience in administration and his ability to encourage interested people to support the St. Paul OIC. Mr. Williams is no longer with the OIC program.

CONRAD BALFOUR. A former Dale Carnegie Instructor, Mr. Balfour began his service with TCOIC in December of 1966, as a Job Development Specialist. He has since been promoted to Branch Director of the Minneapolis Feeder, and Assistant Deputy Director of Operations. Mr. Balfour has been one of the outstanding assets in the TCOIC program during his two years on the staff.

MR. BALFOUR

MRS. WARREN AND MR. WILLIAMS

REV. KING, REV. SULLIVAN, MR. NEWMAN

Community Facilities, General

high purposed group working with a limited staff, and attempting a king sized job, the *Urban Coalition*, directed by Harry Davis. After a year of leadership under Stephen Keating, Pres. of Honeywell Inc. (new president is Dean McNeal of Pillsbury), the group listed as major accomplishments, the political persuasion of Republican aldermen to accept Ronald A. Edwards, a young black militant to the new Commission on Human Relations, the naming of Davis to the Civil Service Commission which dictates the hiring of the all white Fire Department and the nearly all white

Police Department, the landscaping and equipping of 10 neighborhood childrens playgrounds, the Housing Task Force aiding in procuring down payments for 81 poverty-level families to buy houses, the endorsement and aid to 75 minority-race youths to college education, and the proposal to add $225,000 in "seed" money for new Negro small businesses in the area.
The following factual information was provided by the city. It is intended only as a guide to the overall aims and programs of the Minneapolis municipal government for *all* citizens. And it is presented here without further editorial comment.

Christopher W. Gossett (right), fifteen-year-old Minneapolis, Minn., high school senior who was awarded the Bell Telephone Laboratories Achievement Scholarship, tours Bell Labs, Murray Hill, N.J., with Erling Reque (center), his Washburn High School physics teacher, and Gene Jacobi (left) of Bell Laboratories. The four-year college scholarship which Gossett was awarded is based on a national competition.

Harrison Park Summer Recreation
Each summer, as in most Minneapolis parks, many group activities are planned for the neighborhood. Here the kids plan a woods hike.

Glenwood Community Center
These little cut-ups are having a ball smearing paste during Kids' Hour at the Center.

John Robinson,
formerly Juvenile probation officer for Hennepin County, presently Personnel Coordinator with Control Data.

Vice President Humphrey and the boys club strike up a mutual friendship. The Vice President has always been a favorite with the young, from his days as Mayor of Minneapolis.

Jessie Bell,
also formerly Juvenile probation officer, is now with Super Valu and is in public relations part time with the Minnesota Vikings.

A Cool Day at Calhoun Beach
It may surprise some non-residents that Minneapolis can be torridly hot in the summer. This little miss loves it.

Community Housing

The city has recently reorganized its functions under a "program" system and abandoned the standard "departmental" format. It is believed that this approach, which consists of seven general programs encompassing all phases of municipal management, will give a better understanding of the city . . . its government, operations, obligations and service. The seven programs are:

COMMUNITY DEVELOPMENT — Involved here are the planning, designing, building and maintenance of the city in which we live . . . the efficient utilization of land, the continuous programs to create new, modernize existing and rehabilitate old structures and areas. Pilot City and the Model Neighborhood, the extension of the Nicollet Mall, revitalizing of the gateway area, the proposed new civic center, rejuvenation of Hennepin Avenue and a city-wide beautification program are examples of community development. So are the housing projects for the elderly and lower income families, the neighborhood conservation projects which assist communities to up-grade themselves. The city is constantly working to strengthen economic and industrial development to achieve an industrial climate conducive to the retention and expansion of existing industries and the location of new industries here. The city has recently expanded its auditorium and convention facilities, created a new sports area, contributed to the development of the Metropolitan Airport system . . . all calculated to build the city's reputation, services and revenue.

Low Income Apartments
These open-air pleasant high rises are located at 13th Ave. So. and 9th Street, Minneapolis.

Pentagon Apartment for the Aged
This apartment for the aged is the modern new look available for the retired. It is located at 23rd St. and 14th Ave. So., Minneapolis.

Ultra Modern Private Owned Apt.
This apartment owned by Mrs. Francis Travis gives an idea of the new Negro owned housing slowly emerging in the city.

Community Service Agencies

TRANSPORTATION — Involves all phases of movement . . . the public transit system . . . the planning, development, completion and maintenance of our freeway systems, street, highway, bridge, sidewalk, lighting and snow and ice removal programs. It adopts and enforces traffic systems and regulations to establish the efficient traffic flow. It involves our parking meter program and off-street parking . . . every phase of pedestrian or vehicular movement to keep our city "on the go".

LAW ENFORCEMENT — Your safety, and the protection of your life, personal freedom and property are the major concerns of the Minneapolis law enforcement agencies. The prevention, investigation of crime and the apprehension of criminals are carried out by a great many departments and men educated in and dedicated to the protection of the people. Besides the activities involved in enforcement, the police department maintains an emergency service, ambulance service, first-aid and emergency treatment.

The City Attorney's office handles prosecution of offenders and provides for the defense of others.

HEALTH AND WELFARE — This Department is concerned with the health education and information for you, the prevention and control of diseases and health hazards which might affect you personally. The department provides Medical care in the form of home nursing for deserving persons, Maternal and Child Health Education, prepares for and responds to emergencies and supervises the public relief activities of the city.

HUMAN DEVELOPMENT embraces all phases of education, recreation, cultural and social growth. The city maintains first quality elementary and secondary schools augmented with special classes, enrichment programs for the exceptional, vocational training and adult education programs, work training, employee recruitment and job placement services.

The many branches library is open and available to everyone interested in reading for study, enrichment or just plain relaxation.

The Minneapolis Park Board has a comprehensive program of sports, music and drama, crafts and games and unstructured play for all ages. It keeps an elaborate system of parks and playgrounds.

Glenwood Four-plexes
Located on the north side, these units were built for large family, low-income families.

Senior Citizens
The units in the background are also north side apartments for retired couples. Foreground, large family units.

The National Council of Negro Women

The NCNW representing thousands of outstanding Negro mothers, career women, professionally trained, is probably *the outstanding* voluntary, non-profit national organization in the forefront of the Negro drive for equality and citizenship in the country. For example two of its stated purposes to which these wonderful women are dedicated are "to work for the enforcement of laws and for administrative and legal action to protect the civil rights of all and to combat poverty for the many," and "To broaden the base of participation by women of widely different backgrounds to achieve the common goals of respect for their families, their race and themselves."

SOME CURRENT HIGHLIGHTS

PROJECT WOMANPOWER — NCNW is now in the second year of this project, funded by the Ford Foundation, to recruit and train 6,000 Negro women for effective service and action in their communities.

VOLUNTEERS UNLIMITED — Women in three pilot cities — Danville, Virginia, Twin Cities, Minnesota and Miami, Florida — were trained in delinquency prevention with disadvantaged girls.

PROJECT HOMES — NCNW is acting as a bridge between private builders, local housing authorities, the U.S. Department of Housing and Urban Development and local communities in the rural South to make home ownership a reality for low income families. Ground is being broken for the first 200 homes at Gulfport, Mississippi in March 1968.

WORKSHOPS IN MISSISSIPPI — Taking the role of advocacy, WIMS uses workshop methods to close the communication gap between rural and urban poor, government and civic personnel working, on a wide range of economic and civil rights abuses. Received Lane Bryant citation two years running.

WOMEN IN COMMUNITY SERVICE, INC. — WICS is a joint venture by National Council of Jewish Women, National Council of Catholic Women, National Council of Negro Women and United Church Women, finding and screening girls 16-21 for Job Corps Training and providing supportive services to girls in poverty.

CONSUMER PROTECTION — Educational programs enable low income families to make better use of buying, saving and credit where "the poor usually pay more." NCNW is a participating member of the Ad Hoc Committee of National Organizations of the President's Committee on Consumer Interests.

RELIGION

Church Community Keeps Pace

One of the earliest of Negro religious leaders in Minnesota was Reverend Robert Hickman a slave born licensed preacher who assisted a white minister at the Pilgrim Church in St. Paul (organized in 1863) until his ordination in 1877. This church was a *mixed congregation* until 1870 and was re-founded as a Negro church on Cedar Street, St. Paul, with Rev. Hickman as its founder.

The St. James African Methodist Episcopal Church was the first all-Negro Church organized in Minneapolis in 1863, and its first prayer meetings held at the home of a Paul Brown on 4th Avenue Southeast. In 1869, the group procured a building from a white

church at the corner of Sixth Avenue South and 2nd Street. In 1870 a new church and community leader arrived, a Reverend J. Hedgeman, and a new Methodist Episcopal church, in the village of St. Anthony.

Strangely it would seem in a study of Minnesota history the first real lines of segregation, Black from White, occurred of all places in the church. The white community, particularly the building trade unions and politicians semed to feel the need to draw a line between themselves and the Negroes arriving monthly by way of the Mississippi River.

And faced with few friends, objects of open

Zion Church
This very active church group has sponsored many affairs, both religious and social, in the community. The church is located at 621 Elwood Avenue North.

Rev. James Holloway
The Minneapolis religious community was tremendously enhanced when Rev. Holloway accepted the pastorate of Zion Baptist Church. Under his spiritual and economic leadership the congregation has recently moved into a beautiful new church. Rev. Holloway is very active in religious as well as community services.

antagonism of white workers already established and depending almost entirely on the few whites willing to do their part to receive and accept them, the Negro here turned more to his church and looked to his church leaders, generally better educated than himself, for his direction. In 1865, one prominent white leader George W. Prescott, a member of the United States Christian Assn. in St. Paul wrote: "I don't know how you feel on this subject, but my conviction is that the people of this country have a duty to perform to the colored race — to carry out God's plans. These people must be educated, their present necessities must be supplied. I am willing and glad as a Christian to be identified with the movement.*

Thus, religion has been in the past and is in the present the strong foundation roots from which the Negro community grows. From the founding of "Little St. James" A.M.E. church the Negro community of churches in this community has grown to more than 25, representing many denominations and faiths. In recent years church construction has increased, especially active in replacing and enlarging old church buildings as well as building new, modern ones. And Negro churchmen are serving in many inter group faiths throughout the city.

Bishop Joseph Gomez

Bishop Joseph Gomez is the former prelate of this, the Fourth Episcopal District of the African Methodist Episcopal Church. The congregations in Minneapolis under his leadership were St. Peters, Wayman, and St. James A. M. E. Churches. He recently was assigned to a different position and in his place now is Bishop Primm.

Rev. Mrs. Annie Bailey

Rev. Mrs. Bailey was ordained by Rev. W. P. Grossley, who then was pastor of St. James A.M.E. Church. This busy woman, though quite active in many church activities, maintains a lovely home for two of her sons. She frequently receives visits from her daughters who live in Missouri.

Rev. Walter L. Battle

The founder of the Minneapolis House of Refuge is a native Mississippian. He, along with his wife, the Rev. Mrs. W. L. Battle, is fulfilling more than just the spiritual needs of his church's members. Rev. Battle's Sunday night radio program is a must for thousands of listeners.

*The Negro in Minnesota

The Ministry and The Churches

Rev. Carl A. Fuqua
Pastor of St. Peters A.M.E. Church in
South Minneapolis for the past several years. Prior
to his appointment to St. Peters he was in Chicago.
In addition to his pastoral duties in Chicago,
he was also president of the Chicago Branch of
the N.A.A.C.P.

Rev. G. F. Trawick
Rev. Trawick is pastor of St. Mark's
Baptist Church which is a
member of the National Baptist
Convention. He is also the owner
of The Palm Cleaners in
Minneapolis.

This very busy husband and
father is quite active in the
business community as well as in
the religious community of the
city.

Bishop William B. Williams
Is the Pastor of the Fourth Street
Church of God In Christ for the past
20 years. Former Executive
Secretary for the Board of Elders,
Minnesota Church of God In Christ.
He attended Albion College,
University of Minnesota, and
graduated from Northwestern Bible
College. Since being appointed
Bishop his area has been enlarged,
and his duties and activities are
quite numerous.

Louis W. Johnson
The Rev. Louis W. Johnson, minister of St. Thomas
Episcopal Church, Minneapolis, is a member
of the teaching staff for the Institute of Religious
Studies. He will teach the course, "Light on
the Dark Continents (Africa and North America)."
Father Johnson is a recognized authority in the
field of African history. He has been pastor
for the past 20 years.

Bethesda Baptist Church

We want to emphasize that we have come thus far by faith.
Bethesda Baptist Church began as a Sunday School class in Mrs.
Sarah Farr's Hair Shop, 521 Nicollet Avenue in downtown
Minneapolis. In 1889, as the congregation grew, they moved to
Fryer Hall, 505½ Washington Avenue South. Shortly thereafter, an
edifice was erected at this site, 1118 South 8th Street, where we
worshipped until the building was partially destroyed by fire on Palm
Sunday, 1961. On Easter Sunday of that year, we began worship
in the Pillsbury Citizens Building, 4th Street and 16th Street South.
The Lord God was our helper and we were able to erect a church
educational unit at this same site at the total cost of $70,000.00.
Upon completion of this unit, we had our first service here on the
second Sunday in September of 1963.

Rev. John H. Young
is currently the pastor of Bathesday
Baptist Church at 1118 S.
8th Street, Minneapolis.

Rev. L. Johnson and Mr. Roy Larsen are shown closing
a transaction which involved the church. Rev. Johnson is the
former Pastor of St. Peters A.M.E. Church and Mr. Larsen
is Chairman of the Board of Twin City Federal Savings
and Loan Association.

Henry E. Johnson
A minister of Negro ancestry has been named to a
newly created post of community services at
Hennepin Avenue United Methodist Church,
prestigious Minneapolis congregation.

The new minister of community services is the
Rev. Henry E. Johnson, a native of Mississippi.

Mr. Johnson's job according to a story in the
daily press will be to coordinate the church's
activities in the area of urban problems.

Wayman African Methodist Episcopal Church is located on Minneapolis' near North Side. The membership is very proud, and rightfully so, of their new edifice. In this very modern new structure worshippers from all over the city gather. Rev. Hendrieth is the pastor.

St. Peters A.M.E. Church

Located at 401 E. 41st Street, in South Minneapolis, this church has just completed a new addition with the purpose of educating and providing recreation for its young members.

House of Refuge

Action work is a summer project under the direction of Reverend Walter L. Battle, founder and pastor of House of Refuge, Inc., who is a man of strong convictions and believes in creating an answer to as many problems as possible. He holds that Christ is the answer but there is a need for ways of presenting Christ. Action Workshop serves toward exposing an answer to boys. Where many are offering recreation camps, vacations, automobiles, etc., the Workshop is of the opinion that young Americans should begin practicing our way of living. Action Workshop offers work in order to give them instructions and discipline.

The summer of 1959, a 3 acre farm was operated in Robbinsdale, a suburban town 8 miles west of Minneapolis, employing approximately 125 boys and girls plus operating a fruit and vegetable store on 38th street and 4th Avenue, Mpls. The farm gave many of these youngsters a start in life, and now, 10 years later, not one has a jail or police record. Because of this early start they are a step ahead of many of their classmates. The program was resumed in 1968 when there was a threat of a long, hot summer, National guards in riot training, police equipping themselves with more M-16 rifles and too much talk and intolerance towards our youth, especially blacks. Out of necessity the 1969 Workshop was launched with 2 free breakfasts for boys prior to June 23rd, the date work began. The work is cutting and placing house numbers on a finished redwood board. After some of the older boys learn good work habits, they will paint houses.

young bros.
barber shop

Small Businesses Negro Owned

The small business, owned and operated by Negroes, is on the upswing. More and more young Negroes are taking advantage of the changing economic picture in our Metropolitan area. At present, it is estimated there are about 200 Negro owned and operated businesses independent of white supervision. The majority of these are in "foods and drinks". However, recently with the recent emphasis on "Black Power" (meaning economic) there have been ventures into other areas — book stores, fashion shops, beauty salons, superettes, laundries, cleaners, haberdasheries, filling stations, contractors, real estate, catering, art shops, antiques, drugs and sundries, all mainly to serve the Negro community.

The "liberal" thinking white community is also aiding the aspiring Negro merchant with community project, participatory efforts similar to a neighborhood group in Fridley who call in food orders to a North Minneapolis grocer weekly.

This may or may not be a "one time only" quasi movement, prompted only by a momentary emotional feeling of white "recognition" but even if it is "only a start," it is indicative of the coming opportunity being provided, finally, for the young energetic Negro who aspires to own and operate his own business in an integrated economic society.

Why now, suddenly, is the Negro becoming a manager rather than the managed? Why is he evoluting into ownership as opposed to an on the job servitude to a white owner — a sub-status he unchallengingly accepted historically?

The answers to these questions are varied depending on the religious, political, or even psychological frame of reference.

The religious and political arena produce answers or a rationalization that is related in that they are both liberalizing out of a survival need. The Metaphysicist who in the past preached, "Be content on earth for the poor shall inherit the riches of Heaven" and the politician who in the past relied on party solidarity are rapidly being "shouted" out of their demagogic empire. The Black man is ever increasingly insisting on captaining his own ship.

Book Store Manager

Clarence S. Carter gave up a possible academic teaching appointment at the U. of M. to become general manager and part owner of the Challenge Book Center. The main reason for the book store is, by exposing Black literature, to help bridge the understanding gap. Mr. Carter, his wife and children live in South Minneapolis.

The store is an example of the recent local interest in taking up the challenge of community enlightenment in the affairs of the Black man. It offers several hundred books and authors, histories, poetry, songs, famous debates, contemporary prose and novels, all by Negroes. It also plans to handle art and posters of Black subject matter.

Bar-Cafe Owner

Mr. Anthony B. Cassius, a Minneapolis businessman for over 30 years. He is very well known throughout the Upper Midwest. He attends most major sporting events wherever they may be held. He is quite active in civic and social functions. He and his lovely wife are the parents of two children, a son and a daughter.

Mr. Tela B. Burt

A retired postal employee. For more than 14 years, Mr. Burt, head of the T. B. Burt Realty Co., is very grateful to the many satisfied buyers and sellers of homes. Mr. Burt says, "In business I feel that my greatest strength and success is in my natural honesty, sincerity and integrity."

Levy T. Powell

Mr. Powell is the owner of "Mr. Ribs," a food carryout chain, which is developing a franchising program with a goal of expanding throughout the state with a view toward the national market.

Currently, he has three business locations, two in Minneapolis, 1721 Nicollet Ave. So. and 1915 W. Broadway, and one in St. Paul, 602 N. Dale Street.

"Mr. Ribs" is a going thing!

Smithy Norton

Mr. Norton was made available to the Urban Coalition of Minneapolis by the Greyhound Corporation (Minneapolis Bus Terminal—R. E. Leonard, Manager). As Information Specialist for the Urban Coalition movement, Mr. Norton served as liaison representative and coordinator for their community awareness program, "What Do You Care Anyway".

His firm, Lorenze Smythe Norton Associates, Community and Public Relations Consultants, is located in the Times Annex Building, Room 411, 63 South 4th Street.

Small Businesses

These political leaders have provided and will continue to provide the psychological avenue to a pure "equality" economy only if the dissident "rank and file" pressure continues. Thus it is immediately apparent that it is necessary to "keep the pressure on" if the Negro is to become an equal partner in the self-owned world of business.

The ill-informed, traditional oriented dogmatic urban or suburban man on the street with his almost completely selfish motivation obviously will acknowledge, accept and do business with the Negro businessman only if his religious and political leaders set the pace and show the way, and from all available indications this is not the trend in much of this community today. Now is the hour for the enlightened young 21st-century Black man who is gaining an education, formal or informal, to step out—step ahead of this time and accept the responsibility of Negro-owned private enterprise, and the benefits that logically follow in the free enterprise system. There are those in the Black community itself who reject the "white" concept of business and industry entirely, and deliberately. We say let's not get "hung-up" with irrelevant detail and get on with the job. The objective is essentially the same, "militant" or "non-militant." That objective is respect and recognition of the Black man, his abilities, his talents, and his soul.

A Private Nursery
Operated by James and Helen Burns. Designed to give the child an opportunity to participate in a new program of small classes, gain social experience, and supplement and enrich the basic learnings the child has had at home with his family.

Service Station Owner
Ernest Martin is a man with a service. He operates a modern service station in South Minneapolis. With the sincere concern he has for his customers, we are sure that he will be in business for a long time to come.

Clothing Store Owner: Marion Loftis

Mr. Loftis has been in business for the last 22 years in the Mill City. The civic arena as well as community often call on him to perform in various capacities. His response is always immediate and generous. In business, he carries as fine a line or lines of merchandise as any store in Minneapolis.

Mays Superette

Mr. and Mrs. Jesse Mays are in their sixth year of grocery business in South Minneapolis. Both are members of St. Peter's A.M.E. Church. Mr. Mays is a long time member of the Steward Board.

Upholstering Company Owner

Marty Moritz began his venture into the business world after being thoroughly trained and employed by one of the leading firms of its kind. The Moritzes and their children reside in South Minneapolis.

Small Businesses, Food and Drink

Carl's Superette
Located at 1201 Fremont Avenue North, Minneapolis, Minn. Carl began business in the fall of 1960. The business was originally called Carl's Grocery. It was later changed to Carl's Superette after remodeling. The store has recently been moved because of urban renewal. Carl is relocating on the South Side of Minneapolis.

Restaurant Company Owners
Nate and James Smith operate one of the most pleasant eateries in the Minneapolis area. The single set find it very convenient for their location, as well as their taste. The Smith Brothers are adding to their menu continually. Customers come from all over the area to enjoy some real good Soul Food.

Fred Bryan
Has been a chef, bartender, and assistant manager at several of the leading restaurants in the city. Currently at the Peacock Lounge.

Liquor Store Clerk
Mrs. Yvonne Slaughter is one of the most popular cashiers in town. "The lady with a pleasing personality" is what she is referred to by the customers at Lake Street Liquor Store.

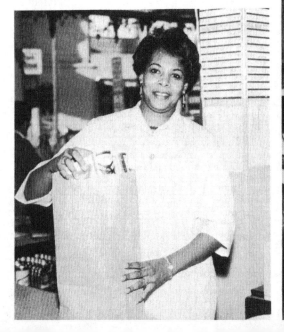

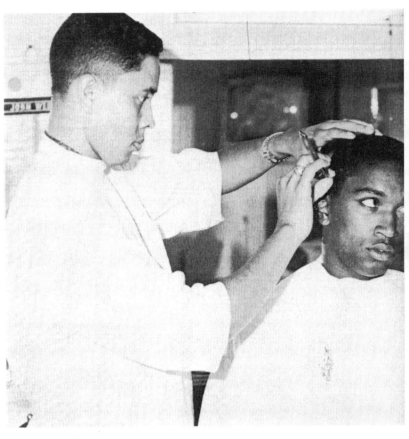

Cleaner and Tailor

Worthy Turner, one of the finest tailors in the city.
He is one of the few Negro Americans in this city who was
located on famed Hennepin Avenue for a number of years.
Mr. Turner, a Texas native, takes quite an active part in
his church, which is Zion Baptist Church.

Barber Shop Owner

John Webb has moved into a new location. In the near
future he plans to add more barbers. This young businessman
is planning to have one of the most modern barber shops
in the city. Mr. Webb takes part in various civic functions.

Contractor..

Herman Barfield has been heading his
painting and decorating contracting firm in
Minneapolis for the past dozen years.
He and his employees can be seen doing jobs
all over the metropolitan area. His jobs
range from the most expensive homes to
some of the smaller priced structures. When
Mr. Barfield is not painting, you may at
times find him on some swinging set.

Small Businesses

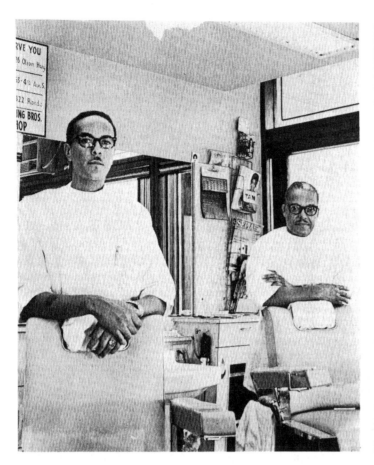

The Young Brothers

Chubby and Fred, operate the shop on the Minneapolis North Side. Chubby and Fred built their present shop in 1960. It is one of the most modern barber shops in the city.

Dickie and Raymond Young

Barber Shop Owner

Warren Watson, a native of Arkansas, a former resident of Michican (Flint), he also lived in the State of Wisconsin. He started his business career in Minneapolis in 1962. He recently purchased a building which covers one half block, located in South Minneapolis.

Charlie Brown

Located on Plymouth Avenue, the heart of the "soul" area, Charlie Brown's Barber Shop is one of the spots of conversation and discourse on the affairs of the Black Community — and Charlie, himself, is a great barber.

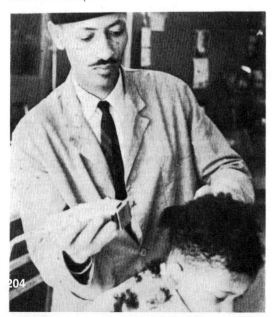

Laundromat Owner
Frank Harvey, Sr. Many bachelors in the city can be seen on their way to and from their jobs dropping off their laundry to be washed. For the past five or six years, Mr. and Mrs. Harvey have been rendering prompt and efficient service to their many customers. Mr. Harvey is an avid sports fan. His son, Frank Jr., accompanies dad to many of the local sporting events.

Oscar C. Howard
President, Private and Industrial Catering. Invented food warming devices. Conducts a Meal Wheels service covering the Twin Cities area. Member of Minneapolis Chamber of Commerce. An officer in Zion Baptist Church.

Restaurant Owner
Mel Hammond. This ex-prize fighter, instead of dishing out punishment in the ring, is now dishing out some of the finest Bar-B-Q in the five state area. His customers come from far and near. Many night people wonder if they will be able to get into Mel's place to be served. Out-of-towners and residents alike will have the treat of a lifetime by eating at Mel's House of Ribs in South Minneapolis.

Cement Contractor
Warfield Griffin is one of the busiest contractors in the city. He often can be seen in all sections of town supervising various projects. In addition to cement work, he also finds time to contract for painting and general maintenance work in commercial and residential properties. When he can find time, Mr. Griffin is more than at home on the golf course.

205

Small Businesses, Services

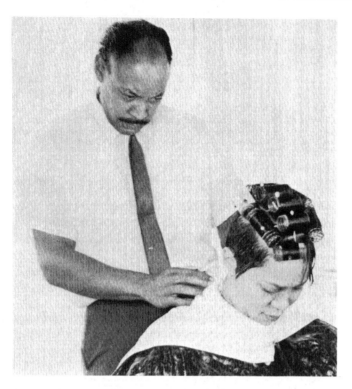

Beauty Shop Owner
Richard Mays. Dick Mays opened shop in 1964.
He received his training at Ritters School of Beauty
Culture (St. Paul). Additional training under Mr. Paul
(one of the tops in his field) and a stint at Summett School
of Beauty Culture in Indiana. He recently moved to
larger quarters in South Minneapolis.

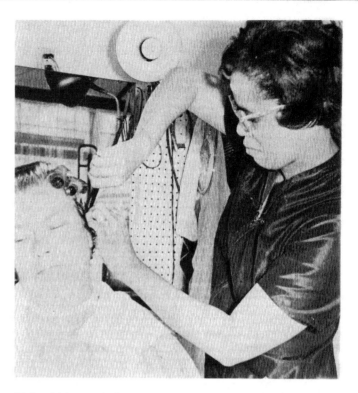

Richard Mayes. Dick Mayes opened shop in 1964.
He received his training at Ritters School of Beauty
Culture (St. Paul). Additional training under
Mr. Paul (one of the tops in his field) and a stint at Summett
School of Beauty Culture in Indiana. He recently moved
to larger quarters in South Minneapolis.

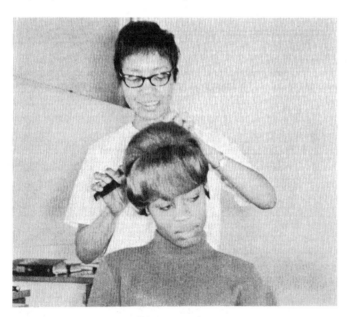

Beauty Shop Owner
Julia Mae Thompson, a St. Louis native, after going
to a college in Missouri for two or three years, came to
Minneapolis. She started her own business after having
worked in a beauty shop on the South Side. She presently
runs one of the better shops in the city. She takes part
in many functions in the city. She is the sister-in-law
to Leo Browne, Sales Manager of the Minneapolis
Negro Profile.

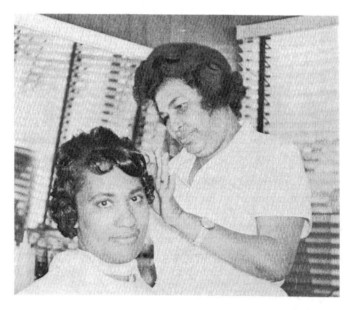

Beauty Shop Owner
Yvonne Jones. Mrs. Jones began operating her own business
in 1950. Prior to that she was associated with Bea Hall for
nine years. She was one of the first Negro beauty shop
operators in the city. She has 18 years of experience of
being in business on her own, and her shop is quite
fashionable. She is a member of the National Beauty Culture
League and Local.

Liquor Store Clerk

Bob Puckett (above) is one of the most popular retail liquor store clerks in the city. A seven or eight year veteran in the business, he may one day own and operate his own establishment. After working hours, Bob can be seen taking in some of the latest movies, or watching some of the late late late TV movies. He holds membership in organizations that are sincerely trying to bridge this vast societal gap. Bob is employed by Chicago-Franklin Liquors.

Liquor Store Clerk

Jack Smith (below). At the State Liquor Store in downtown Minneapolis the clerk who knows the stock is what the people say about Jack. Any brand called for he can direct other clerks or get it himself in a matter of seconds. He has been at his present job nearly ten years and is considered a very able and reliable employee.

Small Businesses

Nacirema Club Officers and Board Members

Charles J. Rhodes
Manager of the Nacerema Club, Inc.,
for 7 years. Was born in Iowa, was
a Golden Gloves and professional prize
fighter, U. S. Army 4½ years (10th
Cavalry). Worked in the Veterans
administration for 4 years prior to
present job. Is a good golfer,
bowler and pool player.

Samuel Gransberry
Mr. Gransberry is on the Board
of Directors of the Nacirema Club.
He has been a Minneapolis
resident for the past twenty years.
He was a former employee of
the N. P. Railroad until his
retirement three years ago.

William Lumsey
Vice President of Nacirema Social Club,
has been connected with the club for the
past six years. He is on the Board of
Directors. The present membership of
the club is six hundred.

Joseph Lewis, Jr.
Mr. Lewis is general manager of Cassius'
popular Bar-Cafe. He is one of the most
popular bartenders in the Twin Cities. He has
many friends from all walks of life. His
congeniality and humor keep his customers
entertained and relaxed. They'll tell you
he's quite a philosopher as well!

Among his many acquaintances are Emmet
Ashford, Jackie Robinson, The Late, "Duke"
Slater, John Wyatt, and other famous names.
Mr. Lewis is a native of Minneapolis.
He is a graduate of South High School.
He has also attended the University
of Minnesota.

Harvey Jones

Operates one of the most popular lounges,
The Peacock Alley, in Minneapolis. Mr. Jones'
career has been varied and interesting in
many fields. He and his charming wife are
what Peacock patrons consider the
perfect host and hostess.

Night Club Owner

Tommy Lewis (below) shown with Benny Fields (the
club's manager), is a very popular Minneapolitan. He has
been in business a number of years. Prior to going in business,
Tommy was an entertainer. He performed with the likes of
Lester Young, Rook Gans, Oscar Pettiford and many other
top-named performers in the Twin Cities area. This famed
North Side night spot will be moving in the near future
to an unknown location. Wherever it may go, Tommy
will see to it that caliber of entertainment will
always remain top shelf.

Rubbish Removal Company Owner (Retired)

Charles Jackson was president and owner of one of the
most efficiently operating firms of its kind. Over 75 per cent
of his customers used his service from the time he
opened shop until his recent retirement. Mr. and Mrs.
Jackson attend St. James A.M.E. Church, where he has
been a Trustee for many years.

 **VIC MANUFACTURING CO.**
1620 Central Avenue N.E. · Minneapolis Minnesota 55413

Sam Dubose

A fabricator at VIC Manufacturing Company, is shown here making adjustments on the nibler for a production run of drycleaning machine parts. This operation cuts through steel sheets, notching them in various shapes. Mr. Dubose has been with VIC since August, 1964.

Gary Brown

Although he is only 21 years old, Minneapolis born Gary Brown exudes that quiet efficiency which so typifies Northrup King people. He is beginning his Northrup King career in the Packet Seed Department where he operates a Jet Press multilith machine which overprints the retail price on many of the millions of seed packets processed at the Minneapolis plant each year. Gary is very active in church work, likes to read and enjoys bowling.

Edd Logan

Edd Logan, Jr. was born in Tuscaloosa, Alabama and now makes his home in Minneapolis. Edd began at NK in 1966. An important part of his job in the Packet Seed Department is to keep track of almost a thousand different varieties of flower seed and styles of packets that are used. Edd is married, an Air Force veteran, a graduate of Elkins Radio School, holds a 1st class radio license and is doing graduate work in electronics. His main outside interests are electronics and Citizens Band radio.

Ambrose Overton

Ambrose Overton began at Northrup King in 1952. His seventeen years of experience are put to valuable use in the Garden Seed Department. Ambrose enjoys sports, church activities and jazz in his spare time, but his chief enjoyment is golf. Ambrose is not only a below-par golfer, he is probably the only person at Northrup King who has ever shot a hole-in-one.

Rudolph Bacquie

If you want to know the latest in sports scores, ask Rudolph Bacquie. Rudy started at Northrup King in 1966 and is now a permanent Warehouseman. His outside activities include reading, baseball, football, basketball and fishing.

NORTHRUP, KING & CO.
1500 JACKSON ST., N. E., MINNEAPOLIS, MINN. 55413

211

The Main Bank
This slender steel structure is a familiar sight in the downtown loop skyline. It is the home office of the First National Bank.

Mrs. Margaret Jones
Mrs. Jones was born in Trinidad in the West Indies but grew up in London, England. She progressed through elementary and high schools there and attended the University of London where she earned a Bachelor of Arts degree in Languages. She speaks, reads and writes Spanish and French fluently.

Mrs. Jones came to Minneapolis on a vacation trip in 1965. Here she met her husband-to-be, Donald Jones. She returned home to London briefly and came back to Minneapolis in January, 1966. She married Mr. Jones shortly afterward. They reside at 1717 Second Avenue South, Minneapolis.

Mrs. Jones had worked several years in a London accounting office and, last year, was employed as an accountant at The Dayton Corporation.

Her parents now reside in Trinidad. She has three sisters and two brothers, some of whom live in London and others in Trinidad.

212

LAND O'LAKES®

Beverly Williams — 34,
Laboratory Technician, came to Land O'Lakes on April 28, 1969. Hers is a responsible position in running bacterial analysis samples in our Control Laboratory. Prior to coming to Land O'Lakes, she had three years experience in the Iowa State Chemical Laboratory and one year at the University of Minnesota Micro-Biology Laboratory.

Carl Russell — 37,
is training to be a working supervisor in the butter printing operation. He started February 27, 1968 as a checker in the butter oil and cheese processing. He was responsible for supplies and supply control. He has held various positions in butter packaging. He attended the University of Minnesota for two years.

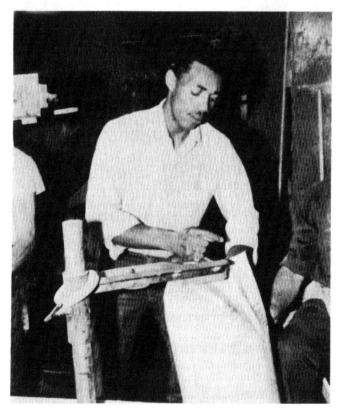

Joe Lloyd — 30,
started at Land O'Lakes September 19, 1967 in the butter print room. He worked approximately one year. Due to illness he took a leave of absence. Upon returning, he was assigned to the feed mill where he has been for the past eight months working as a relief man in various feed operations.

Joseph Felder

Mr. Felder joined Donaldson Company, Inc., as a Laboratory Tester in September, 1964, and was promoted to Technician II that same year. In 1966, he was promoted to Technician I. In March, 1968, Joe was admitted to the Engineering Intern Program at the University of Minnesota. This is a program which Donaldson Company sponsors in co-operation with the Institute of Technology at the University. Interns may obtain degrees in Mechanical or Aeronautical Engineering while working every other academic quarter at the sponsoring company. Joe will soon obtain his degree in Engineering through this program. He is married and resides at 1105 Olson Memorial Highway, Minneapolis.

David Thomas

Mr. Thomas joined Donaldson Company as a Laboratory Tester in 1967 and, within the same year, was promoted to Technician II. The following year, he was promoted to Technician I. He has only recently been advanced again, this time to Office Services Supervisor. This job involves responsibility for all communications, printing, and other supporting functions for the general offices. Dave attended General Motors Institute before coming to Donaldson Company. He is married and lives at 3410 South Girard Avenue, Minneapolis.

Ward Bell

Mr. Bell has been employed by Donaldson Company since 1963. He began as a Research Technician and was promoted to Technical Writer II and Senior Tech Writer in 1968. He works with the Protective Systems Department, part of the Research Division. He is married and resides at 2916 North 18th Avenue, Minneapolis.

DONALDSON COMPANY, INC.

214

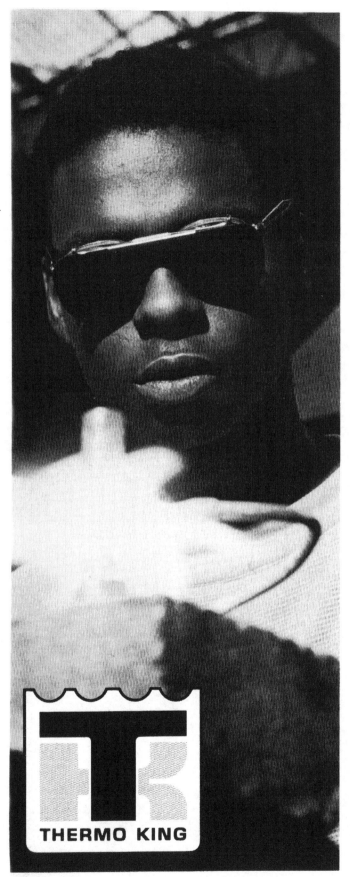

THERMO KING

Ronald Majors

Tube Bender Learner, with company for 3 years, working himself up through a variety of jobs. Learner program is of 520 hour duration. Learning to read drawings and sketches showing layout of bends in tubing, dimensions in inches and degrees and make a variety of adjustments.

Patricia Robertson

Blue Print Machine Operator, operates blue printing machine for shop and engineering requirements. Responsible for maintenance of blue print machine, maintains tracing files, also performs one or more routine clerical operations such as posting, inventory, production, labor or material cost records.

Elbert Clark

Personnel Supervisor, extensive experience in labor-management relations, Human Relations and dealing with problems of disadvantaged, minority and under-employed. Present job includes hiring, screening, counseling and records keeping of all employees. Supervises 5 people.

Roscoe Lacey

Material Scheduler, in and out plant expeditor discusses a parts shipment to our Louisville, Georgia plant.

Small Businesses

Mr. Wilbur A. Buchanan
Mr. Buchanan works as a Supply Clerk in the Plant Services department on the University of Minnesota campus. He is responsible for ordering supplies for 14 physical plants.

Al Simmons
Al is employed by the Western Printing Co.

Norman O. Woods
Is considered one of the best at rebuilding and repairing automotive and standard automobile transmissions.

Alvin Riley
One of the few Negro printing salesmen in the Northwest.

Marquette National Bank

Willie Hale

Has been employed at the Marquette
National Bank since February 23, 1953.
He works in the Mail and Proof Department.
He has the sincere, steady dependability
that is so necessary in the banking business.

217

Eugene M. Shepherd
Of 3620 15th Avenue South, became Dining Car Steward for
Northern Pacific Railway in January, 1964. Prior to his promotion he
served as waiter-in-charge for many years. He has an enviable record
of more than 41 years' continuous service with the company, plus
intermittent temporary employment dating back to 1923.

Jan C. Campbell

Jan joined CDC on January 4, 1965 as an Assembler-B. In November of that year she was promoted to Assembler-General. Although Jan left Control Data in October of 1966, she returned in May, 1967 as a Bindery Helper. She was named an Inspector in June, 1967. As an Inspector, Jan assures the excellence of products by inspecting equipment produced by other employees.

CONTROL DATA
CORPORATION

John Compton

Mr. Compton first came to work for us on a part-time basis, parking cars evenings and over the week-end, since he was employed otherwise by Swift & Company during the day. About three months later, he expressed an interest in becoming a full-time driver of one of our airport limousines and has been so employed for approximately three years.

Leon Valdez

Mr. Valdez first came to work for us as a driver of one of our airport limousines and because of his knowledge of food, distinguished appearance, and desire to improve himself he was transferred to our Totem Pole Dining Room to assume the position of Maitre d'. He is a capable and loyal member of our staff.

Richard Newberry

Head tailor at Kieffer's, is shown taking measurements for a suit to be made. He has worked in his present capacity for nearly 15 years. His employer is quite satisfied with his work.

Bill Orr

Mr. Orr, pictured on The Mall at the Minneapolis Public Library, has been a regular, full-time cab driver employed by Yellow Cab for the past ten years. Bill and his wife Mildred live at 1120 Knox Avenue North.

Ben Mouton

Ben is Bell Captain at the Northstar Inn. He is one of the many residents who came for a vacation and liked it so well that he and Mrs. Mouton decided to make Minneapolis their home.

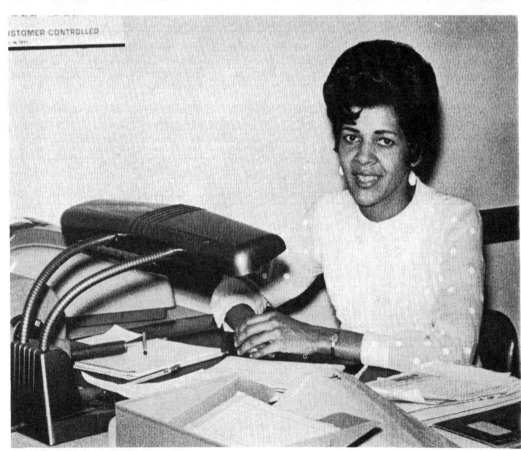

Leola C. Crawford

Secretary-Bookkeeper for the Minneapolis Central Labor Union Council. Has been employed with them for three years. Also a member of the Office and Professional Employees International Union #12.

SOCIAL ACTIVITIES

Negro Society in Minneapolis

By 1900, with most of the Negro population of approximately 7000 persons in the State of Minnesota, concentrated in Minneapolis and St. Paul, a definite social structure began to emerge. In any new society there are attempts to set social standards; and, lacking a long history as a free people, the Minnesota Negro of necessity adopted the standards of turn-of-the-century Minneapolis with some modifications. Inevitably, a rather fluid society resulted; and, except for those few who judged stature by skin color, social criteria was the same as the rest of the population.

Opinions varied greatly as to "who was who" and from the gossip of the day, or "Continuing process of evaluation", a few families stand out as being possessed with the personal magic of leadership — charisma — Careys, Van Hooks, Mitchells, Colemans, Robert Marshall, Srs., Cunninghams, Pierres, Smiths, and many, many more.

Prominent among these families was that of Dr. Robert S. Brown who began practicing in Minneapolis in the 1880s; thereby, starting a family tradition of medical service to the community which has been unbroken through three generations. Both of his sons, Carol and William Donald, continued the tradition until their deaths. Dr. W. Donald Brown, Jr. is the third generation of the family. Another important family was that of John B. Wright, who came to Minneapolis from Henry County, Kentucky, in 1908 and built the home for his growing family which later became the parsonage of Bethesda Church. About 1912, the family moved to Robbinsdale where Mr. Wright had purchased a large tract of land and by the time he died had acquired considerable property in Minneapolis. Many of the homes in Robbinsdale are on land which was purchased from

**Club Presidents Honored
At Council of Clubs' President Ball**

The above club presidents were honored at the Twin City Council of Clubs' sixth annual Presidents' Ball Saturday evening at the Leamington Hotel.

They are (reading from left to right) Leon Lewis (Past Exalted Rulers Council), Mrs. Genevieve Jackson (Unique Cosmetology Unit), Mrs. Amile Cook (Twin City Golf Auxiliary), Dr. Alexander Abrams (Sterling Club), Mrs. Ethel McIntosh (Wednesday Matinee), Joseph Arrington (Club 15), Miss Mae Leonard (Meteors), Carl Claiborne (Untouchables), Mel Jass, MC for the evening, Mrs. Annette Kelly (Paradise), Wilbur Nevels (Royal Twenty), Mrs.

Rosemary Micheau (Les Amies), Willard Jones (Socialites), Mrs. Helen Underwood (Twilight Bowling League), Kenneth Barnes (Les Gentilhommes), Mrs. Fern Hawkins (Amitie), Mrs. Odessa Allen Walker (Mpls. Urban League Guild), and Russel Davis (Ames Lodge).

Also honored but not shown in the picture were: A. B. Cassius (Nacirema Club), Howard Brown (Loafers), Father Denzil Carty (Assoc. Negro Credit Union), Dr. Thomas Johnson (Johnnie Baker), Thomas Lewis (Cato), Mrs. Timma Leah Riess (North Star Branch, NAPE Auxiliary), Lewis Seaton (Twilite Social), Merrill Taylor (Fezzan Temple #26), and Carl Wade (Twin City Reel & Trigger Club).

the Wrights. Mr. Wright was greatly respected for his business ability and strict standards. The third generation of his family still resides in the original home in Robbinsdale.

One of the gracious hostesses of the time was Mrs. Squire B. Neal, who as a wife of a prominent funeral director was known for her warmth and generosity. With one of the most successful businesses in the area, both Mr. and Mrs. Neal were active in civic and social affairs. Generosity to the unfortunate is not a usual characteristic in a new society, especially when it is personal giving. This was an outstanding trait in both Mrs. Neal and in Dr. W. Brown, Sr. The magnitude of their generosity will never be known except by those who benefited by it.

The crosstown rivalry between residents of the North and South sides of Minneapolis was probably founded on misunderstandings gendered by those who sought an artificial means of establishing social superiority. In spite of problems of overcrowded housing, crowded schools, and inadequate recreational facilities, the North Side contributed many outstanding persons to both Minnesota and National society. Mr. and Mrs. Frederick G. Thomas lived on Sixth Avenue in the early 1900s and their son, John Thomas from a beginning in Minneapolis where he was a leader of young people on both sides of the city to his present position as Director of the Intergovernmental

Committee for European Migration in Geneva, Switzerland, has become a world citizen during his lifetime. A nephew, the Reverend Father James Breeden, from president of his class at North High was one of the first Freedom Riders to arrive in Mississippi and has followed the cause of freedom for the black man constantly, to his present position as Executive Director of the Commission on Church and Race of the Massachusetts Council of Churches. Many other families of those early years had descendants such as Hilda Simms who made a memorable "Anna Lucasta", June Hawkins whose magnificent voice was heard in "Porgy and Bess" and "Carmen Jones", Ted Allen, the Harry Davises, the Archie Givens, Sr. and Jr., the Breedloves, Morrows and Browns, William Simms of the National Urban League, Miss Gertrude Brown who is credited with starting the present Phyllis Wheatley House and who probably was the most influential woman in Minneapolis during her time and was constantly visited by a succession of great Negro persons among whom was Mary McLeod Bethune. As an outstanding, lone crusader of her day, it is unfortunate that no memorial has been made to her on the North Side.

But, along with the early struggle to become established there were good times and regularly scheduled events as well as the formation of various clubs and social activities.

Founders of the Acirema Club
located in South Minneapolis as a social and civic center for the local community shown in the photograph are from left to right: Mr. and Mrs. Aaron Arrondonda, Claude Mason, Tom Johnson, A. B. Cassius and John McHie.

The club has provided a meeting place for political and social gatherings and has also sponsored summer programs for young people such as baseball and basketball teams. The club was formed in 1950 and in 1955 purchased and refurnished the building which is the club headquarters for 1969.

Early Events

One of the earliest clubs was the Forty Club which was patterned from the Forty Club of Chicago. The Bachelor's Club, whose members were James Hughes, Sr., Tela Burt, Harold Combs, Morris Gibbs, Raymond Cannon, James Combs, Harry Harper, Homer Cannon, Hiram Gibbs, Charles Terry and Donald Brady, Sr., became members of the Forty Club as they dropped their cherished single status. The Forty Club today gives four social functions yearly, one of which is usually a formal dance.

Outstanding events in the summer were two picnics during the twenties and thirties. One was sponsored by the Episcopal Churches of Saint Phillips in Saint Paul and Saint Thomas in Minneapolis. Usually held at Lake Minnetonka, it was necessary for the picnickers to take a train to Spring Lake Park and the tracks along which they traveled may be seen in front of Lyman Lodge on the lake. The other picnic was jointly sponsored by Minneapolis churches and at its peak attracted throngs of persons from both cities.

The big Spring event was certainly the annual style show and dance given by members of Saint Thomas Episcopal Church which continued until it became too time consuming for volunteers and so on the twenty-fifth anniversary of the show production ceased to the regret of the audiences and the relief of the committees.

Members of the Twin City Chapter of Jack and Jill of America, Inc.

(above) are pictured at an earlier installation ceremony which was followed by a dinner meeting. Officers seated at the table are: Mmes. Richard Stokes, John K. Freeze, Harold Carter, Robert Murray, Morris Gibbs and Tyler Howell.

The Twin City Chapter of Jack and Jill of America, Inc. (left), was started in Minneapolis by Mrs. Carl Rowan and Mrs. Sheldon B. Granger and includes many of the most prominent women in the community among its past and present members.

Mrs. Virginia Lewis, as a member of the National Jack and Jill Foundation Steering Committee is shown installing officers of the Twin City Chapter on September 13, 1968. From left to right are shown: Mmes. Frank Wildersen, Andrew Hudson, Claiborne Neal, James Bowman, Conrad Reed, Tommy Braddock, Harry Davis and Mrs. Virginia Lewis. Another officer, Mrs. Arthur Royster, is not shown in the picture.

The Minneapolis Socialite Club

is pictured at the dinner honoring the twenty-fifth anniversary of the club's founding in 1935. The Socialite's annual Christmas dance is one of the main events of the holiday calendar. Identified in this picture taken in 1960 are the couples Mr. and Mrs. Paul Mayes, Edward Robbins, H. Eugene Underwood, Richard Session, James Bailey, Percy Hughes, Jr., Phillip Blackwell, Wilson Johnson, Willard Jones, Claude Mason, Mrs. Roberta Singer and Mr. Donald Session.

Mrs. Bernyce Welling,

president and founder of Gamma Tau Chapter of Iota Phi Lambda, is shown flanked by Miss Pearl Mitchell, left, and Mrs. Charles W. Johnson, right, at the reception honoring Mrs. Charles Johnson's selection by the sorority as "Woman of the Year". Miss Mitchell and Mrs. Wreatha Maxwell (not shown) were selected by the judges as runner-ups. The three women were judged for their civic contributions to society during 1967-68. The sorority awarded the three honorees with handsome bronze statues symbolizing the particular field of endeavor.

Gordon Parks, and Hilda Simms

famous photographer, composer, writer and moving picture director is shown being interviewed by Hilda Simms. Mr. Parks, author of "The Learning Tree" is currently in Hollywood directing the picture based on the books. Mr. Parks is the first black producer to make a major picture for a major studio in the history of Hollywood. In addition to writing the book based on his early life in Kansas, he has written, produced and directed the film and has composed the musical score. Both Miss Simms and Mr. Parks are former residents of Minneapolis.

Fraternities and Sororities

The Omega Fraternity, XI Chapter was for many years in the leading position when it came to entertaining. Probably the greatest sponsor was the 10th Regional Conference in May 1947 when many of the Brothers had returned from service in World War II. Memorial Day weekend had become known as Omega weekend and this year when Brothers Allen, Jordan, Jenkins, Kyle, Butler, Maxwell, Jones, Stephens, Mallory, Shoffner, Wallace, Carmichael, Murray, Bradford, Benjamin, Schuck, Ward and Hall, most of whom were returning veterans, celebrated their return in memorable style. An especially popular trait of the Omegas was their policy of inviting the high school graduates so that often this was the first formal dance a graduate would attend. It sometimes happened that on Monday following the formal one might see Brothers in formal clothing still on the way home from the dance. Roy Wilkins was the first Basileus of XI Chapter.

The Kappas and the Alpha Kappa Alphas sometimes gave a formal together in the late spring while the Alphas gave one during the winter season.

House parties were always in vogue and it is interesting that often they too were formal.

With the number of good jazz pianists around, there was usually live music even at home and one of the most popular pianists was Gordon Parks whose rendition of Poor Butterfly was very much in demand. The high school group met at the Mallorys, the Bradys, over on Columbus Avenue at the Mann and Mason home and often down at the Carter's house on Oakland Avenue where the two families lived in a double bungalow which could easily accommodate the whole crowd.

Phyllis Wheatley House was the scene of intramural basketball tournaments with the fraternities furnishing their best often with more fervor than skill but the balcony was always packed with the faithful and at the dance afterwards it was hard to remember the imprecations which had preceded.

Today, the same events are held annually by the fraternities, sororities, fraternal organizations as were held then. In addition, there are many new clubs holding social functions and there is much home entertaining among different social sets. Bridge clubs are plentiful, both for men and women and a number of dinner clubs exist. Certainly there is something for almost everyone. Only among the very young is there a lack of organized clubdom, but perhaps they will continue toward National trend of a more service-oriented society.

Barbara Sybil Cyrus

71 years of service to the community — A tradition of service Dr. Robert S. Brown, 1898-1927. Dr. W. Donald, Sr., 1927-1968. Dr. W. Donald Brown, Jr. — present. Dr. Carol Brown, brother to Dr. Brown, Sr., practiced during the same period.

Omega Psi Phi (below)
Brothers of Omega Psi Phi Fraternity, Epsilon Rho chapter are shown as hosts to the 10th District Meeting in April, 1965. Founded in 1911 at Howard University in Washington, D.C., Omega Psi Phi is the second largest Negro fraternity in the United States.
From left to right in the first row the members are: Tyler Howell, Ray Pleasant, Thomas Stovall, William Benjamin. Second row: Dr. Thomas Johnson, James Horris, Albert McClure, Earl Kyle, William White. Back row: Wilbur Cartwright, Robert Mitchell, Boyd Wright, Ron Johnson, Maceo Moody, John Sims, John Work and Rozmond Kennon.

Alpha Phi Alpha (right)
Included in this picture are Cornelius Tucker and Charles Nichols in the front row, The Honorable Judge Stephen Maxwell in the rear, Rufus Webster, Clyde Hatcher, John Warder, Walter Goins, Jr., Sandy Stephens, Al Duran, Geo. Wardlow and William Cassius (front left).

The popular Percy Hughes Band
of the fifties featuring vocalists Judy Perkins and Dickie Mayes. These were swinging days in Mill Town.

Officers, Fezzan Temple No. 26
(First row): Lela Mae Stewart, Cecile Doty, Clarence Smith, Gertrude Greene. (Standing): De Vaughnia Simmons, Viola Madden, Leota Perkins.

Organizations, Patriotic, Civic

As in most American communities, the Negro veteran returned from service of his country to participate in the solution of his community's problems. For the most part he found it necessary to join segregated Negro veterans' posts and organizations to make his presence felt. Nevertheless, Negro patriotic organizations fulfill a definite need in their communities. Here in Minneapolis they have gone quietly about the work of patriotism and community service. Having lost so many buddies, brothers and friends in some foreign land, they are fiercely dedicated to Negro veteran recognition and citizenship.

Patriotic participation
(upper right) a Negro post commander addresses the State American Legion Convention, (below left) delivering groceries to the needy and the poor for Christmas, (below right) the Boy Scouts of America learn how to make Mulligan stew.

Social activities involving Negro citizens in our urban and suburban Minneapolis area are not confined or restricted to its ethnic boundaries — as in other large, congested industrial areas where the more unfortunate "Ghetto" Negro historically has been ignored by both the white and the Negro middle and upper class.

The Minneapolis area, fortunately, enjoys the product of its history — that of relatively little social discrimination and economic, educative and cultural equality, particularly in its community-sponsored yearly festivals.

This relaxed atmosphere has produced an integrated society — both industrial and social — where people participate generally because of their personal preference rather than their racial image. There is very little of the open confrontation of ethnic groups in these programs.

This ubiquity is generally true, and the generalities that are violated (more than occasionally) are either by pragmatic choice — or by some emotional pre-judgment. But again, as a general rule, the Black and white people mix comfortably and continually in our Minneapolitan society.

Minneapolis has become quite famous for its Aquatennial each summer with its many parades and store-sponsored entertainment, its bands, its water carnivals, and its competitions. Negroes participate in most of these areas. They also provide much of the accompanying entertainment through concerts and group activities. African culture, for instance, was promoted rather extensively in the past year throughout the community. And Afro-American culture is on the upswing through the youth movements in the Black community.

The Twin-City Observer, important local negro newspaper, endorsed this float in the Minneapolis Aquatennial Parade.

ITT

Louis Moore
A Wonder Bread salesman at our St. Paul Agency
for one year, is making a delivery for our
Hotel and Restaurant Division.

Homer Boyd
Acting pie shop foreman, has been with the Company
for four years. Here he is supervising Robert Renfro,
an 18-year veteran in the making of pie crust. Mr. Nathaniel
Martin, a 23-year man, and foreman, was on vacation.

Frozen Foods

Hostess Cake

232

UNIVAC

Mrs. James (Geraldine) Mills

(left), a computer assembler at Sperry Rand Corporation's UNIVAC Data Processing Division facility in the Roseville Space Center, suburban St. Paul, Minnesota, since December 1966, hand-wraps a wire connection on a principal component of UNIVAC Model 1108 Computer System. Mrs. Mills, 1021 Morgan Avenue North, Minneapolis, is employed in the final assembly area. She is a graduate of Minneapolis Vocational High School and the mother of two children.

Ray O. Pleasant,

a senior standards engineer (seated, second from left), tackles another engineering problem with professional associates employed by the Sperry Rand Corporation's UNIVAC Data Processing Division facility in the Roseville Space Center, suburban St. Paul, Minnesota. Pleasant, 9841 Xerxes Curve, Bloomington, Minnesota, joined UNIVAC in 1955, after two years' service as a U. S. Army corporal. Married and the father of two children, he received his bachelor's degree in electrical engineering from the University of Kansas.

Minneapolis Central H.S. Band
and majorettes perform at half time ceremony at Central Field in the North H.S. football game.

The Ames Lodge Drum and Bugle Corps
originated January 16, 1940, under the then Exalted Ruler, Major M. O. Culbertson, with Theodore Nixon as director and Leon T. Lewis as assistant director. The Ames Corps has been parade award winners in the Aquatennial Parade many times. Their list of achievements includes many trophies and a number of plaques and they are constantly adding to their collection.

Art Frazier, 12 years with us, expertly operates and adjusts this complex machine. It shaves tiny fibers of steel from 650-lb. coiled sheets — to make fine steel wool for industrial use.

Art and his wife, Meridythe, live in Brooklyn center with their three children.

Roosevelt Elliott, welder, adjusts his torch before neatly fusing together steel parts of a power sweeper — destined for use, with others, in more than 50 countries around the world.

Roosevelt, once a hospital worker, studied welding at Vocational to help prepare himself for his interesting job with us. He's been with us 2 years.

TENNANT COMPANY

ESTABLISHED 1870

701 N. Lilac Drive, Minneapolis, Minn. 55440

World's Largest Manufacturer of INDUSTRIAL FLOOR MACHINES

The Negro voter makes his choice

In the recent national election, Minnesota was
blessed with two of the four candidates for
President of the United States.
Both Eugene McCarthy and Hubert H. Humphrey
were well known and respected by the Black
community. And although neither were ultimate
victors, both were warmly endorsed and
even more warmly consoled when they returned
recently to their State. The Negro choice was
overwhelmingly for H.H.H. But being the spirited
citizen that he is, the Negro hopes to work
with and continue the progress made with the
Nation's choice, Richard M. Nixon.

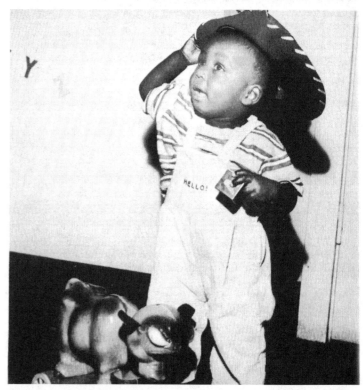

He wants a Mama and Papa

This cute little fellow, left alone and nameless,
is one of the children whom the state has
for adoption. He needs a mother and father and
we'll bet he would love them lots and
bring them great joy and happiness.

BEAUTY ENTERTAINMENT

Fashion and Photographer's Models

As has been previously mentioned in the Arts section of this book, the problem of Beauty for hire in advertising has been slow in solution for the talented young Negro woman, at least locally. Many such ambitious lovelies as Lenore McKenna, Jewel Gill and Elaine Person have sacrificed their personal limited finances, studied hard and tried even harder to find the reward that usually comes to talented in this field. The problem in the use of Negro models is in finding a willing sponsor. Still most of the girls shown here have enjoyed an occasional job as fashion models. And with the new emphasis on the Negro market the future looks brighter for them than the past.

Each year many Negro girls come out of school, looking for that ever evasive rainbow. In many of the larger cities some have found it.

We contend that Minneapolis could do much more to help the local model. Recently there has been several groups, interracial and racial, formed to try and cross this barrier. The companies of course could lead the way by insisting on the use of the local Negro model in advertising their products.

It should no longer be necessary to prove that beauty is more than "skin-deep". We salute these girls for their pride and ambition and wish them the best.

Model
Jewell Gill. A recent arrival on the modeling scene is this very pretty lady. In addition to her profession she likes to sew and read. With her ability we're sure you will be seeing her gracing your television screen real soon.
This beautiful lady hails from Duluth, Minnesota.

Olivia Rhodes
A graduate of Central High, and attended Minneapolis School of Art for three years. This very pretty young lady plans to become a fashion coordinator and she has an inkling to design clothing as well. She is the daughter of Mr. and Mrs. Oliver W. Rhodes.

Lenore McKenna
This very beautiful woman is a lovely example of looks, talent and versatility. She is a wife and mother, a homemaker, and a very talented model with the famous Ellie Morris agency. She and several other Negro models, including a sister, are pioneering the first break-through locally in the use of the Negro Beauty to sell T.V. and magazine advertising.

Elaine Y. Person
A native of Memphis, Tenn., Miss Person was graduated from Vocational H.S. in 1966. She specializes in the needle arts, which includes dressmaking and tailoring. She has been employed at Justers. She attended the Minnesota School of Business, qualified as key punch operator and recently was employed at TCOIC. She is also a photographers' model.

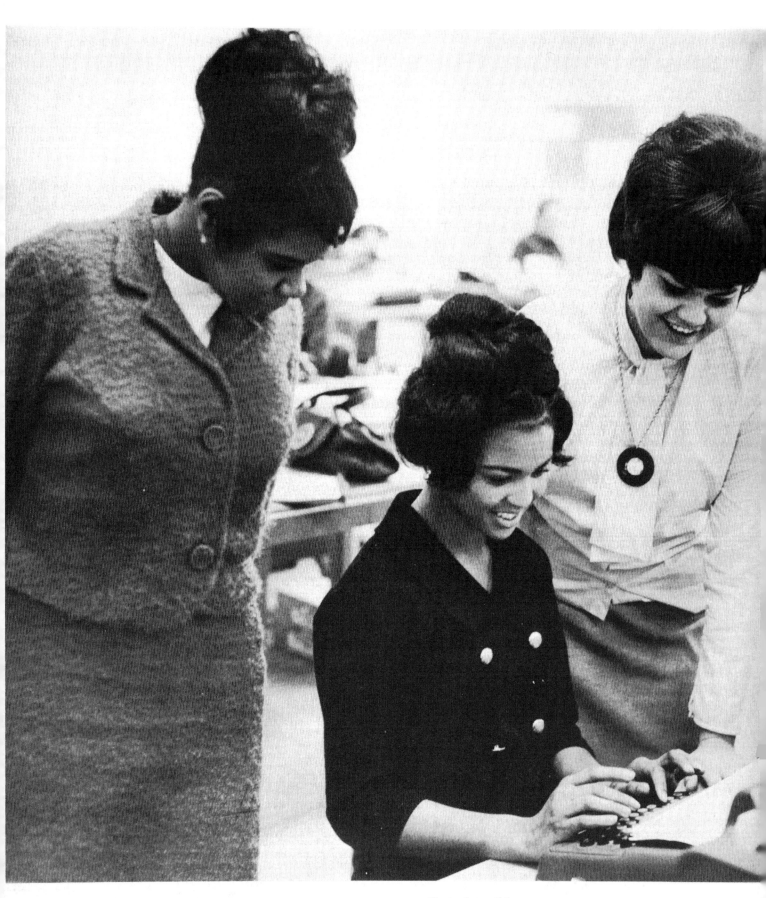

Willy Ruth English

and friends. This lovely young lady held various positions after receiving her business training. Since this photo was taken she has taken time off, to be married and become a mother.

Linda Lee Jones

Miss Jones has resided in Mpls. for two years. She is currently employed by Honeywell and has attended the Mary Lowe Modeling School for Professionals. She has modeled for the Star and Tribune. Art directors and photographers take notice.

Terry May Bluitt

is a pretty 18-year-old senior at Minneapolis Central H.S. She plans to train as a Registered Nurse upon graduation.

Two of Minneapolis' lovelies,

Cheryl (left) and Lynn Davis, daughters of Mr. and Mrs. Danny Davis. Cheryl attends Augsburg College and Lynn attends Regina High School. Their father, a famous ex-prize fighter, also appears in this book.

Deborah Lewis

Miss Lewis, age 23, was born in Minneapolis and has lived both here and in Edmonton, Alberta, Canada. She has appeared recently in local fashion shows and in television. She currently is employed by the National City Bank of Minneapolis.

Entertainment, Musical Groups

The entertainment scene in Minneapolis today is probably as varied as are the tastes and inclinations of members of the black community. It is evident, at least visually, that the trend toward engaging more black artists of talent has resulted in more regular and more representative attendance in all places where these artists appear.

Once Michael Babatunde Olatunji was introduced at Dayton's, his troupe was enthusiastically taken up and subsequent appearances at Walker Art Center, The Guthrie Theatre and in Saint Paul were sold out. Jazz concerts, wherever they are, are always sold out. And it is also interesting that when the Minneapolis Institute of Arts presented the Black Artists Show in this area there were more Negroes there than I have seen in many years of constant attendance at the

Institute. It is now history that the Art of the Congo sculpture show at Walker drew unprecedented crowds, many black people being there for the first time.

In the world of jazz, the story is a little different, however. Minneapolis, in its early history, was blessed in having a number of gifted musicians who were born and incidentally stranded here during the lean years for black musicians. It was also a time when the Negro in Minnesota was so completely ostracized that he was allowed to own and run his night clubs in his own way and his own time just as long as he kept away from downtown. As a result, the native-born Negro in Minneapolis is often heard lamenting the "Good old days". On any weekend night on the North Side one might hear Oscar Pettiford, Adolphus Alsbrook, Rook Ganz, Vernon Pittman and many

Buddy Davis Trio
This swinging trio consists of Buddy Davis, Maurice Turner (bass), Jesse Lopez (drums). For the past year Buddy and his group has been appearing at the Thunderbird Motel and Supper Club. This popular trio has appeared at the

city's leading night spots. It would be a great thing to reserve an evening to hear Buddy Davis do "his thing." Buddy is featured on the X77 Hammond Organ and the vibraphone and piano and also does a fine job of vocalizing.

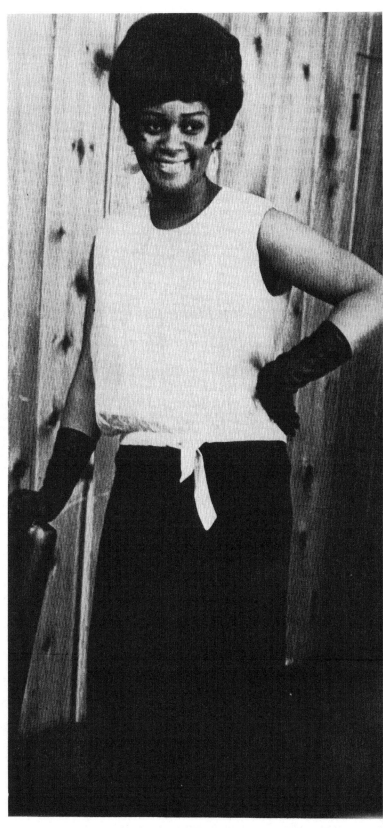

Jimmy Bowman
is a former Chicagoan but now makes Minneapolis
his home. Wherever he appears the crowds
are large. They come to hear him when working
as a single; also attendance is great when
the Jimmy Bowman Duo is on the stage.
His recording of Wine and Roses was quite a hit.

Shirley Witherspoon,
a brilliant local talent, is really
doing great things on the local jazz scene.
The local jazz buffs have acclaimed
her as one of the finest singers to hit
the scene in a long, long time.
It won't be too much longer before
she hits the National scene.

others who after finishing engagements downtown come out the Clef Club, the Benganzi, Twenty Limited, the Elk's Rest, Howard's Steak House or others.

But wherever one ended the evening, Saturday nights always started at the Dreamland where Florence and A. B. Cassius ran a "tight ship" being "home folks" but where one usually had the best possible time. It was here that notables in the city usually came for meals and to absorb something of the black community, and in 1947 when the Cassius's moved downtown to what had been Bell's and opened the Bamboo Room, the whole crowd went downtown with them. The Bamboo Room was an innovation in Minneapolis in that it was the first legitimate

Negro-owned spot downtown where liquor could be served and where good entertainment was to be heard. Here on Saturday nights a combo of Rufus Webster, Oscar Frazier, Irving Williams and Ronnie Newman usually played and on occasion other good musicians might appear.

There are certainly many fine young musicians around today with Michael's Mystics, Dave Brady, Jr. and others playing to tremendous followings. The Bobby Lyle group plays to huge crowds whenever they are at the Nacirim on Sunday. There are many of the younger set, "Rhythm And Blues" and "Soul Groups" who have yet to be recognized. However, (and perhaps it is unfair) Dickie Mayes downtown is

CONTINUED ON PAGE 247

Rook Gans
is a native of Kansas City. He still plays for dances and parties. He was a member of some of the biggest name bands in the country. His close friendship with people in the entertainment world entail a full page of names. Rook has resided in the city for over 30 years.

Percy Hughes
and his band has been appearing at the Point Supper Club for the last 10 years. His saxophone playing (tenor and alto) is still rated high on the list. When not on the bandstand, Percy can be found catching up on some long-overdue reading and just plain relaxation.

Judy Perkins
is known as a singer's singer; this lovely lady seems to get better and better. When she is not singing she is doing her first and most enjoyable role as being a housewife. In private life, Judy is Mrs. Percy Hughes.

John Work
recently moved to the East, but here in Minneapolis he really began to come to the front. We're certain that it won't be too much longer before we see him on Broadway.

The Cassanovas

Typical of several new fast rising Rhythm and Soul groups
with an eye on future fame, among the northsiders are
The Cassanovas, a combo formed last year at the home of
Mrs. Thompson on North Oliver St. This group
of self-taught young soul brothers plays and composes its
own sounds and has caught the fancy of the community,
having recently played The Way, T.C.O.I.C., Augustana College,
University of Minnesota, and outstate small towns in
Wisconsin and South Dakota. They have also played adult
dances as the older crowd catches on to the latest thing.
Pictured left to right are Roy Thompson, Keith White,
Edward Brown, Leopold Williams and John Jefferson. Missing
in this photo are Cecil Nelson III, organist, Troy Williams,
sax, and singers Bruce Pearson, Larry Brown and Steve Shannon.
Below: Dance time at the Way Center and the young "brothers"
and "sisters" do the Soulful Strut and get themselves together!

Shari Farris

Miss Farris has been an exciting jazz vocalist for several
years in this community. She is formerly from Duluth,
Minnesota, and has been billed in the past with Count Basie,
Les Elgart, Glenn Miller, and the Playboy Clubs.
She is a mother and a housekeeper and is currently attending
school here. She plans to renew her singing career
in the near future.

not the same as Dickie Mayes at the Flame when he made those tremendous entrances leaping onto the stage and belting out those hard blues numbers before a near-hysterical audience of Percy Hughes followers. An over-amplified Muddy Waters at the Guthrie is not the same as Muddy Waters at the Cozy Bar or the Blue Note where his style is most appreciated.

Any jazz sophisticate knows that the rapport between the audience and the entertainers in a black-owned club is something different and that the give and take or call and response is not to be found anywhere else.

There is something to being "at home" and to knowing that there won't be "too many of them" which usually results in a change of management or policy or going out of business.

It is not that it isn't wonderful to be able to go anywhere one chooses but it is simply that one seldom finds the true jazz experience anywhere but on one's home ground.

In music, it may be only temporary but as of now, integration and relocation have ruined the day!

Barbara Sybil Cyrus

Miss Doris Hines
This vivacious local young vocalist is known as a Brown Bombshell in the business with torrid vocals and heart-stirring soul music renditions. She has just recently returned to the city from national engagements. Her recent appearance at the Golliwog Lounge at the top of the Sheraton Ritz downtown was "Out of Sight."

Dickie Mayes
is one of the most popular singers around—not only in the city but around the country. Listening to Dickie, whether it be in concert or night club, is a lovely way to spend an evening.

Choral or Religious Groups

Negro church and religious song groups have for decades been the original proving ground for many of the musically talented youths who have many times gone on to national popularity and fame, sometimes in religious song (as Mahelia Jackson) or in a more rythmic popular song or "Soul" music (as Aretha Franklin). Most ballads, blues, Soul music or rythmic groups have, originally in Negro history, been fostered by the Negro Church Choir, both Gospel and Choral.

The Negro painfully or happily sings from his heart.

Minneapolis has had many such fine groups, mostly voluntary and non-profit who have made themselves available to the community to spread good will and promote good race relations regardless of religious affiliation or denomination. From its humble beginning to its recent proud recognition, "Soul" music knows no color barrier. It is simply, *one* sincere man talking to *another*.

(Above) **Zion Church Senior Choir**
in the beautiful setting of their new church give a stirring rendition of a Negro Spiritual.

SPORTS

The Black Athlete

Recently, much of the nation's attention has been focused on the affairs of the Negro athlete, both professional and college, particularly as a result of the "closed-fist" incident at the 1968 Olympics in Mexico City by Black track team militants on the U.S. squad. It would be foolish to ignore the obvious implications of this incident. In fact, to call it merely an incident would be foolish.

The Negro has contributed much to this Nation's highly competitive image of athletic supremacy, as viewed by the rest of the world. This is especially true in the view of the athletes themselves, who have amassed an impressive collection of Gold, Silver, and Bronze medals each Olympic year. With a simple look at the total U.S. points each year, one could not escape the conclusion that the U.S. games record at least would be far below many of their friends' and even the Iron Curtain countries if it weren't for the Black American. And this is not to question the motives of the Black militant athlete himself. His loyalty throughout the years is without parallel.

It does indicate, though, that all is not golden in his view at least with the system as it remains. Many feel that they have been used as an instrument to create an illusion and have been ignored in the benefits, they feel rightly belong to the victor. Many come from very poor families and lack the funds to develop their talents. Many of the Athletic Clubs have accepted them as team representatives but have denied them Club membership or financial encouragement after their competitive days are over.

Locally many Negro athletes reach a high plateau of recognition, only to disappear into relative obscurity after their prime. Many potential youths in the Black community feel it's all a waste of time. There seems to be no benefits due them after their retirement. Still, in sports the Negro is traditionally a *fighter*, and many of them here, militant or otherwise, *do* continue to produce enviable records, for themselves and their schools.

(Above) **Earl Bowman,** then the football coach at Minneapolis Central H.S., and his fighting team

Jim Marshall
All-Pro defensive end, Minnesota Vikings

Alan Page
star, All-Pro defensive tackle, Minnesota Vikings

Carl Eller
All-Star, All-Pro defensive end, Minnesota Vikings

Charlie West
Defensive back, Minnesota Vikings.

Clint Jones
All-American halfback, Vikings

The Bronze Amateur Open

Unquestionably, one of the most widely known nationally, and locally in the Negro community, and probably least heralded sports event locally in the white community is the Jimmy Slemmon's sponsored "Bronze Amateur Open" Annual now in its 28th year of production. It has year after year attracted the outstanding non-professional Negro golfers of the Nation to Minneapolis each summer and traditionally has offered this somewhat unnoticed and unappreciated talent a moment of glory, at least in their groups. Such illustrious names as Joe Louis, Charlie Sifford, Pete Brown and Ted Cook have participated in past years. Golfers have journeyed here from Chicago, Milwaukee, Peoria, St. Louis, Gary,

Cleveland, Dallas, Indianapolis, Detroit, and from as far away as Los Angeles and Miami, Fla. just to enjoy Minnesota summers and participate in this Negro tournament. Traditionally it has been in the past held at the tough Theodore Wirth Park course, however last year it was changed for the first time to the Hiawatha Public Course. As many as 250 Negro golfers have participated in each two day affair, which includes a social party, a dance and many hundreds of prizes for amateur play, given by local merchants and companies. Mr. Slemmons promises a bigger and even better tournament in 1969. Let's back it!

Ted Cook One of the first recognized Negro professional golfers in the United States is from Minneapolis

Mike Fitzgerald ex-Viking

Ersal Mackbee defensive cornerback, Vikings

Gene Washington All-Star flanker, Vikings

Archie Sutton ex-Viking

The Minnesota Twins and Vikings

Much has been written about the magnificent and heroic exploits of the Negro stars on the Minnesota Twins and the Minnesota Vikings. There is the fantastic hitting of super star Tony Oliva, ex league batting champion, the daring play and running of Rod Carew, ex league rookie of the year, the all around play at many positions of Cesar Tovar, the solid generalship of John Roseboro, the ex L. A. Dodger, all Twins. Some others have gone to other teams as sometimes happens in this National pastime, like Zoilo Versalles, and Mudcat Jim Grant, both players on the League Champion Twins of 1965. And who can forget the lamented but memorable wrong way touchdown of Big Jim Marshall back when the Vikings were the fledgling newcomer to the N.F.L. This year, 1968, the rest of the league, especially the mighty Green Bay Packers knew they had grown up — champions of the all tough Central Division, edging the Chicago Bears for that title on the last day of the season.

And not enough can be said about the greatness of our front four, Marshall, Page, the youngster, Eller, the all pro, and Larson, the equally great white member of the defensive quartet. And also there's the antelope-like darting of Gene Washington, off to pick off passes amidst a swarm of defenders on third and long yardage. And All-American Clint Jones, who has yet to reach the full promise of his No. one draft choice rating. Teamwork was the word for the 1968 Vikings and the Negro members of the team really lived up to the word as did their white mates. Next year, the Super Bowl maybe?

(Right) **Tony Oliva**

Rod Carew

Cesar Tovar

John Roseboro

The Gophers and Other College Stars

Many Negro All-Americans, Stars and Super Stars, have gained their first national recognition while playing their hearts out for Minnesota universities and colleges. The list is long and glittering. Names like Horace Bell, Sandy Stephens, Bobby Bell, Aaron Brown, Carl Eller, Lou Hudson, and Archie Clark, just to name a few were stars of the past on nationally ranked Gopher teams at the University of Minnesota. More recently new names like Ray Stephens (Sandy's younger brother), Wayne Barry, Al Nuness, Leroy Gardner, Charlie Sanders, Hubie Bryant and at North Dakota State, Paul Hatchett, locally from Minneapolis and a Little All-American, have given this area a brilliant history in college sports achievement. It is generally accepted that many of the state's outstanding teams could not have gained their recognized measure of success nationally or in their conferences without these Black athletes. The Minnesota Gophers alone certainly can attribute their recent success in the Big Ten in football and basketball and track

Ray Stephens, Basketball

Ray Stephens, Football

to their Negro athletic recruiting programs, as can most of the other schools in the conference. The University of Minnesota was one of the conference leaders in the encouragement and play of the Negro athlete. This is also true of the other smaller schools and colleges in the State. Recently as in other schools throughout the nation, Negro athletes at State schools have demanded a greater role in the affairs of the school and its athletic programs.

For instance, it has been logically pointed out by the athletes that they are still quite a minority in enrollment, have few or no representation on the coaching staffs and feel that they are being used to promote the school name without having much influence on its policies and decisions. It is a fact, certainly, that although Negroes do achieve national recognition as players for Big Ten schools and smaller colleges, very few of them are selected as members of coaching staffs or athletic directors, or even teachers or staff members in the school's Physical Education curriculums. This seems to tarnish an otherwise brilliant record of inter group team play. Through the use of boycott and pressures of a sympathetic student body, the Negro athlete hopes to change this condition by the mid 70's. By then, hopefully, we may see a Negro coach nervously pacing the sidelines and biting his nails at the Rose Bowl on New Year's Day.

Hubie Bryant

Al Nuness,
captain U. of M. basketball, 1968-69

Wayne Barry

Leroy Gardner

Track, Bowling, Boxing

As in most northern cities, in Minneapolis sports activities on the local level are seasonal. With the exception of hockey, ice skating and skiing, Negro athletes participate in most of them and are outstanding in some. Negro bowlers participate in local team competition, and a few of them on mixed teams. Several have competed on TV prize shows and have been winners.

In track the Black athlete is supreme, both in high school and college, particularly in the dashes, jumps and middle distances. Local organization-sponsored baseball teams have won State championships. Since most of the Negro population in

Al Frost received a plaque commemorating his Hamline scoring record during half-time ceremonies of the Hamline-Concordia basketball game. Presenting the plaque was Clarence Nelson, (right), Hamline athletic director. Piper coach Howie Schultz, and Earl Bowman (left), one of Al's high school coaches at Minneapolis Central, look on.

(above picture) The Starlite Bowling League

Gerald Bailey, Sr.	Elbert Clark	Robert Green	Andy Clark	Fred Lee	Mattie Hill
Muriel Gardner	Bessie Green	Edna Judy	Helen Underwood	John Burrell	

the state is concentrated in the Minneapolis-St. Paul area, the public schools of this community have been represented by many fine players from the Black community. As yet however have they appeared on the powerful suburban teams such as Edina and St. Louis Park who have heavily endowed sports programs much more extensive and better coached than the city program. Even so, the youthful Negro athlete has more than held his own.

In boxing, a sport dominated nationally by the Black fighter both amateur and professional for more than 40 years, Minneapolis has done equally well. During the twenties, Minnesota enjoyed its finest hours in the fight game. St. Paul was considered the boxing capital of the world around 1927-1930. It had fighters like the Gibbons Brothers, Billy Miske, Light Horse Harry Wilson, Bill Tate, Tiger Flowers, Harry Wills, the Black Panther, who Jack Dempsey refused to fight. The Boston Tar Baby also fought in Minneapolis, St. Paul. Then there was Battling Siki who won the title in Dublin, Ireland on St. Patricks Day who fought from out of the Twin Cities. Billy Daniels and Art Laskie were Minneapolis contenders during the '20's and early '30's.

In later years there were the Hammond Brothers, Eddie Lacey, and Danny Davis.

Under the tutelage of Harry Davis, an outstanding Negro ex-prize fighter himself, Minneapolis enjoyed its finest years in Golden Gloves, in the 30's and 40's. He had championship teams year after year at the Phyllis Wheatley House, and attracted crowds at the Auditorium of ten to twelve thousand avid fans. Some of these outstanding fighters were Wally Holmes, Danny O'Shea, the Rodrigues Brothers, Jim Beattie and others.

To the left—Danny Davis was a fast, clever fighter with explosive hands. He is one of many local boxers who carved their names indelibly in the history of the fight game, both nationally and locally in Minneapolis.

The Former Minnesota Pipers

Last year the Twin Cities were hosts to the Champion Pipers. The big switch in the American Basketball Assn. (ABA) had seen the 2nd Place Muskies move from here to Florida, and the Champion Pipers move here from Pittsburgh to become the Minnesota Pipers. Thus the Twin Cities had gained a proven winner with a record tough to match. The Piper team had a 54 win, 24 loss record with a .692 percentage and led the league by 4 games. The team also won the ABA playoffs over New Orleans, 4 to 3. There were several new stars in addition to the players shown here. Now the Pipers make their home in Pittsburgh and the Minneapolitans wish them the best of luck.

Left to right, (first row) Willie Porter, Tom Washington, Leroy Wright; (2nd row) Charles Williams, Chico Vaughn, Arvesta Kelly, and (far right) the league's most valuable player and highest scorer, Connie Hawkins.

MINNEAPOLIS·MOLINE®

Walter Jones

Mr. Jones was born in Wichita Falls, Texas, is married to Doris Nadine, and is the father of three. He is ambassador-at-large for M-M, company car for delivery of RUSH, EDP section, data processing material between the Hopkins plant and other plants and offices in Minneapolis. He also carries all correspondence and confidential material interplant and executive personnel between plants. He says, "If I were asked what a young man or woman could do to assure a good future, I'd say simply 'Stay in school, because your future depends on what you make of yourself.' "

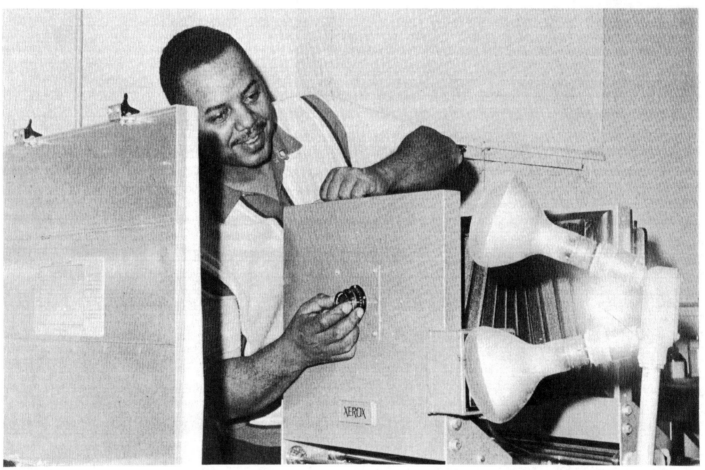

Kenneth Earl Grigsby

After service (1954-57) in the U.S. Army Paratroopers, Ken worked at Veterans Administration and later at the Minneapolis Post Office before joining Minneapolis-Moline in 1966. With experience in Army communications, Kenneth began in M-M's internal photolithing and stationery department

Born in Louisiana, he was married to Marie Bellard in 1957. They live with their four children, Samuel, Maxine, Angela and Kenneth Jr. at 701 Penn Avenue North in Minneapolis.

After graduating from Minneapolis Vocational High School, he matriculated at Augsburg College where he studied before enlisting in the Army.

Learning the fine points of photography and photolithing, chiefly "on the job" at Minneapolis-Moline under the

direction of Kenneth Dumas, Kenneth says, "Any boy or girl who wants to get an education leading to a better job can do so. Without an education, things will be pretty tough these days. Success in any work is not automatic.

"Whether it's a profession like medicine or law or engineering, or mechanical work or office work, you have to put out a lot of effort to learn the basics and then improve as you develop," he continued. "But, I've found that there is no greater satisfaction than doing my job well. My wife Marie and I are doing our best to get across to our children this idea of ambition, self-respect for themselves and for others and a sense of personal responsibility as the best assurance for a happy life."

![Onan logo]

Melvin Goodman

Mr. Goodman, age 53, has been employed at Onan for 32 years, one of our first employees and the first Negro employee. Mel is an inspector in our Quality Assurance Department. He is married and has 5 children, lives at 907 Penn Avenue North.

Alphia C. Black

Mr. Black, age 38, is one of our newest employees. He also is a first, the first Negro electrician at Onan. He works in the Electrical Maintenance Department which repairs and installs all electrical work at Onan. Alphia is married and has 4 children, lives at 3948 5th Avenue South.

PHILLIPS & SON

Mr. George Riddles
Mr. Riddle is employed with the Ed. Phillips & Sons Co. in the production department. He is attending night school at North High School. Mr. Riddle is married and the father of two children.

Mr. Ira Smith
Mr. Smith is employed as an order filler with the firm of Ed. Phillips & Sons Co. He has been with the firm since 1957. He has 3½ years of college. He is married, and the father of six children.

HOLIDAY INN

The matre'd at this famous place of entertainment has welcomed hundreds of Negro organizations in regular and holiday festivities throughout the years. This downtown inn has done much to encourage Negro participation in luxurious dining and dancing.

Keeping Twin Citians "On The Go"

Above: Charles Banks, a 29 year veteran, is a mechanic in the Overhaul Shop, specializing in keeping cylinder heads in the 635 buses purring like a kitten.

Center: William Massie, a 21 year veteran is part of the crew of 850 that keeps the 635 buses travelling a distance equal to two "Round-The-World" trips daily.

Below: Clarence Perry, a 20 year veteran, who started as a bus driver, is assistant Personnel Director searching for the talent that keeps the buses "On The Go."

Twin City Lines serves more than 1,000,000 passengers a week. It takes a lot of people with a lot of talent to meet the demands of this kind of service. These men are members of the team that keeps Twin City Lines "On The Go" in Minneapolis and St. Paul.

Summary

The editors and publishers of this book wish to thank the many hundreds of friends, associates and companies, whose assistance, advice and contributions helped create what we believe to be a valuable, useful, and informative publication. A limitation of space does not permit us to name each of them individually. We do wish to acknowledge the following persons, who, in addition to those listed as staff members, have contributed specific and detailed facts in the different divisions of this book: Mr. Ashby Gaskins, Mgmt. Consultant, Mr. A. B. Cassius, Mr. Wilbur Rogan, photographer, Mr. Charles Stanifer, Mpls. Chamber of Commerce. Thanks also goes to the Minneapolis Board of Education, the office of the County Sheriff, the Minneapolis Police Dept., the County and City Attorneys for providing photos and information. We also thank Governor LeVander and Mayor Naftalin for the encouragement their letters of endorsement gave to the project.

Equal Opportunity Employers

Finally, we offer a special endorsement and vote of thanks to the firms that proudly bear the title, "Equal Opportunity Employer". Without their support and assistance, this project would not have been possible.

The following are E.O.E. companies who have participated in this book. In the order of their appearance they are:

General Mills Company
Electric Machinery Company
International Milling
  Company
Northwestern Bell
  Telephone Co.
American Telephone and
  Telegraph Co.
Western Electric Co.
Gambles
Apache Corporation
Minneapolis Star
Minneapolis Tribune
IBM Company
Baker Properties
Twin City Federal
Northwestern National Bank
Pako Corporation
Dain, Kalman and Quail
  Company
Farmers & Mechanics Bank
Super Valu Stores
Piper Jaffrey and Hopwood
Sears Roebuck Co.
Northern States Power
  Company
Minnegasco
Honeywell Inc.
Donaldson's Stores
American National Bank

Midwest Federal
WCCO Radio and TV
Bemis Company
Dayton's
Pillsbury Company
Northwestern National Life
Cargill, Inc.
Colwell Press
Ford Motor Company
North Central Airlines
Napco Industries
Great Northern Railroad
Investors Diversified
  Services
Northwest Orient Airlines
Vic Manufacturing
Northrup King
First National Bank
Land O'Lakes
Donaldson Co.
Thermo King
Marquette National Bank
Northern Pacific R. R. Co.
Control Data
Univac
Tennant Co.
Minneapolis-Moline
Onan
Twin City Lines

Future Publications

We sincerely hope this book meets with your approval. We hope you have enjoyed the contents. And above all we hope that the information we have gathered, requiring *months* of painstaking care and inquiry, will serve the purpose we originally envisioned, namely, to promote a healthier understanding of the Black Community, eliminate some of the false concepts of shiftlessness, ineptness or failure of the Black Citizen, and educate the Negro youth to their vast potential and the past accomplishments of their elders right here in Minnesota.

With this purpose in view, the Scott Publishing Company plans to extend future publication service to other communities. We hope to do similar profiles with local approval and endorsement on the Negro Communities of St. Paul, Milwaukee, Chicago, Cleveland, Detroit, Gary, Indianapolis, Cincinnati, St. Louis, Omaha, and Denver.

Mr. Leo E. Browne

Mr. Browne started with Mr. Scott in September of 1958. He is the Public Relations man for the book. With Mr. Browne's help publications were made possible. When the company begins to expand, Mr. Browne will be responsible for its operations in other cities in the United States.

Northrup, King and Co.

Mindless Racism Has Expunged The Negro From History

"We hold these truths to be self-evident," wrote Thomas Jefferson in 1776, in the Declaration of American Independence, "that all men are created equal; that they are endowed by their Creator with certain unalienable rights, and that among these are life, liberty, and the pursuit of happiness."

"But, sir," Benjamin Banneker protested, in a 1791 letter to Jefferson, "how pitiable is it to reflect, that although you were so fully convinced of the benevolence of the Father of Mankind, and of His equal and impartial distribution of these rights and privileges, which He hath conferred upon them, that you should at the same time counteract His mercies, in detaining by fraud and violence so numerous a part of my brethren, under groaning captivity, and cruel oppression . . ."

Banneker, these lines make plain, was a Negro, one of the most distinguished of his day; he is described as follows in "The Black Power Revolt," a collection of essays edited by Floyd M. Barbour: "One of a team of three who determined the boundaries of the present city of Washington, Banneker published annually after 1792 a widely used almanac devised by himself."

In fact, Banneker seized the opportunity to chide Jefferson in a covering letter for a copy of the almanac which he was sending to the great Virginian, who undoubtedly welcomed it with the interest he showed for anything scientific. It is too bad that so few today, white or black, know anything about this remarkable early American.

That is true also of, say, Dr. John S. Rock, a Boston physician who also became, before the Civil War, the first black man admitted to legal practice before the Supreme Court; nor do many Americans realize that a black man came over the Atlantic with Columbus, well before the Mayflower, another explored the West with Lewis and Clark, and another went to the North Pole with Peary.

Tom Johnson of the New York Times has just returned from several months in Vietnam, during which he made a close study of the attitudes of the black soldiers who make up more than 60 per cent of the Army there. One of his most curious findings was that many of them believed that in Vietnam Negroes were for the first time getting a chance to prove themselves as fighting men, and that this belief pushed many of them to excel as soldiers.

Few of them knew, Johnson found, that thousands of Negroes served under George Washington in the American Revolution and Andrew Jackson in the War of 1812; that black troops acquitted themselves well on both sides in the Civil War; and that a large number of the storied cavalrymen who cleared the Indians from the Old West were black men.

This is just one more result of the all-white orientation of American society and culture — that most deepseated and unquenchable form of racism which is neither malignant nor expressed but unconscious. It is this orientation which has virtually eliminated from American education any study of the origins, the development, the cultural and social contributions, and even the simplest history of more than 10 per cent of the population.

This all-white education (a matter quite distinct from the question of pupil segregation) has been responsible for what James Baldwin called "a feeling of no past, no present and no future" in Negro children; it has made black soldiers in Vietnam unaware that they are part of a long and valorous tradition; and it has obviously been a large factor in the lack of self-esteem noticeable in many older Negroes.

It is equally obvious that the practical expunging of the Negro from the record of the past is bound to have had its subtle effect on white attitudes. If white men do not know that black men helped win American independence and pacify the continent, it is a lot easier to talk glibly of "giving" the Negro his rights only when he has "earned" them.

Rep. James Scheuer of New York has been looking into all this with a view to establishing a commission on Negro history and culture. No doubt that would help; but the greater need is for school boards, teachers' associations, and textbook publishers to take some direct, practical action against this kind of mindless racism.

The above article was written by Tom Wicker of the New York Times Service and appeared in the Minneapolis Tribune last year during the period of the "Long Hot Summer" protests in this city and others throughout the Nation. It is as appropriate an answer we know as to why this book was written and published.

The Heroic Negro Soldier

Since World War I, the Black American communities have given many thousand lives in defense of their country. Today the American Negro soldier still fights for his freedom, fighting many thousands of miles from home in Vietnam, for the cause of democratic concepts to be offered to his Oriental brethren. Many of these same concepts have yet to be realized by his own family at home. Let us make amends and give him the just reward of complete first-class citizenship that he has earned.

<u>Not</u> for discriminating people

MINNESOTA'S

BLACK COMMUNITY

MINNESOTA'S

BLACK
COMMUNITY

MINNESOTA'S
BLACK
COMMUNITY

SCOTT
PUBLISHING COMPANY INC.
MINNEAPOLIS, MINNESOTA 55407

SCOTT PUBLISHING COMPANY INC.
Walter R. Scott Sr. . . . . .President-Publisher
Anthony R. Scott . . . . Executive Vice President
Walter R. Scott Jr. . . . . Vice President
Chaunda L. Scott . . . . Secretary-Treasurer
Alvin W. Riley Sr. . . . . Production Director
LeClair Lambert . . . . Executive Editor
Ashby D. Reed Jr. . . . . Art Director
Litho Technical Services . . . . Printing

DEDICATED TO:
*the maximal development of
all Black children in the
state of Minnesota and the
United States of America*

CONTENTS

Walter R. Scott, Sr.
Publisher

Dear Fellow Citizens:

In the spring of 1945 the Governor's Interracial Commission submitted to Governor Edward Thye a report on the condition of Black people in Minnesota. It was later published as a booklet under the title, *The Negro Worker in Minnesota*. The supply of copies has long since been exhausted, and many requests have been made for a new edition.

Yet, during the past thirty years there have been considerable changes in the condition of the status of the Black population and in the attitudes of the majority population. It seemed to us, then, that current data should be collected and presented.

For that task my son and I secured the following information to be put into this pictorial resume. With the limited resources at our disposal, we collected the data and prepared the material for this book. The changes during the past thirty years have been so significant that the two of us judged that this book should carry a new title for this Bicentennial celebration, "Minnesota's Black Community."

We now submit our effort to you. In it an earnest attempt has been made to present pictorially, not merely facts, but facts in their proper proportion and perspective.

Respectfully yours,

Walter R. Scott, Sr.
Publisher

LeClair G. Lambert
Executive Editor

PUBLISHER'S STATEMENT

Any attempt to separate the Black people from Minnesota's history would be as difficult as trying to divorce the stars from the stripes on the American flag. The stars on Old Glory represents today's 50 states and the stripes represents the 13 original colonies. Without the 13, there never would have been the 50.

In precisely the same way, without the Black man, there never would have been a modern Minnesota—bustling, growing, expanding, innovating, and rolling with the punches of the 20th Century.

Mr. Frederic Jones, chief engineer at the United States Thermo Control Company in Minneapolis—now known as "Thermo King"—worked many, many years with this company. Acclaim came to him by inventing the automatic mobile refrigerator, making it possible for servicemen to have fresh vegetables, meat and ice cream on their menus in the most remote and obscure places on the battlefront. Mr. Jones was elected to the American Society of Refrigeration Engineers and was called to the Bureau of Standards in Washington to consult with the office of the Quartermaster General. Mr. Jones was given credit for being one of the first exploring in the field of sound equipment. It was said that 75 percent of the theatres in the Northwest, at one time, used sound equipment developed by him.

Despite the remarkable episode in Minnesota's history written by Mr. Jones, little is known about this extraordinary man, few realize that he was a Black man. No one has dedicated himself to the compilation of a volume which chronicles the barriers which Black people found in their paths in the pre- and post-Frederic Jones era.

This is why the *Minnesota's Black Community* was published. It is unfair to the nearly 50,000 Blacks now living in Minnesota to hide their historical link to the state. It is equally a disservice to white Minnesotans who are anxious to know more about their fellow Black citizens. Thus, after years of research, compilation, and editing, the *Minnesota's Black Community* has become a reality and provides in one volume, reasons why the Black man in Minnesota as a "worker" has not reached his potential.

This is a reference book and is not intended to be a historical narrative. Because the staff felt that the most pressing area of understanding lies in the role of the Black worker in Minnesota today, we have made this our editorial emphasis. However, we have woven into our pages historical information—editorially and pictorially—crucial to an understanding of the state and its growth.

We chose to follow this approach mainly because we have great hope that *Minnesota's Black Community* will become a bridge toward understanding in these days of enormous unrest and racial provocations. Basic to most of the enmity between blacks and whites is an accumulated ignorance on both sides. Blacks are all too often unaware of significant inroads they have made in the state's political, economic, educational and cultural development.

Our effort reveals that a few Blacks are "almost" everywhere in Minnesota life and their presence is by no means, at the bottom rungs of the ladder. There is hardly a field of endeavor in which they are not represented and in many areas, they have climbed to high echelons of responsibility and status. Pictorially, presenting this progress in certain areas, the staff feels, will not only provide highly significant resource material for the student of race relations, but will also have vital psychological and inspirational impact on the Black population, especially the younger element which is increasingly impatient and demanding.

At the same time, white Minnesotans are woefully ignorant of the great positive contributions which Blacks have made to Minnesota's historical development. Nor are they fully aware of the continuing role of the Black man in Minnesota's growth. This gap in understanding is a major cause of the racial problems which grip Minnesota, as it does every other state in this nation.

Because of this gap in understanding, the staff of *Minnesota's Black Community* have put under one cover what is without question the most complete compendium of Black activity ever published on the Black people in Minnesota.

On the following pages, editorially, will be a collection of material pertaining to the Black worker in Minnesota. You will also find profiles of Black people today whose influence and achievement have been outstanding. There could be many more but the plan for this book is such that long narratives are not consistent with its format. Thus, you will find on the pages ahead many such profiles.

Indeed, as complete as is our presentation of Blacks in Minnesota, there will be many oversights, omissions, and we fear, some errors. For these, the publisher accepts complete responsibility and assures you, "I have made every possible effort to make this book worthwhile."

It is my fervent hope that this volume will serve its purpose: generate greater understanding between the races, and, as a result, help close the gap which keeps white Minnesotans and black Minnesotans from clasping hands to "work" toward a United America. I believe that this book will be a vehicle in the achievement of this goal.

Walter R. Scott, Sr.
Editor-Publisher

EARLY BLACK SETTLERS

Stephen Bonga

George Bonga

EARLY BLACK SETTLERS

What is now the State of Minnesota was first explored by the French in the mid-1600's. As they penetrated the wilderness, the French found hundreds of lakes, streams and waterways—the most famous of which is the Mississippi River. Located in the center of North America, Minnesota gets its name from a literal Indian translation, "Sky-tinted waters." And from its heartland, the majestic Mississippi River begins its 2,470 mile trek to the Gulf of Mexico.

The Mississippi was of utmost importance to the early migrations of people to Minnesota—fur traders, hunters, French entrepreneurs, and the early black settlers who came up from the South to make a better life for themselves. Certainly among the earliest of all people (excluding the Native Americans) to this "fertile and hearty country" were Negroes who came with the French and later with the British as they traded and settled in the Minnesota territory.

Among the early black settlers who arrived in 1800 was Pierre Bonga, a Negro servant. Pierre eventually married a Chippewa woman. Their son, George Bonga, became a voyageur for one of the fur trade companies. George Bonga later became an independent fur trader and acquired much wealth and prominence in the settlements.

Others of black heritage came as servants or slaves of the officers and agents, and tradesmen who lived at the Fort Snelling military post. By 1827, James Thompson, a free Negro at Fort Snelling was able to donate land for the first Protestant church in St. Paul, and even supplied some of the building materials. Thompson is said to have helped build the first residence in St. Paul.

During this period, the most famous Negro in North America came and lived briefly in the Minnesota Territory. Dred Scott, well-known runaway slave in history books, arrived here in 1836. As the story goes, Scott had to return to his slave master, but he came back as a free man, and married a servant of a Fort Snelling Officer.

Three years before Minnesota entered the Union to become the thirty-second state, its people generally had the same Northern attitude about servitude in the United States. Antislavery was the issue at a territorial convention in 1855. Antislavery protagonists organized and issued a platform which called for a repeal of the Fugitive Slave Law, including a denouncement of the extension of slavery.

Nevertheless, many Southerners still were invited as guests with full knowledge that slave-servants would travel with them, much to the chagrin of some Minnesotans. Although small in number, the Negro in Minnesota had already become an issue—particularly in the territory's bid for statehood, for control of the legislature was based on antislavery issues.

In 1861, three years after statehood, Minnesota was the first state to volunteer troops for the Union Army when Fort Sumter fell to the Confederacy. Governor Alexander Ramsey was in Washington on that day and offered the War Department 1,000 Minnesotans for the Cause. "The Negro population of the state also responded to the call of arms and sent 104 soldiers to the Union color.", If these figures are correct, almost half of the Negro population volunteered to serve. According to the 1860 U.S. Census, the Negro population in Minnesota was 259.

At the end of the Civil War, a few Southern Negroes returned with the Minnesota volunteers and were "mustered out" at Fort Snelling. As the

Mrs. Dred Scott
from Frank Leslie's Illustrated Newspaper
June 27, 1857

Dred Scott

(All photos in EARLY BLACK SETTLERS courtesy, Minnesota Historical Society)

steamboats docked at the river towns in Minnesota, an increasing number of blacks were on board, many porters, stewards, and workmen debarked and stayed. The chance for a brighter future seemed eminent for many Afro-Americans in the new state to the North and West where the land was fertile and the pioneering spirit of the people was strong in their cause for social and political freedoms. Industrialists also encouraged skilled bricklayers, carpenters, and plasterers to come. Towns were growing, construction was at a peak, so they came, and they settled.

Among those who came and settled was Mary Doris who owned the land on which the St. Paul post office was established. The founder of the Minneapolis Urban League and local chapter of Alpha Phi Alpha Fraternity, Raymond W. Cannon, recalls that his maternal grandparents settled in Northfield in 1857 and his paternal great grandfather was a runaway slave from Missouri who made it to Long Lake about 1863, then accomplished the next to impossible task of going back and collecting most of his children—many of whom had been resold and their names were changed.

Frederick Mc Ghee, the first Negro to practice law in Minnesota.

But the encouragement to come and help build this new "free" state also planted the seed for discrimination in job opportunities. This influx of a rival labor force became a threat to the economic security of the European immigrant working class. So racial friction was not uncommon. Although the Negroes then (and blacks in Minnesota today until only recently) were not "quite in the mainstream of totality," they were here to stay. Racial friction was not totally new, but different was no real restrictive legislative laws on the books.

Among the newcomers in the Civil War period was John W. Cheatham, a former slave in Union County, Missouri, who arrived in Minneapolis, with his parents shortly after being freed in 1863. He became a member of the Minneapolis fire department, was appointed a fire captain in 1899, and served in that post for many years. John Alfred Boone left Wilmington City, North Carolina, before the Civil War as a freeborn Negro, served with a Missouri regiment during the conflict, went to Le Sueur County after the war, lived in Northfield for some years, and died in Minneapolis in 1914. John Green, a former slave

Robert Hickman, founder of Pilgrim Baptist Church, St. Paul.

Maurice Hickman, 1893

who was brought north by a Major Saunders, settled in Le Sueur in 1865.

As Minnesota's black population continued to grow, and as the state continued its social and economic buildup, skilled black craftsmen were among the people who came to ply their talents. Many liked it here and stayed to raise a family. Among them was Benjamin A. Stephens, the grandfather of Jeanne Cooper, publisher of the black newspapers, the *Twin City Observer/St. Paul Sun.* Stephens was recruited from Marietta, Georgia to do masonry on the state capitol. Today, his great-granddaughter, Teresa, is a page there.

By 1880, the black population had increased to 1,564 — 24.4 percent of them were native-born. (Overall population was 780,773.) They concentrated in Hennepin and Ramsey Counties, in the area which now comprises Minneapolis and St. Paul. The third largest concentration was in Duluth. Even today, this trend has not changed.

Into the 20th Century, the population increased to 7,084 by 1910 as more people migrated from Chicago

F.D. Parker, first editor of Western Appeal

and other parts of the Midwest to work in the meat packing plants and from all over to work on the railroads as St. Paul became a railroad hub. Although some 500,000 blacks migrated to the northern states between 1910 - 1920, a little over 1,000 came to Minnesota. Thus, the population stood at 8,809 in 1920, with 88.52 percent living in the three urban areas where industry was highest. Although much social progress had been made by the turn of the century, this concentration of people and transition into different life styles effected some social problems which arose from race contact, and the struggle for full liberty, equality and recognition continued for another 50 years.

Since the first black arrived in the Minnesota Territory over 175 years ago, the black population today has grown to over 30,000. Some new arrivals recently settled here and assimilating into the community are Debbie Rosemond, Marcus Williams, Rudy Russeau, Michelle Dejoie, and Denise Martin. In many ways, they too are pioneers. Their decision to live here aligns itself with the positive attitude of the early black settlers and the natives who choose to remain.

Dr. R.S. Brown, one of the first Negroes to practice medicine in Minnesota.

ARTS

THE ARTS

Blacks were in and into the Arts long before they came to American soil. With them from Africa and the Caribbean they brought in their hearts and souls their own music, dance movements, the vivid earth colors of their paintings, and their chants and folk tunes. The aesthetic culture of the heritage of blacks — particularly in music and dance — has been thoroughly assimilated into all American life. As the Negro came up the Mississippi on the steamboats, his songs came with him and his music was being listened to or played by the bands that came out of Louisiana, Missouri and Kansas.

These two great contributions to American culture are so vividly expressed today in the spirituals sung by the Minneapolis Zion Baptist Church Choir, the Mt. Olivet church choir in St. Paul, and most other churches in the Black community. Spirituals, folk songs of religious expression in melody, were outpourings of suffering and anguish during the days of slavery. "Nobody knows the trouble I've seen, nobody knows but Jesus," is such an example. Many of

Kim Livingston, from the Children's Theatre production, AFRICAN TALES, "Kalulu and His Money Farm." A St. Paul Marshall High graduate; turned down a San Francisco Ballet offer to sing. Studied classical voice, U. of Minn. and N.Y. Vocal Arts Foundation, and now with Janice Hardy, Minnesota Opera Co. She starred at a February Guthrie performance, "From Now Till Sunday," with the Sounds of Blackness backed by Roberta Carlson, and a ten-piece jazz band.

These animal masks, worn by members of the Children's Theatre Co. in "Kalulu And His Money Farm" are modeled after authentic tribal African masks.

Anthony Elliot, principal cellist, Minnesota Orchestra, gained national prominence through the Toronto Symphony and Radio Canada. He teaches cello at the U. of Minn. and Macalester College. Honored in the World Who's Who in Musicians. Member, AAMOA, he plays on a Tecchler cello, dated from 1703.

these songs, still sung in Minnesota today actually began as a means of conveying messages to runaway slaves, letting them know when and where to be in time to head North and be "delivered from bondage."

The troubled, syncopated music of jazz is as distinctive a contribution as the spirituals. The Negro has expressed so perfectly in music the bafflement of humans at the tempo of industrial and urban life that jazz and the jazz age have come to be regarded as belonging, not to the Negro, but to America generally and to the whole present world of western industrialism.

Jazz is modern American life caricatured by the expressive new race.[3]

Prevalent in most Negro communities during the early 1900's was the anticipation of looking forward to Saturday night when people could relax and enjoy themselves after a hard week of working as servants or at whatever task they had to earn a living. Being confined to specific places for their own entertainment may be looked upon as a positive mode of segregation. For out of this, the desire for blacks to express themselves through their own music (particularly jazz), song, and dance created an art that is

Maxwell Glanville as Mr. Parker, CEREMONIES OF DARK OLD MEN. Gerry Black as William Jenkins.

Shown are **Ron Glass** as Tranjo, and **Barbara Bryne** as the Pedant in Shakespeare's THE TAMING OF THE SHREW, a '71 Guthrie production. An old scholar is persuaded to masquerade as a wealthy father and a servant masquerades as his master in the complicated plot.

Michele Shay plays Katrinia, the Shrew, in the Guthrie's 1971 Summer Festival production of Shakespeare's THE TAMING OF THE SHREW.

289

unsurpassed even today. That art form, now called entertainment, will be discussed later.

The innate expression of black creativity has been carried over into other aspects of the Arts. Blacks in Minnesota are still growing into the finite aspects of classical music and opera. The number of individuals who perform or are studying are few, such as James Murray, Dr. Geneva Southall, Ermine Allen Hall, and Kim Livingston. But the innate expression of black creativity in drama is very strong here. Specifically, this was conveyed so well in the recent University of Minnesota play "My Kingdom Come," written by local black playwright, Ernest Hudson, directed by University of Minnesota black drama instructor, Horace Bond, and performed by the well-known black actors and actresses, Lou Bellamy, Danny Clark, Edna Duncan, Tisch Davis, Ronald Hall, Sharon Walton, Phil Blackwell, and Estelene Bell.

Likewise the Shoestring Players' recent performance of "The Emperor Jones" and other performances by other black artists add much life to the Minnesota stage.

In Minnesota today, the impact of blacks in the Arts may be seen in the works of many examples on

Ermine Hall Allen, contralto, grew up in St. Paul, began singing around World War I at public gatherings. A familiar artist in concert halls around the country, she had formal training at Macalester College, Minnesota College and the Mpls. College of Music. Noted for her renditions of spirituals, she is 20 years a soloist at St. John the Evangelist Episcopal Church and sings at First Baptist, Pilgrim Baptist and Christ Episcopal Church. Her grandfather, a slave, who escaped from New Orleans, died in St. Paul years later from a wound received during the Civil War Merrimac-Monitor encounter.

Gary Lewis as Rumpelstiltskin. From the Minneapolis Children's Theatre Co. Production of TWO AFRICAN TALES: "Kalulu & His Money Farm" and "Rumpelstiltskin."

James Murray, baritone; studied voice, MacPhail School of Music, Mpls. and with Madame Mady Ziegler, St. Paul. Has played leading roles in "Green Pastures"; "Showboat"; "Finians Rainbow"; and toured with "Porgy and Bess." A recent work was Scott Joplin's "Treemonisha," directed by Luther Stripling. His new recording is dedicated to his wife, Lavinia. They live in St. Paul.

view at the Minneapolis Afro-American Cultural Arts Center. In works by Seitu, Kush Bey, Alvin Carter, Alonzo Cotton, Don Walker, Tim White, and Jackie Richardson, paintings and sculptures are exemplified through their exhibits—particularly at community centers around the Twin Cities. Hakim Ali's coordination of bringing art to the community through the auspices of the St. Paul Arts and Science Center adds greatly to this.

Only a few of Minnesota's black people in the Arts are depicted here, but art is alive — as alive as the recent film premiere of the Twin Cities own Gordon Parks' "Leadbelly." As alive as "The Sounds of Blackness" can express it. As alive as the Uwachi Dancers or Arlene Vann's Hallie Q. Brown Dance Group, or John Work's compositions. It is even alive in the words and writings of young poets and essayists as Kristie Lazenberry, Robert McClean and Michael Rosemond. It is also indicated in Mutima, the new black theatrical ensemble in the Twin Cities and by the recent Third World Artists Exhibition in Minneapolis, emceed by the football star, Carl Eller.

Alvin M. Stafford, cultural arts director, Hallie Q. Brown Community Center, St. Paul. B.A. Degree, English, Journalism, College of St. Thomas. He is responsible for creating, developing and implementing all cultural activities in the performing and visual arts in the Martin Luther King Center, including "The Death of Malcolm X." Shown here, he is surrounded by props for "Slow Dance On The Killing Ground." He is Board member, Mayor's Cable TV Task Force; Director, Summit-U Arts Festival; Board, Neighborhood Arts Coalition; former Board member, St. Paul Urban League. Single, he is the sixth of 13 children.

AUTHORS

AUTHORS

The writers in Minnesota's Black Community today are many. They can be found working in all categories of the work force. Unfortunately, authored works would require much lengthy research to designate many of them. This is particularly true of early black settlers. For historical records are few and to publish would have been a costly venture, although much was written in the black newspapers in the last two decades of the 1800's and during the early 1900's. This will be mentioned later.

Many published papers and dissertations are written in Minnesota by blacks, but are usually confined to specific professions. But Minnesota can claim a few authors who have briefly lived here such as the Urban League's late Whitney Young, Jr. who with William Seaborn, compiled data and prepared the material for a 1949 Governor's Interracial Commission report on *The Negro Worker's Progress in Minnesota.* Young was also noted for his book, *To Be Equal.* Another author who now lives in California is Robert Staples who authored, *The Lower Income Negro Family in St. Paul.*

Conrad (Connie) Balfour grew up in Boston, studied at Drake and Boston Universities, then headed West to North Dakota to work as a radio announcer. While in North Dakota, he was hired by Dale Carnegie Courses, the job that led him to Minneapolis. He became the director of minority programs for Dayton's, and then he was asked to apply for the position of Minnesota's Commissioner of Human Rights. From January, 1970, to April, 1971, he worked for prison reform, rights for gays, fewer restrictions on abortion, and better hiring practices by the state. Since his term as commissioner, Connie has continued to work for human rights through the Urban Coalition, and as a consultant and writer. He is now working on a book about the Sioux Indians of Minnesota.

Robert L. Williams is author of the book, *Educational Alternatives for Colonized People.* Williams focuses on manifestations of racism that present formidable barriers to quality relevant education for colonized children. This gives rise to conditions that limit the life styles and reduces life-chances of poor people. He is an assistant superintendent, Intergroup Education, Minneapolis Public Schools.

Carl T. Rowan, nationally syndicated columnist, on the *Washington Post* staff, and prize-winning reporter. From Minneapolis, he was Ambassador to Finland, head of the United States Information Agency, and Deputy Assistant Secretary of State under President John F. Kennedy. His book, "South of Freedom," has been widely read.

Mahmoud El Kati, college professor, writer, essayist, is another Twin Citian commited to recording black history. His dissertations on Afro-American life and his unique insights about the black experience are a meaningful contribution to published works by blacks in Minnesota.

There are other black Minnesotan authors of reknown. Briefly depicted are Mary Jackson Ellis, Robert Williams, and Joy Ellis Bartlett. Another for example, is Carl T. Rowan, who still retains a Minneapolis residence. As it stands, more blacks in Minnesota will probably become authors. Taking to heart Rowan's words in his introduction of Earl Spangler's book, *The Negro in Minnesota:* "Hopefully, those taking pride in the Negro's growing achievements in Minnesota will be aware of the fact that men, not anonymous forces, make progress. If this record of the past will inspire just one youngster to brighten the Negro's future, then it will have helped to refute the cynical crack by George Wilhelm Hegel: 'We learn nothing from history.' "[4]

Mary Jackson Ellis (deceased, March, '75), was the first black teacher in Minneapolis, 1947; one of her students was state treasurer, Jim Lord. Author of 70 children's books, including *Gobble, Gobble, Gobble.* Recipient of many awards and honors, she was a master teacher at the '64 N.Y. World's Fair. A West Virginia State graduate she was in Who's Who of American Women and Who's Who in the Midwest, and mother of Twin Cities residents, Dr. Susan Crutchfield, Joy Ellis Bartlett, and Carter Ellis, III.

Author, Joy Ellis Bartlett, and education TV personality, wrote *Tiny Peoples' Circus Unit,* a teaching aid. Co-authored *The Courtesy Units* with her mother, Mary Jackson Ellis. The recipient of Minnesota Education Association School Bell Award, and 1st Annual Outstanding Young Educator Award, she is a West Virginia State graduate and is completing graduate studies at the University of Minnesota. She lives in Edina with husband, Jeffrey and two sons.

BUSINESS

BUSINESS

Blacks and other minorities own some 300 businesses in the major urban areas of Minnesota. Much to the surprise of many people today, many ex-slaves who came up from the South and the free Negroes who came, where skilled in some specific jobs. Many were barbers, shoe repairmen, and laundrers. For some who were skilled at carpentry, and masonry, and other labor roles, their working was restricted. They were seen as competition for the European laborers already settled here. Many had to find other means of earning a living, for they had not the capitol to start their own carpentry or construction shops nor the customers to patronize them if they did.

This plight of the Negro goes back three hundred years as slaves were brought to this country and the status of the black population first became a psychological anathema.

In the eyes of many, and adverse to the laws of nature and mankind, many people still believe that blacks are a shade less than other people. For some reason, whether they are rich or poor, certain groups

D. Sam Gransberry Independent businessman. Born in Louisiana, he is a Minneapolis resident for thirty-five years. Retired from the railroad a few years ago, Gransberry is quite active, along with his wife, in many social and civic organizations.

Richard C. Estes, of Estes Funeral Chapel, has been in business in Minneapolis for 13 years. A graduate of the College of Mortuary Science in Los Angeles, he served his apprenticeship under John M. Estes Funeral Home in Des Moines.

Skip Belfrey is the successful owner of Skip's Bar-B-Q, at 1729 Lyndale Ave., N. Mpls. In business for 12 years, he started out in his backyard and now boasts the biggest barbeque pit in the Midwest. Skip says "The secret is in the sauce," originated by a distant uncle who was a slave.

Jim Fuller, owner of the Cozy Bar, one of the most popular night clubs in the Northwest. Mr. Fuller attended Wilberforce College. Many of the areas leading entertainers have gotten their start directly from or through Mr. Fuller's efforts.

of people have to feel that they are "better than" other groups. In order to ensure this, blacks in particular have been the brunt of blatant discrimination and subtle racism in jobs, housing, in public facilities and against their own person.

This age-old concept became obvious early in Minnesota's history, although not to the degree in which it was carried out in other parts of the country. The antislavery and pro-slavery factions waged many battles here; so did the proponents and opponents of Negro suffrage. Fortunately for the small Negro population (and for the overall population as well)

Minnesota came into the Union as a free state. And its people on a third try in three years, voted yes, for the Negro's right to vote — two years before the ratification of the U.S. Constitution's 15th Amendment! Thus, on an equal basis in many ways, some Negroes opened their own shops and conducted business with all Minnesotans. Others catered exclusively to an all-black clientele.

Opportunities for jobs were not overwhelming for some newcomers, unless their skills were specific enough for the building process in the urban areas. But the black population increased as people came to

Thomas H. Tipton, pres., Vanguard Advertising. BA, English, Morgan State; TCOIC dep. dir., '68-'70; writer, prodr., "Gospel Erupts," WCCO "Black Sounds. . .," "Dat Feelin'," Guthrie, '72. '75 testimonial/ minority scholarship fund in his name.

Dr. Hayward McKerson, pres., The McKerson Corp., specializing in chemical products for industry, medical facilities, and business. The company also supplies technical grade chemicals to other businesses for germ and pollution-free use.

William Rowe National Locator Service.

Dawson Limousine Service, **Bill Dawson**, owner. "An invitation to excellence." Experienced, excellent and courteous limousine service 24 hours.

seek better lives for themselves. Though small in number, their influence on the overall population of Minnesota was a very important one.

Employment has always been an economic problem for blacks.

But throughout Minnesota's history, the barbershops, beauty parlors, small food stores, funeral homes, and recreation and relaxation halls survived. The idea for founding one of the Twin Cities' leading black social agencies today, for example, came out of the late S.E. Hall's barbershop where contacts for

jobs were made through the white businessmen who patronized the shop.

Small businesses for blacks in Minnesota are now quite diversified. No longer are they confined to the personal service fields. Individuals are into flight instruction, advertising, construction of hospitals and other public and private conglomerates, clothing stores, record shops, fine restaurants, chemical supplies, private and franchise-owned gas stations, office supplies, clothing boutiques, and many other successful privately-owned businesses. One of the top com-

Norman Welch (left) is congratulated upon receiving his pilot's license from his instructor, Rev. Linton Scott pres., Flight Unlimited. The agency provides scholarships and aviation training for minorities.

Rev. Linton L. Scott, inner city minister for Mt. Olivet Lutheran Church, Mpls., conducts a regular radio broadcast to the people of the Metro Area. His broadcast, known as "Words of Inspiration," has been aired continuously for 12 years. He is president of Flight Unlimited.

John Brown, Sr., pres., Brown's Office Machines, will celebrate 25 yrs in '76. In the Summit-Univ. area since '65 he is a member, St. Paul Chamber of Commerce; advisory board, HELP Dev. Corp.; board, Nat'l Office, Machine Dealers; Knights of Columbus.

Curtis Varnado, owner of Pilot City Printers, uses ideas that recognize the black community as a potential business field.

mercial photographers in his field with major accounts across the country, for example, is Gene McMiller of the Twin Cities.

Much of the success of the black small businessman is the dedication of some key minority-oriented social agencies to the task of increasing the economic development in the black community, the support of major Twin City corporations through MEDA (Metropolitan Economic Development Association), The Small Business Administration, and the Office of Minority Business Enterprise.

Opportunities for private black ownership are increasing for those who aspire to own and operate a business in an integrated business society. In the words of Edwin Embree, author of *The Brown Americans*, published 32 years ago, "One of the best hopes for the Negro in America is the growing co-operative movement through which Negroes, and others, can organize their economic resources to help themselves. The history of many of these co-operatives has proved that low-income groups generally can raise their level of living by buying co-

Luther Prince, pres., Ault Inc.; custom designed electronic power systems; manufacturing and testing facility for electronic components. Estab. in '61; employs 110 people. Customers include Univac, Honeywell, Control Data, Western Elec., Ford Motor Co.

Charles W. Poe, Jr., president, Metropolitan Economic Development Association (MEDA), a Twin City business community sponsored effort to provide management and technical assistance to minority and disadvantaged business people.

Born in Yonkers, a New York City suburb where he grew up, Poe spent two years at Allen U. in South Carolina, majoring in business administration. He enlisted in the Air Force in '52, was commissioned a 2nd Lt., and received his navigator's wings. After service, he began pilot training, received his wings and became an instructor in jet aircraft at Laredo Air Force Base.

Poe contracted polio in '59, was retired from the Air Force, and returned to school at the U. of Denver, where he received a BSBA in political science; then a Juris Doctor Degree from the U. of Denver College of Law. A member of the Colorado Bar, Poe was a staff attorney for the Small Business Association there in 1965.

In 1970, Poe became executive director of Ramsey Action Programs (RAP), the community action program for St. Paul and Ramsey County. He assumed his present position in 1972. He was appoined by the Governor in April 1972 as a member of the Minnesota Adult Corrections Commission, a position he maintained until June 1973. He is a member of the Executive Committee of the St. Paul Urban Coalition and was appointed by the Mayor to serve as Chairman of the Citizens Committee for reviewing municipal appointments in September, October, and November 1972. He serves as a Board Member of the Minnesota Accounting Aid Society, is a member of the St. Paul Better Business Bureau — Arbitrators Council, and a member of both the Minneapolis and St. Paul Chambers of Commerce.

His hobbies are flying and photography and he lives in West St. Paul.

Thomas H. Johnson, III (left) President of West African Gold, Inc., a Minneapolis-based trading company. The primary business of the company is the exportation of grain and sugar. Johnson is a 1971 graduate of Augsburg College of Minneapolis. A former member of the Minneapolis Grain Exchange, he spent a considerable amount of time in West Africa developing the company. West African Gold is represented both in Newark, N.J. and Monrovia, Liberia.

operatively and selling to themselves at far better prices than they can get as individuals. Co-operatives bid fair to become very important as new economic forces and as means whereby investors, managers, laborers, and consumers may find common ground and common interest. To Negroes they are one of the clear ways out and up."[5]

According to Dr. Herrington Bryce, Director of Research at the Joint Center for Political Studies, "The future of black business depends on a great number of forces. Without question a central factor is the economy in general. The principle of last in, first out holds. Because they are so dependent upon the black consumer for their business, black firms are highly vulnerable to recessions since blacks are usually the worst hurt. But inflation also has a devastating affect on these firms. Many companies report that they are in difficulty because they cannot meet the rising costs of materials and machinery. In bad times credit becomes hard to come by and loans —even short-term loans often used to tide the businessman over—are difficult to obtain because of high interest rates. Even as the economy improves these loans frequently can be hard to get because

Cassius Bar and Cafe, A. B. Cassius owner. William Cassius (Photo Above).
Cassius has been in Downtown Mpls., 318 S. Third St. for 27 years.

George Ford, owner of Ford and Son Janitorial, has the majority of janitorial contracts (since 1968), among them Pilot City and D.K. Carter (Laundry Mat.) He moved to Minneapolis from Jackson, Miss. in 1943 and worked for Pullman Co. to 1948; Mpls. Gen. Hosp., '48/'55; owned a farm in Anoka County, '56/'61; then moved back to Mpls. in '61 where he now lives on the south side. A Doepke House Mover from '63 to '68, he is now self-employed.

Richard (Ricky) Davis, Vice President, in charge of small business procurement at Ivorytower Media Company. The advertising firm specializes in serving the Black Oriented Radio listening audience in the Minneapolis-St. Paul Metropolitan Area. It in association with Pharoah Production Company fight a battle with companies and advertising agencies for a fair percentage of the advertising dollars made available to a great extent by black consumers.

banks and other lenders do not necessarily consider black firms good risks."[6]

For blacks to make more gains in business, Bryce further states that "...one of the things we shall have to do in order to grow in the business world is to create larger firms. This is an economy in which large amounts of capital are needed if we are to enter the more important kinds of production and if we are going to benefit from economies of scale. It is a general truism that larger firms have larger markets and hence lower unit costs. In this day of bigness, however, 93.6% of all black-owned firms are sole proprietorships. Smallness is not a virtue."

"Capital, management skills, markets, all of these factors are needed if black business is to prosper," he adds. One of the ways in which markets are going to be developed and attained is by building firms which have broad appeal across the nation and across racial lines.

"Federal programs should be aimed at helping minority firms expand. Too often aid to minority firms comes too little, too late, and is aimed at keeping them small."[7]

Marion Loftis is the owner and manager of Loftis Tailor Shop at 3751 Nicollet, Minneapolis. In business for 30 years, he works with men and women's clothing and also does dry cleaning.

Odell Sumpter, Jr., record shop owner. He has two stores in Minneapolis, one on Chicago Ave., and one on Plymouth.

Ransom Simmons, gen. contr., Ransom & Sons Construction; home builder, remodeler, 12 yrs.

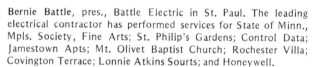

Mpls. grow from offering only one product in 1969, to an impressive array of 29 products, and from 800 sq. ft. of space to the present 10,000 sq. ft. Molar Building. The company supplies building maintenance products, leather cleaners and germicidal products.

Bernie Battle, pres., Battle Electric in St. Paul. The leading electrical contractor has performed services for State of Minn., Mpls. Society, Fine Arts; St. Philip's Gardens; Control Data; Jamestown Apts; Mt. Olivet Baptist Church; Rochester Villa; Covington Terrace; Lonnie Atkins Sourts; and Honeywell.

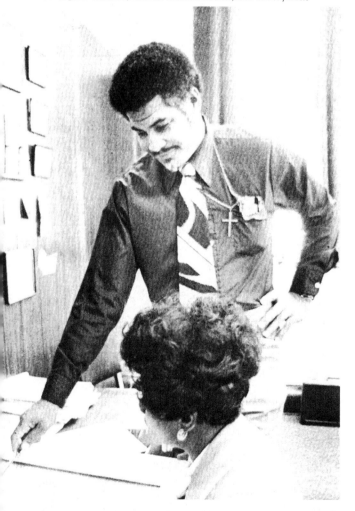

C. Edward Thomas, pres., Narthex Recording, Inc. custom recording for radio and TV commercials; producer of albums by nat'l and locally known singers, instrumentalists, and choirs. Sound system installation in buildings such as those at Cargill and Pilot City.

Robert Thompson, pres., board chairman, Community Electronics Corp. Miami U., Ohio grad; board, North-Gro, United Way, Abbott-Northwestern, TCOIC. Appointed State Athletic Commission. Mbr., Assoc., Computing Machines; Math. Society, Amer.; Masons. He is published in electronics journals.

Moss Printing was established by **Eddie Moss** in St. Paul, 1969. Family owned and operated, it is equipped with offset and letterpress printing and was recently expanded to give better service and more versatility. His wife and two sons work there.

Otha Nash, pres., Nash Construction. General contracting, high rises, commercial and industrial complexes, construction mgnmt. and design.

Joe Buckhalton, owner, Thrifty Mkt., Big Joe's Serv. Station in Mpls. U. of Illinois Bachelors Degree, he entered the U. of Minn. Law School, but finances delayed that. He had a car reconditioning business, was a car salesman, then owned a tire company.

Robert "Bob" Patterson, photography studio owner, started in business part-time, in 1943. He went into business full-time 10 years later. Patterson, a former pilot, still flies occasionally, while being involved with his modeling agency. Many of his models have been featured in local and national media. He also does aerial photography. Patterson left the bachelor ranks three years ago; his wife's name is Karen.

Kali Glover, Graduate of Metropolitan State University, is president and founder of Intimate Greetings Corporation — 1976 — produces black expressions in greeting cards and stationary items. This native Chicagoan and professional photographer, as recognized by the professional photographers of America Association, has begun making an impact on the greeting card industry.

Young Brothers; Raymond, Merle, Sylvester, "Chubby" Richard, "Dickie" Fred, John (seated).
A family of barbers, they have lived and worked in the Twin Cities for many years.

Lee Swearington (right of radio personality, Pharoah Black), president of Central Park Nite Club & Dinner Theater. Has promoted in the Mpls. area, such stars as The Spinners, David Ruffin, Willie Hutch, Leroy Hutson, Edwin Starr and Blue Magic. Born in Houston, Texas, Lee became the largest seller in the Midwest while a car salesman at Hansord Pontiac in Mpls. He produced here the first Black Dinner Club Play — "The Great White Hope" receiving raves from critics, black and white, during its eight-week stand.

Frederic Jones, Chief Engineer at the United States Thermo Control Company in Minneapolis — now known as "Thermo King" — worked many, many years with the Company. Acclaim came to him by inventing the automatic mobile refrigerator, making it possible for servicemen to have fresh vegetables, meat and ice cream on their menus in the most remote and obscure places on the battlefront. Mr. Jones was elected to the American Society of Refrigeration Engineers and was called to the Bureau of Standards in Washington to consult with the Office of the Quartermaster General. Mr. Jones was given credit for being one of the first exploring in the field of sound equipment. It was said that 75 percent of the theatres in the Northwest, at one time, used sound equipment developed by him. (Mr. Jones is deceased.)

Leon Rankin, Rankin Electric, Mpls.; electrical contractor and master electrician. Customers include Knox Lumber, Control Data, Honeywell. Estab., '69.

Edward Thomas, an officer of the NACIREMA Club, and an active golfer. When he can find the time, Mr. Thomas, enjoys visiting friends and relatives all over the country. The Nacirema Club is a facility where other clubs and community groups hold their meetings and fashion shows. The Club is located in South Minneapolis.

Isabel White owns and manages the 46th St. Dairy Home Store. Shown here assisting a customer, the community market has been there since 1971.

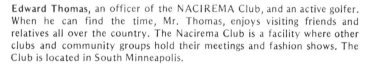

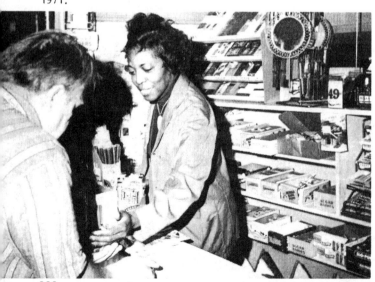

Al's London House, proprietor, Al prepares a special dish in his restaurant, one of finest in North Minneapolis.

Timothy T. Bender of Timothy's Pizza, the only privately black owned pizza house of its kind in Minnesota. Bender started in business in 1949, and then to the Armodila Restaurant on Plymouth Ave., Mpls., in 1955. He had the first black charcoal broiler in the state at the Nicollet Hotel, under the supervision of Neil Mersack, Sr. Presently located at 1106 W. Broadway, Bender is a native of Hattisburg, Miss., and is the son of the late Dr. and Mrs. J.C. Bender.

Satin Doll Hair Fashion Salon, owned by Pauline "Pollie" Young and son, John. Located, 1918 Plymouth Ave., Mpls. As part of a family affair, her husband and his five brothers are barbers at different locations, owned by Pauline in the Twin Cities.

Shown here, Agnes Garibaldi sews and designs fashions for Garibaldi's Boutique, a women's retail shop owned with her two sisters, Alfreda and Debra. She is a Xavier U. graduate, elem. ed., and teaches at Hill School, St. Paul.

Cement contractor, Warfield Griffin also contracts for painting and general maintenance. His business of many years is located in Minneapolis. He also owns Griffin's Service Station in south Minneapolis.

U.S. Upholstering Co., manufacturers of custom built furniture in Mpls., at 4209 E. 38th St. Custom built furniture and reupholstering. Genuine and imitation leather. All fabrics. Cstmrs. include Equbane Night Club; N.W. Nat'l Life Insur. Co.

Charles Arnett, owner, Arnett Upholstering, Mpls. Office and home upholstery. All types of fabrics including vinyls and leatherettes. Pickup and delivery. Established in 1953; two employees.

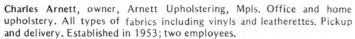

Selbert Athias is owner of Athias Ornamental Iron Co. in Mpls. His company supplies railings, gates, and other metal ornaments for Northwestern Bank, Willow Nursing Home, and others. He has been in business in Mpls. since 1963.

Millie Simmons, only Black realtor, St. Paul. Dir., Mary Bethune Montessori School/Day Care for minority children, ages two and a half to six.

St. Paul Taxi Cab Co., Maurice Turner, pres., 1009 N. Concord, So. St. Paul. Ten cabs, radio dispatched.

Johnny Jones established his rubbish and general hauling operation in 1964. He and three employees work primarily in residental sections of Minneapolis.

Booker T. Daniel, owner, Auto Repair Service. Over 3500 sq. ft., devoted to repair of domestic trucks and cars. Engines, front and rear ends, transmissions, brakes, electrical, towing. Estab., '55 in Mpls.

Ben Vincent is owner of Ben's Standard Station at 36th St. and Nicollet, Minneapolis. He also provides winter starting, towing and minor repair service.

Alfred Davis, mgr., Northside Metro Gas Station. An ex-offender, he has made the once "losing" station a profitable business, in spite of obstacles. Meeting those obstacles, he now owns a car care shop.

Walter J. Hall, Jr., auto and misc. repairman. From Kansas, lived in the Twin Cities 12 yrs. He helps the young use their time wisely and likes assisting adults any way he can help.

Lee Britton owns Lee's Freeway Station at 39th St. and Nicollet in Minneapolis.

Henry Moore's specialty is in the automobile cleaning. He owes his thriving business in Minneapolis to Minnesota's adverse weather.

COMMUNICATIONS

COMMUNICATIONS

Blacks in the field of communications are not new to Minnesota. The Civil War had been over for about ten years and Minnesota's statehood was going into its second decade when Negro newspapers began to appear. Their editors, among them D.E. Butler, Frederick D. McCracken, J.Q. Adams, and A.G. Plummer, took an active part in politics and daily life of the Negro community of the 1870's through pointed editorials and observations on equality and decency.

The real impact of these newspapers was shown through the establishment of the *Western Appeal*, the *Afro-American Advance*, and the *Twin City Star*. Of import was the *Appeal* because it was consistent in its "lengthy fight for equality and recognition" of Negroes in the Twin Cities. The ministers and other Negro leaders—mostly professionals who had moved here from other states, and the newspapers played a large role in racial development and equality at the turn of the century. The same was true some 40-50 years

Cecil E. Newman (1903-1976), founder, editor and publisher, 42-year old *Minneapolis Spokesman* and *St. Paul Recorder* newspapers. He was founder, editor, The Twin City Herald (1927-1934). Nationally and locally known as a vigorous crusader for human rights from the late '30s through the 60s, at one point, he spent more time in community work than with his newspapers. At the time of his death, (Feb., 1976) at the age of 72, he still devoted much time to the newspapers and to counseling youth who sought his advice and guidance. The first black to head an established professional news organization, Minn. Press Club, he watched such notables as Carl Rowan, Gordon Parks, Edward Blackwell, and Sherrie Mazingo get their starts on his newspapers. He left the black community and Twin Cities a legacy of history, and through him, much progress in Civil Rights.

later when the late Cecil Newman was able to make some changes in hiring practices of Negroes in the war defense plants through editorials in the *Spokesman/Recorder*. He was also able to turn about police brutality in Minneapolis by publishing on the front page, stark pictures of blacks who had been subjected to police beatings.

The need for such a voice began back in 1827 when the first black newspaper, the *Freedom's Journal* was published in New York. It was the first message ever disseminated by a black communications medium. The *Journal* became a reality to defend the animosities and denigrations cast upon blacks, especially by white newspaper editors. The black editors in the first issued stated, ". . . we deem it expedient to establish a paper . . . for the moral, religious, civil and literary improvement of our injured race." And from the third issue, ". . . we think there ought to be some channel of communication between us and the public, through which a single voice may be heard, in defence (sic) of five hundred thousand free people of colour."[8]

The *Western Appeal* mentioned earlier was actually a second *Western Appeal* newspaper which began in

LeClair G. Lambert, information and research; assistant to executive director, St. Paul Urban League. Writer, editor, graphics. B.A., Hampton (Va.); other studies Boston and Munich, Germany. A *Time/Life Books* researcher, left NY to live, write in Europe. Taught biol. and Eng. Lit., Tripoli, Libya. Came to St. Paul in '73. An incorporator, *S-U Free Press;* convener, Twin Cities Theatre Guild; choreographer and prog. writer/designer, '75 Miss Black Minn. Pageant; a '74 "Black History Focus" writer; consultant, HELP Dev. Corp. and Intercul. Progs., U. of Minn. A KEEY radio host. He is a member of the National Public Relations Council and St. Paul Urban Leaguers. Lambert is the executive editor, researcher and writer for *Minnesota's Black Community.*

Yusef Mgeni, program supervisor/producer; community affairs, director, KUOM radio-TV, U. of Minn. "On The Black Side" producer since '72; executive producer. "Random Access" (WTCN-TV) and "Radio For Black People" (KUXL). Founding president, Twin City Black Communicators; a native of the Twin Cities. He has committed his life to "communicating to Black people."

1885. It was taken over by the active and outspoken editor, J.Q. Adams in 1887, who remained its editor for 35 years. But probably the first *Western Appeal* was actually the first black newspaper in Minnesota, according to an article in a September 23, 1876 *St. Paul Daily Dispatch* which stated, "...It is small in size, but neatly printed, and its literary execution is highly creditable to its conductors...." It is likely that the first *Western Appeal* black newspaper did not survive because it went the way of many others—bankruptcy. Even today, usually the biggest problem faced by black newspapers is to keep the money flowing in, mostly through advertising from larger or more successful firms that can afford it.

So, the channel for black communications was established at least 100 years ago in Minnesota. Today, there are over 230 black newspapers in the United States with more than two million subscribers. Five of these can be found in the Twin Cities: The already mentioned *Minneapolis Spokesman* and *St. Paul Recorder*, The *Twin City Observer* and the *St. Paul Sun*, and the *Twin Cities Courier*. You might ask, "Why do black newspapers exist?" They exist to give a complete report of blacks and their activities.

Born in Orangeburg, S.C., **Kate M. Williams** is a general news reporter for Minnesota Public Radio, KSJN-FM and is a professional freelance photographer. Her photographic specialty is people. She is a graduate of the University of Minnesota in Photojournalism and Broadcastjournalism. Her hobbies are filmmaking, swimming and tennis. Her parents are Physical Therapist Erle Williams and University of Minnesota Home Economist Professor Gloria Williams.

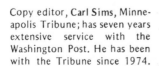

Copy editor, **Carl Sims**, Minneapolis Tribune; has seven years extensive service with the Washington Post. He has been with the Tribune since 1974.

They also exist because, too often the white media is not consistent in equally and fairly reporting the news of the black community.

A brief note about the five black newspapers in the Twin Cities: The *Spokesman* and *Recorder* were founded by the late Cecil E. Newman in 1934. Newman, through his newspapers led the fight for civil rights in Minneapolis—and assisted in the whole state as well—against discrimination in jobs, housing, and in use of public facilities. Many of today's blacks in communications in Minnesota received some training with these papers or with the *Twin City Herald* a

black newspaper which Newman edited before he founded the *Spokesman/Recorder*.

In touch with Minnesota's black history is Jeanne Cooper, publisher of the *Twin City Observer* and the *St. Paul Sun.* Her uncle, Milton G. Williams started the newspapers some 35 years ago. Her great-grandfather Benjamin A. Stephens was one of the black settlers here (see EARLY BLACK SETTLERS text). The *Observer and Sun,* like many black newspapers, may on occasion, exemplify the need for more blacks in the communications field. Mrs. Cooper, for example, must sometimes get her paper

Alvin McFarlane, Jr., is publisher of the North Minneapolis, *Insight Magazine* and owner of Insight Communications. He is an editor and writer, and in public relations and promotion. Originally from Kansas City, McFarlane attended the U. of Minnesota School of Journalism. He is former director, urban journalism workshop, U. of Minn.; participant, MEDA Business Leadership Training Project; and member, Metropolitan Council, community advisory committee. He lives in Mpls. with his wife, Bobbie, and children, Selene and Batala.

David Coleman, Jr., Corp. insurance manager, finance department, *Minneapolis Star and Tribune,* joined the company in 1969.

written, edited, and ready for publication with only a skeletal staff. "One of my difficulties," she says, "is finding enough people permanently dedicated to reporting the news and communicating with black people."

The *Twin Cities Courier* is the fifth Twin Cities black-oriented weekly newspaper that details events and activities in the black community. Its editor, Mary Kyle (pictured in the BLACK WOMEN section), every week presents a candid eye on news in the community, as well as commentary, and even interviews with visiting well-known blacks to the Twin Cities. Some black reporters that add zest to the paper are Estyr Bradley Peake, Lillian Warren, "Little Herbie," Dan Welch, and James Brenfield. The *Courier* recently celebrated its 10th anniversary of disseminating information to much of the Twin Cities black community.

But the communications field is broad and entails more than the newspaper media. Take television, for example. Black Minnesotans are employed by TV stations, as depicted here. More are needed. Perhaps a stronger need exists for more input by racial minorities to present their views on what the viewing

Visions of Total Reality Corp., a young and dynamic videotape and graphic arts company; promotes and coordinates varieties, festivals and gatherings. Shirley Calloway is Corp. president. Its biggest asset is the ability to communicate specifics to a wide range of people. Others pictured are: Gamba Kambon, Amandilo Mmelika Cousin, Guy J. Cousin, Rickie B. Cousin and Peter Cousin.

audience is interested in. The question arises, "Are one or two half-hour black-oriented local shows enough for one week?" "Are there enough information sources for social individual and community uplift in employment, housing, and educational needs (advanced learning courses, for example), or even on culture?" Looking ahead, there is room for more blacks in television in Minnesota, so is there more attention needed to be given by television for social concerns.

And likewise for radio. Too often air time is wasted on the constant replay of the so-called top 20 records (of the last six months) by many stations— every two hours! Radio should at some point be a part of captivating communication, not abounding abomination. But how does this relate to Minnesota's Black Community? Much worthy effort is seen in talk shows conducted by blacks; and so are some of the hours devoted to music expressly played for blacks in the community. But much more is needed. Both radio and television have a responsibility to the total community, granted, needs and interests of particular groups are involved. But accomplishing the task of communicating to everyone can be done effectively

T.J. Jones, soul radio specialist, KUXL; president, Pharoh Productions radio advertising co., and producer, the "Pharoh Black Show." From Brooklyn, N.Y., he graduated, Minneapolis Central High and the Brown Institute. He and wife Kathy Lee have two children.

Morabik Abdul, broadcaster and musician; is heard on WCAL-FM's "Black Voices, Black Sounds" every Saturday from Northfield and St. Olaf College. At Brown Institute, '69 to '70, he is also percussionist and background vocalist for the "Prophets of Peace." He is a St. Paul Monroe High graduate and Vietnam veteran.

321

through programming to particular groups within the community, thus strengthening the ties of the total listening and viewing population. Blacks do have pride in their heritage, and that pride can become more distinctive through media exposure. That heritage, that black experience can be more understood as other groups of people are exposed to black and other minority contributions. Minnesota's broadcasting must take a more in depth look at this, for black people cannot be ignored. They are as much a part of Minnesota as the Swedish, German, Irish, and other ethnic groups that make up the population here.

Much of the negligence might have to do with certain station owners who apologize by stating that they have to cater to the whims of the masses. Others often blatantly ignore FCC rules. On the other hand, there are stations in Minnesota that do provide programming for segments of the population and even throw in some public service time for equal opportunity.

Minnesota is not unique in this aspect. Although major cities in other states do have black-oriented

Toni Hughes is a WTCN-TV weather reporter and news analyst.

Curtis G. Chivers (deceased), vice president, Spokesman/Recorder Publishing Co., worked with the newspapers since 1938 as ad solicitor, then advertising manager. He was active in political, civic and church circles and was one of the 1st blacks elected to the Jaycees in the U.S. He was a leading figure locally and nationally in the NAACP.

radio, this does not necessarily mean that their programming is quality broadcasting. Nevertheless, Minnesota's blacks in radio, television and other media are usually of a high calibre. They work hard at maintaining it.

Over the years, communications in Minnesota and the role blacks play in the field have both changed greatly. A transition from the 1930's to the late 1960's and 70's has seen many blacks who grew up here, or came to and through Minnesota, go on to other places to work; among them are Carl Rowan, Gordon Parks, Jacqueline Carty, Roy Wilkins, Milton Coleman, and others. Many stay here; others come and stay. Yusef Mgeni is a good example. Having grown up in Minnesota, he has chosen to remain in the Twin Cities and dedicate his life to communicating for black people.

And like Yusef, communications is a way of life for many blacks in Minnesota who are involved in television, radio, public relations, publishing, editing, audiovisual communication, journalism and photo-journalism, and videotaping. Among these are Pat McKinnie (public relations), Bill Davis (photo-journalism), Jewel Sawyer (community newspaper),

Part of the WTCN-TV team are (l. to r.) William Nash, custodian; A. Michael Young, engineer; and Harold Maupin, floor director.

Norma Jean Williams, is a news clerk and receptionist for the *Spokesman and Recorder.* A graduate of Sawyer Business School, she enjoys meeting the public.

Nick Coleman and Mike Hall (reporter), Cheryl Eaves (copy desk), Kakayi Ampah (photographer), Tom Johnson (promotion), and . . . Bengie McHie. Others are Perry White, Lou Latson, Joe Odon, Denise Johnson, Guy Cousins, Dave Early and more.

Communications in Minnesota for blacks is an open field. Cable TV has only been talked about, videotaping can be expanded, reporters are few, telecommunications is new, and not enough blacks are recording the true and present history of blacks.

In the words of James D. Williams, Communications Director for the National Urban League, "Blacks . . . need a press which is directly responsible to them and which serves their needs. . . ."* Likewise all facets of communications to blacks and by blacks in Minnesota must speak to this pressing issue and be extended.

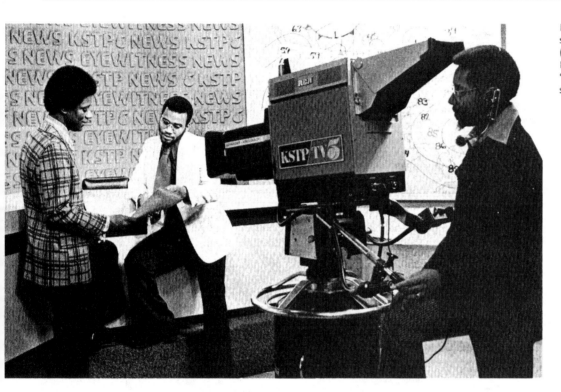

KSTP-TV men involved in on-the-scene reporting and studio work are (l. to r.) Lou Harvin, reporter, and Ray Wells, ActionCam editor for "Eyewitness News" and Al Sanders, studio cameraman.

Professional office worker, **Imogene Mabone**, *Spokesman and Recorder* newspapers, is interested in learning all phases of newspaper publishing. She has a wide knowledge of the Twin Cities community and is a valuable addition to the staff.

Key men at WCCO-TV are (l. to r.) **Harvey Clark**, CBS news intern; **Frank Mitchell**, reporter; **Bob Lackey**, news photographer; and **Sam Ford** CBS News, intern.

Bill Davis, ace *Pioneer Press* photographer, is shown at work in the studio. He captures on-the-spot scenes for the daily St. Paul paper.

KTCA-TV representatives are Alberta Murray (Above), member, Board of Trustees; **Ralph Greenwood**, producer-director; and **Thomas Clark**, engineer (Lower Photo).

Sherrie Lee Mazingo, Ph.D; journalist; communications researcher, achieved many honors as a former *Minneapolis Star* reporter. She is a Washington (D.C.) Journalism Center Fellow; lecturer and consultant, U.S. Office of Education and the U.S.I.A. A St. Paulite, her doctorate is from Michigan State (Mass Communications); M.A., Syracuse U. (Public Communications); and B.A., Howard University.

Estyr Bradley Peake, columnist and staff writer, *Twin Cities Courier;* the only black columnist to have written continuously in the Midwest since 1927. A native of St. Paul, she is a member, Minn. Press Women; Clerk, Vestry, St. Philip's Episcopal Church; Vice pres., St. Paul Urban League; Chairman, St. Paul Blk. Legal Defense Fund; Treasurer, St. Philip's Gardens. A widow, she has three sons.

At her desk, Mary Jane Saunders, writer, reporter, *St. Paul Dispatch/Pioneer Press,* edits her copy for the Family section. She is 1974 recipient, St. Paul Urban League's Community Service Award for dedication to and progressive reporting of the black community.

Jerold Jackson, public relations coordinator, VA Hospital; free lance writer and poet in the Twin Cities. A former reporter and feature writer, *Milwaukee Journal*, he came to Antioch College for his B.A. in Mass Communications. Has contributed to many local publications, including the *Greater Minneapolis Magazine*, and the *Minnesota Daily*.

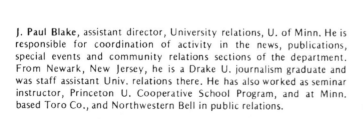

J. Paul Blake, assistant director, University relations, U. of Minn. He is responsible for coordination of activity in the news, publications, special events and community relations sections of the department. From Newark, New Jersey, he is a Drake U. journalism graduate and was staff assistant Univ. relations there. He has also worked as seminar instructor, Princeton U. Cooperative School Program, and at Minn. based Toro Co., and Northwestern Bell in public relations.

Gerri Williams, publications editor, Peavey Co. She spent her youth in Mpls., attended Carleton and has a Communications Degree, Simmons College, Boston. Member, Twin City Black Communicators and National Association Business Communications.

VA Hospital switchboard operator, Charles Posey, is a Vietnam veteran. He was in the U.S. Army for three years, with the rank of Sp/4. He has attended welding and auto mechanics school; is a member, Twin Star Post No. 885 and enjoys fishing and mechanics.

BLACK WOMEN

BLACK WOMEN

Black women as a group have emerged in the last 15 years as a social force in all facets of American life. As professionals in the first half of the century, most of them were in education—teaching and molding the minds of our youth. Today, they can be found in all fields of endeavour. Nationally, Barbara Jordan and Shirley Chisholm in politics, Janice Kissner in social services, and Eleanor Holmes Norton in human rights, are just a very few representatives of black women making a viable impact on the country.

Truly representative is Mary McLeod Bethune. She founded a Negro college (Bethune Cookman College) in Florida; strived for upgrading the role of black women; voiced her feelings nationally about the importance of education; and was a loud voice for civil rights, equal education and social reforms long before the 1960's when it was not fashionable to do so. A memorial to her is now located in Washington, D.C. and erected by the National Council of Negro Women.

For a long time now, black women have gotten up early to get their husbands off to work, their children

Shown here are 15 of the 26 Links, Inc., members, Twin Cities Chapter. They provide services to Youth, Freedom and the Arts, and National and International trends and services. They are left to right, Front Row: Dr. Joyce Jackson; Mrs. Wenda Moore; Mrs. Rosemary Davis. Second Row: Mrs. LaRue McClung; Dr. Ida-Lorraine Wilderson; Mrs. Diane Smith; Mrs. Lenora Charles; Mrs. Phyllis Ellis. Third Row: Miss Wilma Allison; Mrs. Cynthia Tyson; Miss Sandra McGee; Mrs. Beverly Thompson; Mrs. Jean Hudson; Mrs. Shirley Kaiser; Mrs. Marion Kennon.

Not pictured: Mrs. Christine Dunham; Mrs. Sylvia Adams; Dr. Iris Butler; Mrs. Mabel Cason; Mrs. Myrrhene Crawford; Mrs. Patricia England; Mrs. Martha Goss; Mrs. Delores Henderson; Mrs. Fanney Posey; Mrs. Matsolonia Pullens; Mrs. Irece Winans; and transfer member, Mrs. Gwendolyn Goodman.

off to school, then got themselves off to work in every job imaginable. "I was not raised to be somebody's wife, I was raised to do something with my life," states Eleanor Holmes Norton, New York City's Chairman for the Commission on Human Rights. Her words speak for a majority of black women. Generally speaking, black women get out of the home and into the work force (except those out of work or not seeking work) to supplement their husband's salary; as a single parent-head of household; or as a single or married career woman.

Not the case a hundred years ago in Minnesota. The numbers of Negro women were few. And the few derived their livelihood from working as cooks, maids, general cleaning women, and taking care of their employer's children. Strong, hard-willed, and dedicated, most of these women had to come home after a long 10-12 hour day and repeat these duties for their own families.

Early in Minnesota's history, a few Negro women made themselves known. One of the first to be mentioned in the archives is Harriet Robinson, a

---

Laura Grevious Gaskins, is a Hennepin County Welfare Supervisor and very active as a Minneapolis social worker. She holds an A.B. Degree from Kentucky State and graduate work at the Atlanta Univ. School of Social Work. The first Black Supervisor for the Hennepin County Welfare Department, she is a member of many social work groups, NAACP, National Council of Negro Women, and Alpha Kappa Alpha Sorority.

Wenda Weeks Moore, Regent, University of Minnesota. Former staff assn't., Gov. Wendell Anderson. M.A. Degree, Southern Cal.; B.A., Howard U.; researcher, Washington, D.C. libraries. She was honored in 1971 as Outstanding Woman of America. A member of the Links, she is married to lawyer, Cornell Moore. They have one child.

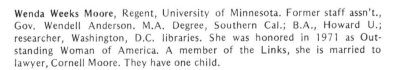

Allie Mae Hampton, from St. Paul, is exec. dir., Ramsey County OIC. She is a nat'l board member, Women In Community Service, and Nat'l Council, Negro Women; board member, St. Paul United Way, Urban Coalition, Benjamin E. Mays Learning Center; and member, State Advisory Special Needs Program. Recipient 1975-76 Community Leader and Noteworthy Americans. Mental Retardation Award and 1970 Leland Douglas Award for the handicapped.

servant of Major Lawrence Taliaferro, the very equitable Indian agent at Fort Snelling. Incidentally, Taliaferro respected the rights of the Indian; he often placed their immediate needs above the traders and hunters. Young Harriet Robinson married the historical figure, Dred Scott. Another person of note was the aforementioned property owner, Mary Doris, whose land was used to occupy the post office in St. Paul. One other woman found in the sporadic records is Mrs. Eliza Winston. Involved in a much publicized event, she was the first Negro in Minnesota and among the few slaves elsewhere to be individually freed by court order. Mrs. Winston's lawyer rested his case on the fact that slavery in Minnesota was illegal, although her opponent used the famous Dred Scott Decision for testimony.

During the influx of Negroes to Minnesota shortly after the Civil War, most of the people that migrated here were single men who came seeking better job opportunities, or married men who came to earn more pay and hoped to send for their families. But some women did come with families later in the 1890's and settled in rural areas of Fergus Falls. Meanwhile, the urban black women continued to

Regina Reed is editor and publisher of a new national black political magazine and a talk hostess for KUXL. A former State Republican vice-chairperson, she is Outreach chairperson for the state Republican Party Women's Federation; publicity person for the Women's Assoc., Breck School; a trustee for the Afro-American Cultural Arts Center; member of the Board, American Lung Association; member, National Council of Negro Women; and former state Interfaith Coordinator, United Negro College Fund. Born in Mississippi, she attended Harris Teachers College in St. Louis. Widowed, she has two children and lives in Minneapolis.

Rosemary A. Davis, State Ethics Commission, appointed by Gov. Wendell Anderson; former chairperson, U.S. 3rd Dist. DFL Party; married to Dr. Curtis E. Davis.

Nancy L. Bannister, biologist, U.S. Fish and Wildlife; from Amelia, Va. M.S., Degree, Ohio State; B.S., Va. State; enrolled part-time fishery biol., U. of Minn. At work, she studies land and water devlpmnt. projects. Corres. sectry., St. Paul Urban Leaguers; Zeta Phi Beta.

Mrs. Dorothy M. Hawkins, denominational repres., Church Women United, Mpls. Council Churches. The wife of Rev. E.A. Hawkins, a member of NAACP; Nat'l. Council Negro Women; pres., Grant Missionary Soc., St. Peter's A.M.E. Church, extending its arm to the needy in the community.

World traveler, **Earlene R. Johnson**, has visited six continents. Northwest Airlines personnel for seven yrs.; Continuing Educ., U. of Minn., nutrition. She writes about food and travel, *Summit-Univ. Free Press.* Orig. from the Southwest, she does St. Paul community volunteer work; adores children; is the aunt of athlete, Vida Blue; likes interior design, and collects antiques.

Jeanne V. Cooper, pblshr., black-oriented *Twin City Observer/St. Paul Sun.* A St. Paul native, grew up in Chicago; graduate, U. of Minn. Became exec. mgr., family-owned nwsprs. in '66, then pblshr., in '67. Member NAACP; Urban League; UNCF; Minn. Advsry. Committee U.S. Commission, Civil Rights; YWCA; St. James A.M.E. Church Choir; recip., Community Service Award, Pan-African Inst; citat., Blk. Community, '75. She has three children.

Worthy Grand Matron, Marilee Parks Lynn, Prince Hall Order, Eastern Star. Mbr., Como Temple #128 IBPOEW since 1929. Served in many offices; twice elected and present Daughter Ruler; Loyal Lady Ruler, #47 Order of Golden Circle; Imperial Deputy, Isisecettes.

Beatrice Shuck Bailey, supvsr., Science and industry Room, St. Paul Library. A St. Paulite, she is a U. of Minn. grad and was a librarian for three Negro colleges. Amer. Assoc., Univ. Women; Minn. Library Assoc.; Alpha Kappa Alpha; Unity Church; Coll. of St. Thomas Women's Auxillary.

Willie Mae Wilson, 1st women exec. dir., St. Paul Urban League; admin. deputy, '72-'74. Course work completed, M.A. Degree, Public Affairs, U. of Minn.; B.A., Knoxville Coll.; Knowledgeable about minority economy and housing trends. Active voice, St. Paul issues, she is first black and woman chirprsn., Brd. of Commsnrs., HRA. Co-chairprsn., SECAC—Sec. School Desegregation; pres., 75-member Council, United Way Exec. Dirs.; vice pres., St. Paul Ramsey Arts and Science. Board, Community Devlpmnt. Corp.; Citizen's League; Minn. Women's Polit. Caucus; Iota Phi Lambda; Delta Sigma Theta, among others. Married with two children.

Lillian Parks Thomas, a proj. dir., Ramsey Action Prog., St. Paul Pres., Internat'l. Continentals; moved from Kansas to St. Paul with her brother, Gordon Parks (famed photog. and film producer). She is on many boards and committees: St. Paul Urban Coalition; Mayor's Mnpwr. Comm.; "400" Committee, Bethune Memorial, D.C.; and past pres., Nat'l. Urban League Guilds, St. Paul League Guild; Natl. Council., Negro Women; Cameos; Eastern Star; St. Philip's Episcopal Church.

work mostly as maids, cooks, and domestics. They were few in number, but their presence was made through their attempts at establishing some permanent ties with their families.

According to the dissertation *The Lower Income Negro Family*, by Robert Staples, "Before 1940 the greatest number of Negro migrants were solitary Negro males. From the first census of Minnesota's Negroes, males greatly outnumbered females. It is around 1950 before we see signs of any appreciable female migration and also the opportunity for many males to have a stable family life."[9]

The close of the 1800's and the beginning of the 20th Century saw much social progress in the Negro communities. Leaders in the community were conerned about themselves as a group and promoted the "highest ideals of all home life among Negroes." The ideas for founding social agencies were instilled in the minds of the leaders when individuals found it difficult to meet the needs of the people. Other Negroes who came here were welcomed and encouraged to live in this state that did not "generally discriminate against its citizens." But they were also told to respect the women, respect themselves as men, and thereby they would be treated as men.

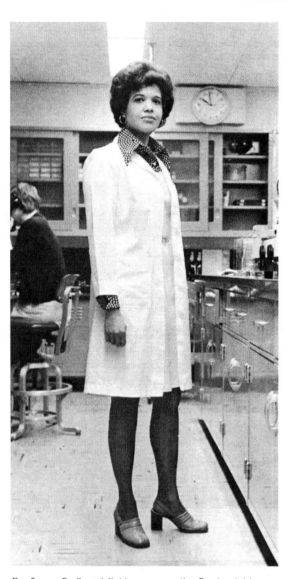

Dr. Susan E. Crutchfield, an assoc. dir., Prudential Insurance Co. From Charleston, West Va., attended Mpls. Central High; B.S. Degree, U. of Minn., then became one of the youngest — age 22 — to earn her degree from the U. of Minn. Med. Sch., '63. Mbr. Amer. Med. Assoc., Amer. Acad. Family Pract., Ramsey Cty. Med. Soc.; Who's Who of Amer. Women.

Doris J. Bailey is shown checking banking records by means of an electronic microfiche reader unit at First National Bank of Minneapolis. Mrs. Bailey, Brooklyn Center, began her career at First Minneapolis in 1950 and now is Operations Officer and manager of the Collection and Coupon Division.

Victoria A. Borom, a branch chief, local Housing and Urban Development (HUD). M.S. Degree., U. of M. B.S., Spellman. From Atlanta, she is active in community and civic orgs.; pres., UNCF; St. Paul Urban Leaguers; mbr., Nat'l. Assoc. Housing Specialists; Delta Sigma Theta; and a trustee, Pilgrim Baptist Church. She has one child.

During this period many young people were beginning to enter college, women included. The first black woman to graduate from the University of Minnesota in 1904 was Miss Scottie Davis. Another graduated two years later and became an instructor at Tuskegee. Macalester College's first Negro graduate was Catherine Lealted who graduated in 1915 with the highest scholastic rating in her class.

Many young black women were also a part of the social consciousness movement. Negro sororities were organized and some all-women Negro colleges were flourishing in the South. The women in the coed schools were also involved in this philosophy of devoting themselves to honor, dignity and scholarship. The Negro sorority, Alpha Kappa Alpha for example, was established on the University of Minnesota campus in 1922, and in less than four years its membership ranked highest scholastically among all the Greek organizations there![10]

Some 50 years later, and in a speech made during the 1975 International Women's Year, Eleanor Holmes Norton went a step farther. She stated that black women and men should remain united in an enduring relationship for, "The repair of the black

Juanita Nevils, U.S. Dept. Agriculture, accounting technician. Born in Minneapolis, Minn. she was appointed the first Federal Woman Coordinator, Minn. Administrative Branches. An EEO Counselor-at-large, 1973-75, she is presently on the local EEO Advisory Committee. She is pres., Helper Club, raising funds for charitable progs. such as Sickle Cell Anemia.

Alfreda Garibaldi, Upward Bound Dir., Macalester College; has a B.A., French Educ., Xavier U.; completing courses for Ph.D., educ. psych., U. of M. Taught French six years at Harding and Central, St. Paul; a counselor last two yrs. Ethnic Concerns Committee, Archdiocese, St. Paul; National Urban League Board of Directors, St. Paul Urban League Brd., Nat'l Alliance, Businesswomen. Co-owner, Garibaldi's, Minneapolis.

Shirley Calloway, pres., Visions of Total Reality, Corp. and a producer, WTCN-TV "Random Access" by and for black people. In communications for six years, she feels that communications cannot win the battle alone, but the battle cannot be won without it. Shirley, who feels her biggest personal asset is an "overwhelming love for people," gives a message to all women of color: "Take care to preserve your femininity and still do a dynamic job."

condition in America disproportionately depends upon the succor of strong families which can defend against the forces that prey most menacingly on unprotected black men, women and children."[11]

Pictured here are only a few of Minnesota's committed black women, representatives of a proud, responsive, viable, and dedicated group of Minnesotans. Some of the many others not pictured here are Nellie Stone Johnson, Barbara Berry, Lorraine Hale, Betty Zachary, Katie McWatt, Laura Scott, Vivian Stone, Dolphine Robinson, Ann Darby, Janabelle Taylor, Sylvia Carty, Parthenia Jones, Willa

Mae Dixon, Ruth Benner, Patricia Collins, Beulah Flowers, Louise Gooden, Josephine Luna, Joyce Johnson, Lena Weston, Mary Lou Williams, and Ione Brown. Others are Nancy Burrus, Faye Keye, Marceline Donaldson, Teresa Fatoba, Mabel Evans Cason, Thelma Mann, Katherine Harris, Mary Kay Boyd, Connie Price, Dolly Spencer, Paralee Milligan, and many more.

These women have an inner strength ingrained in dedication to making life just a wee bit better for other people. In their own individual way, black women are weaving a web of kindred souls to bring about a end-product of unity and understanding.

Mattee Robinson is employed by the Minnesota Department of Public Welfare. She holds a B.A. Degree from Antioch College and is working on her masters degree. She is also a vocalist.

Mary J. Kyle, editor and pblshr., black-oriented *Twin Cities Courier*. Pres., Sentinel Pblsng. Co.; commentator, KMSP-TV and WLOL radio; and lecturer. Born in St. Paul, grew up in Mpls., she went to Central High and the U. of Minn. Minn. Press Club (1st woman pres., '75); AFTRA; Minn. Press Women; and local and nat'l. nwspr. associations. Chamber of Commerce; NAACP life member; Mpls. Urban League; Board, YWCA; Safety Council; State Council, Eco. Educ.; and others. Wife of Earl Kyle, Sr., they have four children.

Pilot Valerie Price begins a new era for black women in Minnesota. She is the first black woman pilot to be trained by Flight Unlimited a Minneapolis based organization founded by the Rev. Linton Scott to provide scholarships for young blacks who are interested in learning to fly. Ms. Price enjoys the freedom of flying and plans to become a Flight Instructor. She is also a teacher at the Mpls. Street Academy.

EDUCATION

EDUCATION

The question of education for Negroes was evident before the Civil War. As early as 1837, children of Negro settlers in Mendota were going to school with their Caucasian and American Indian counterparts. It was also recorded that any teacher coming to town should be entirely free of prejudice on account of color, "... for she would find them all among her students."

But keeping into account America's "psychological anathema," and the emotional basis upon which people base their attitudes, as the migrations of Negroes into the Minnesota Territory before statehood increased, so did an anti-Negro sentiment. As Negroes concentrated in the urban areas, the insistence on a separate school was great. In fact, one did exist in St. Paul in 1857, but closed because the black teacher, Moses Dixon, had no black children to teach. Many of them continued to go to, or re-entered the public schools.

Assn't school supt., James E. Phillips, Ph.D., Indiana U.; M.A. Degree, Columbia U. Began teaching in St. Paul, '55, he is now dir., secondary instruction. Brd. mbr., Minn. Assoc., Secondary School Principals; Title I Advisory Committee, State Dept.; Educ. TV Advisory Committee, Afro-Amer. Studies. He is a Master teacher, Twin City Institute for Talented Youth.

Veterinarian, Dr. George Berry, born in St. Paul; attended Hamline U., Fisk, and Iowa State; USDA 37-yr. employee; circuit supvsr., Meat and Poultry Insp., Minnesota. First black elected to St. Paul School Brd.; named civil servant of the year, '69. Life mbr., Minn. PTA; vestry, St. Philip's Epis. Church; brd., Hallie Q. Brown; and other memberships.

Robert L. Williams, Ed.D., U. of Minn., M.Ed. and B.A. Degrees, Adams State (Colo.); an assoc. supt., Mpls. Public Schools. Member, Amer. Assoc. Sch. Administrators; Phi Delta Kappa; Phi Theta Kappa.

Earl W. Bowman,, Jr., Master's and B.A. Degrees Macalester College. Dean of Students at Macalester, he is shown here at the 1975 Freshman Orientation Day with parents of new students.

The action to separate schools was authorized by the Board of Education because "The board believed that they had a duty to extend educational facilities to Negroes," but "that no children of African descent be thereafter admitted into any . . . schools."[12]

Although the school was not a success, the superintendent of schools informed the board that another "colored" School would open in 1865. Eventually, the school received complaints about the dilapidated condition of the building and poor attendance. It was officially closed by the superintendent in 1867, but evidently continued to operate for

another year. Finally in 1869 the legislature abolished separate schools by withholding funds from any public school that denied education to anyone "on the grounds of color, social position or nationality."[13]

Here again, the presence of the Negro in Minnesota had won out, but the problem was not solved. Many young black students stayed away. Although only 13 applied for school in 1869 and 13 were admitted, the problem was obvious. Legally, all students could go to the same school, but the American psychological anathema still existed and legislation could not remove attitudes.

W. Harry Davis, assn't. vice pres., public affairs, *Minneapolis Star and Tribune*. He has devoted years to public service with the Mpls. Brd. of Education; Governor's Crime Commission; Human Rights Commission; Phyllis Wheatley Center; AAMOA; NAACP; Chamber of Commerce; 1st Plymouth Bank; Minn. AAU; and honored by many Merit Awards. L.L.O., Macalester College, 1973.

Herman P. Bailey, Ph.D; assoc. prof., College of St. Thomas. Doctorate from St. Louis U.; Master's, U. of Minn.; B.A., Lincoln U. (Pa.). He was an Artillery Officer, U.S. Army; taught high school math; educ. and math at Hampton Institute. Life mbr. and Polemarch, Kappa Alpha Psi; past Board member, St. Paul YMCA.

Ralph Crowder, B.S., Hampton Inst., Coord., Black Student Affairs, Augsburg College and counselor, Center, Student Development; advisor, Black Student Union; He is in the Ph.D. program, U. of Minn.

343

Not to be deterred, many Negroes were being educated, and for families who could afford the transporation costs, their young people were being sent East and South to the Negro colleges such as Howard University, West Virginia State, and Hampton Institute. And those who had been to other schools such as Knoxville College and Tuskegee came to live and work in Minnesota.

The population of students who had gone away to college and the newcomers who brought a new sense of worth and active leadership heretofore was at a minimum. Shortly thereafter, the first Negro gradu-ated from the University of Minnesota in 1887. He was Andrew Hilyer, who later became a leader in black business associations. The first Negro woman student, Miss Scottie Davis, graduated from the University in 1904. In spite of the odds, and the few setbacks that even exist in public education today, education for the black population had gone the way of Negro suffrage. Blacks, who were now as much a part of daily life in Minnesota as the French, British, Swedish, and Irish immigrants, had only to be determined to usurp racial attitudes. On the books, the right to go to school anywhere in the state and

Minority Groups Student Center Dir., Mankato State **Michael T. Fagin**, recruits and coordinates facilities to meet the needs of minority groups. From Detroit, he is a member of many Natl. orgs., including the Nat. Assoc. for Study of Afro-American Life and History. M.S. Degree, Mankato; doctorate studies, U. of Minn.

James L. Tanner, MA and MFA Degrees, U. of Wis.; has taught ceramics and glassworking at Mankato since '68. Nationally known for his work with glass; shown in major collections; Brd. member Minn. Crafts Council; and lives in Good Thunder with wife, artist Sandra and two sons.

Richard and Mae Gaskins discuss their team counseling at Gustavus Adolphus College in St. Peter. He has an A.A. Degree in liberal Arts, Boston U.; A.B., psych., Wilberforce, and working on the M.BA, St. Thomas. Mae has a B.S. Degree, educ., Boston U. and teaches in Bloomington.

the right to vote was there. Doing it was the important step to take.

In spite of the fact that Minnesota ranks very high among the educational echelons of this country, and that its educational system is sometimes referred to as "progressive," a crisis exists today in educating the black and minority youth — 90 percent of whom still live in the three major urban areas or "inner cities." Schools are still racially imbalanced and oftentimes racials attitudes of the 1860's still have not changed. Much effort is being done to correct this such as the Minneapolis Plan — studied and used even by southern educators.

The plan urges a policy that no school should have a greater percentage of students of one race than the percentage of students of that race in proportion to the overall population. School administrators are constantly looking at district boundaries and changes to include students from all races and all economic walks of life. They use tests that depict racially mixed situations, and recruit teachers who are more qualified and more sensitive to changing times. Likewise,

Bernard LaFayette, Jr., Ed.D., Harvard U.; degrees from Boston U. School of Law, Fisk U.; Amer. Bapt. Theol. Sem. (BA). He is dir., Peace Educ. and prof., Gustavus Adolphus College. Worked at Harvard Grad. Sch., Educ.; natl. prog. admstr., SCLC with Dr. Martin Luther King; founder, MLK Ctr. Justice and Social Change, Panama; exec. staff, Dr. Martin Luther King; he was a freedom rider and co-founder of SNCC; mbr., Fact-Finding Team, Vietnam, '70; the author of *Pedagogy for Peace and Non-Violence.*

Frank Jones, Jr., grew up in NYC; graduated, Central State U., '72; pursued an ed. psych. M.A. Deg., U. of Minn (Duluth) and worked for Lutheran Social Services. Employed by Metro State U., was a "Jet" in the recent Shoestring Players' "West Side Story" production. He lives in Selby-Dale.

John H. Taborn, Ph.D., Ed. Psych., U. of Minn.; Assn't Prof., Continuing Education Expert, U. of Minn. Taborn is a member of many civic and professional organizations; State Board, Human Rights.

St. Paul has a "Cluster Program" of key centralized voluntary study and recently completed a desegregation plan by the Secondary Education Advisory Committee of which Mrs. Willie Mae Wilson, a black woman, was a tri-chairperson.

Names in the school administration such as Harry Davis, Joyce Jackson, and Marvin Trammel are household names in Minneapolis today. These black educators, as well as other pictured in this book bring to Minnesota some of the best minds in education, at least in the Midwest, to promote learning as a tool for progress for blacks, and for all Minnesotans.

But racial disagreements still crop up, some teachers have to be more of a disciplinarian; and some school district residents do not want to abide by the wishes of the Board of Education; Many black young adults are graduating from high school, but some can only read on an elementary school level. In 1976, education for much of the young black population and for, other groups as well, must make some drastic changes before it moves ahead. The educators depicted here are trying to do just that.

William C. Thomas, M.S. Degree, Loyola U.; B.A., Northwestern; Harvard U. Mgmnt. Cert. Personnel dir., U. of Minn.; was assn't dir. employee relations since '73. A former columnist, Twin City Observer; former host, "Random Access," Black oriented TV show.

Frank B. Wilderson, Jr., Ph.D.; vice pres., Student Affairs, U. of Minn.; M.S. Degree, U. of Michigan. An educator and lecturer, he is married to Ph.D psychologist, Ida-Lorraine Wilderson. They have four children.

Mel Henderson, assn't. prof. and field educ. dir., Metro. State U., holds a Mankato State M.S. Degree, in rehabilitation counseling; B.S., U. of Minn. A Twin Cities native, he is married and has one child.

Rufus Lee Simmons, B.S. Degree; dir., Coffman Union, U. of Minn.; former dir., Martin Luther King Student Ctr., Delaware State College; citizenship award, work in student life, '69-'70. Many sports awards home State of Ohio; member, Association of College Unions, including its '73 Conf. Planning Committee.

Afro-American Studies U. of Minn. dept. head, **Geneva H. Southall**, Ph.D., is also a prof. in the Dept. of Music, Afro-Amer. Studies and member, the Graduate Faculty. Her doctorate is from the U. of Iowa in music lit. and piano performance. An accomplished pianist, she has given many local and national recitals.

George E. Ayers, Ph.D; vice pres. and Dean, Academic Affairs, Metro. State U. Widely known for developing nontraditional educ. programs, he is a teacher, counselor, administrator, and lecturer; published over 40 articles in professional journals.

347

Bernard Raphael, Normandale Community College assoc. dean and instr. On staff when it opened in '68. In the Ph.D. prog., U. of Northern Colo., he holds the M.A. Degree, St. Thomas, and B.A., Xavier U. Phi Delta Kappa; Minn. Council, Teachers of English.

Developmental disabilities specialist, Geraldine L. Carter, Pilot Ci Mental Health Services, Mpls. Ph.D. in educ. admin.; and M.A educ. psych., U. of Minn.; B.A. Degree, Concordia. Grew up Mpls., she went to North High. She assesses special learning ar behavioral problems of inner city children. Wife of Eugene Carte two children.

Melvin L. Bates is a science teacher at Edison High School in Nor east Minneapolis.

Walter Cox, assoc. dean, Student Services, Normandale Community College; he heads counseling, orientation, and activities areas there. Has a M.S. Degree, Kansas State and B.S., health and phys. ed., Southern U. Extensive work in recreation and occupational therapy.

Assistant principal, **Cornelius Tucker**, works at Anthony Junior High in Minneapolis.

Joyce T. Jackson, Ph.D., is principal of the Minneapolis Central High School. She holds doctorate from the U. of Minn.; and B.A. and M.S. Degrees from Southern Illinois Univ. She came to the Minneapolis schools in 1952. A qualified certified psychologist, she is active in community affairs. Dr. Jackson is the wife of Dr. Thomas Jackson, also an educator.

Iris C. Butler, school psychologist, works closely with Minneapolis public school students and their parents.

Richard R. Green, West Area Superintendent, Minneapolis Public Schools, was former principal, North High School, Minneapolis.

Charles L. Smith works as a human relations specialist for the Minneapolis Public Schools.

Berlene Turner is project director for ESAA in the Minneapolis Public Schools.

Charles Nichols is director of Vocational, Technical and Industrial Education in Minneapolis.

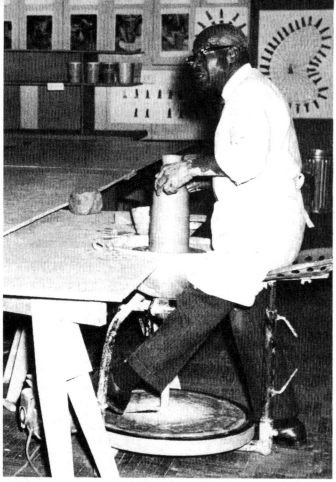

William Artis, assn't. prof., art, Mankato State; one of the nation's leading black artists; exhibited Nat'l. Portrait Gallery (Wash.); Walker Art Museum (Mpls); Slater Memorial (Conn.); Harmon Fndtn. (NY). Holds the MFA and BA Degrees, Syracuse Univ.

Katrina V. Green, B.S., Degree elem. ed., U. of Minn. A teacher, she became assn't to the supt., Urban Affairs, St. Paul Public Schools in '73. Active in quality educ. for minorities, and working on her grad. degree, she is married with two children.

Charles Breese, affirmative action dir., State Univ. System; M.A. Degree, Bus. Admn., U. of Ill.; B.S., Morgan State. Was advertising dir., N.J. Med. Coll.; vice pres., Hyman Assoc. (adver. and PR); consltnt. and fund raiser. Member, Pub. Relations Soc., Amer. Affirmative Action Association.

Baritone, Luther Stripling, is a Macalester College assn't. prof. of music and head of the department's vocal studies. He directs the Pilgrim Baptist Church Choir (St. Paul) and has given many performances with Twin City groups.

Yvonne Corker Condell, Ph.D., Biol prof., Moorhead State; visiting scientist, Minn. Acad., Science, '65; Advisor, Human Genetics, Cass Cty. Mental Health Assoc.; Danforth Assoc., '75-'77; and member, many prof. orgs., including holding office in Amer. Assoc., Univ. Women.

Kate Bulls LaFayette, M.Ed. Degree, Early Child Educ., Tufts. Child development specialist, Minn. Reg. IX Council, Coordinated Child Care, Mankato. She offers tech assistance and trng. to child care progs.; married to Dr. Bernard LaFayette, Jr.

Ida-Lorraine Wilderson, Ph.D., is special education administrator for training programs and a U. of Minn. Liaison. The producer of a teacher training film titled "Mainstreaming," she is active in many educational programs; a member of The Links; and the wife of Dr. Frank Wilderson, U. of Minnesota.

Planning a St. Paul Urban League Street Academy proposal for next year, Antoine M. Garibaldi heads the school for disenchanted youth. M.S. Degree, social psych. of educ., U. of Minn., and Ph.D. candidate. From New Orleans, he is pres., Midwest Reg. and local Assoc. Blk. Student Psychologists. Active in Blacks in the Catholic Church, Catholic Diaconate, and mbr. St. Peter Claver, St. Paul.

351

Marion C. Kennon, 1st Black teacher, Breck Prep School, St. Paul. B.S. Degree, U. of Omaha; M.S., candidate; completing Elem. Remedial Rdng. certificate Phi Delta Kappa; Amer. Assoc. Elem. Sch. Tchrs.; Minn. Rdng. Assoc.; Alpha Kappa Alpha; founder, Twin Cities Links Chapter.

Minneapolis born Donald McRaven, Jr., is assn't. prof., art, minority studies, Moorhead State. M.F.A. Degree, U. of Minn., was a "Black Voices" announcer; photographer; and sign painter. He has exhibited throughout the Twin Cities, in Winnipeg, and Fargo, North Dakota.

Ph.D. candidate, James LeRoy Haynes, is Macalester College's newly appointed director, counseling and minority programs. He is studying psychological foundations of education at the U. of Minn.

Edgar West, welding instr., Hennepin Cty., Vocat. Institute, Brooklyn Park. From Waterloo, Iowa, he worked odd jobs before and after the Air Force; came to Mpls. in '65; worked for Butler Mftg. Co., then went to TVI. A Big Brother, he works with youth to help them advance, Big Bro. Appreciation Award, '73; letter of apprec., Pres. Nixon, '71.

Photographed by Maureen Lambray

"My father works 12 hours a day putting down rails so I can become a lawyer. Now my school is running out of money."

BUILDINGS

BUILDINGS

Blacks have owned buildings and land since Minnesota was a territory. As previously stated, James Thompson, an ex-slave freed by the missionary, is reported to have given the land for the first Protestant church in St. Paul. Most of the buildings (houses included) used in early Minnesota by Negroes were acquired from previous white owners. These included the first Pilgrim Church, then located in 1870 on Cedar St. in St. Paul and St. James A.M.E. Church in Minneapolis on Sixth Ave. SE and Second Street. Most of the black-owned buildings today are in the urban communities dominated by blacks. This outcome is the result of a trend that began one hundred years ago to confine Negroes to specific areas.

As early as 1869, Negroes were settled in what is now the commercial section of St. Paul. Maurice Jernigan, a barber, lived on Jackson Street between Sixth and Seventh Streets. Robert Stockton lived on Fifth Street between Market and Washington. Henry

Moffatt lived on Fourth Street between Franklin and Exchange. Thomas R. Hickman, a calciminer, lived in the rear of the northwest corner of Twelfth and Cedar Streets. Fielding Combs lived on Cooper Street and then moved to 86 Temperance Street in 1880.

Often these early settlers occupied houses which white families left for better homes. These houses were situated so far back from the graded streets that they were designated as being in the rear of certain numbers or east of certain corners.

According to the older members of the Negro community, it was only about 1890 when a movement was noticeable to restrict Negroes on Rondo, St. Anthony, and University Avenues, below Dale Street.

In Minneapolis, the Negroes apparently settled near what is now known as Seven Corners and then moved toward the Loop district. Later they moved to North Minneapolis. The last change was to the southern part of the city.[14]

The majority of Minnesota's black population (about 30,000) live in the metropolitan area of the Twin Cities, and most of them within the city limits, not far from the business sections of town.

Although much change is now taking place with redevelopment, poor housing for Negroes in the past was commonplace. It was a direct reflection of their poor working conditions. Though critical, and even today, parts of the Northside of Minneapolis and the Selby-Dale area of St. Paul are called "ghettos" by some, others of authority have stated that some of the old once-elegant homes and structurally sound buildings could be called North Oaks or Beverly Hills when compared to the real ghettos of America.

Beautiful well-kept homes are found in the urban areas, and many privately owned or black-operated buildings are present. These include the Plymouth Avenue Medical Center, First Plymouth Bank, Mt. Zion Baptist Church, and Pilot City in Minneapolis and St. Philip's Gardens, Mt. Olivet Baptist Church, Camphor Methodist Church, Control Data-Selby Operations, and the Martin Luther King Center in St. Paul, are only a few signs of progress for building and development for or by blacks.

Discrimination against where to live or what to occupy and where has been outlawed for many years now. The pride and need for decent housing and public buildings is strong — so indicated by new construction developing in the North side of Minneapolis and in the breathtaking new home with three bedrooms, a 30 ft. ceiling and a 16 ft.-wide fireplace in the livingroom, recently planned and built by a young black named William Newsom, on Minneapolis' Cedar Lake. The vast wastelands left by "urban removal" in the St. Paul inner city are rapidly being replaced by split-level homes built by private owners, specifically around the new Denzil A. Carty Park, and by the black developer James Milsap north of Freeway I-94, East of Dale Street and South of University Avenue. Soon to be constructed is a 32,000 ft. black-owned shopping center there through the auspices of H.E.L.P. Development Corporation.

Owning buildings and land in America is one of the pinnacles of stability. A commonplace "American Dream" is to own a home and acquire property. Nothing wrong with that! And Minnesota's Black Community is renewing its efforts in this phase of economic development.

RELIGION

Four Minnesota pastors of the African Methodist Episcopal (AME) Church hold a proclamation signed by Gov. Wendell Anderson designating a day as Richard Allen Day in Minnesota. Allen founded the AME church in 1787 in Philadelphia after he and other blacks were told they could not worship in a white Methodist Episcopal Church.

Allen also started schools for blacks. With the proclamation are, from left, standing, the **Rev. Amos T. Chester**, St. Paul, and the **Rev. Noan S. Smith**, Duluth, and seated, the **Rev. T. Edison Cooper** and the **Rev. E. Alexander Hawkins**, both of Minneapolis.

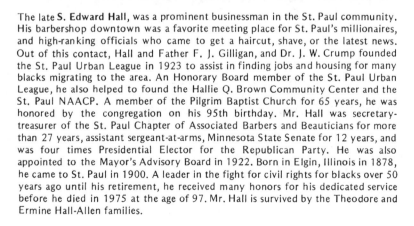

This Annual Report is dedicated to S. Ed Hall, & the forty-five persons who met at Pilgrim Baptist Church in 1923 to organize the St. Paul Urban League.

The late **Rev. Denzil A. Carty** was rector of St. Philip's Episcopal Church in St. Paul for 25 years and died at the age of 71 shortly after his retirement in 1975. A leader for civil rights in St. Paul, he was constantly fighting for "dignity and equality, in education, jobs and housing." Five and one-half years after he came to Minnesota his parish was dedicating a new church, thanks to the persuasions he made with the church board and Episcopal Bishop. Rev. Carty was able to found an apartment complex for better housing at St. Philip's Gardens. Born in St. John's Antigua, British West Indies, he attended high school and General Theological Seminary in New York. Later while working in Michigan and after World War II as an Army Chaplin, he earned a degree in clinical psychology at Wayne State. A progressive minister, one of Father Carty's deacon's and still at St. Philip's is Rev. Dr. Jeanette Piccard, one of the disputed six American women ordained in the Episcopal Church. Carty was a St. Paul Urban League Board member, and received their Distinguished Community Service Award in 1975. He served on the Boards of the Episcopal Community Services and the Minnesota Council for Civil and Human Rights; NAACP; Hallie Q. Brown Community Center; and many other religious and civic groups. He is survived by his wife Sylvia and three daughters, Celeste Myles, Denise Carty Bennia, and Jacqueline Carty.

The late **S. Edward Hall**, was a prominent businessman in the St. Paul community. His barbershop downtown was a favorite meeting place for St. Paul's millionaires, and high-ranking officials who came to get a haircut, shave, or the latest news. Out of this contact, Hall and Father F. J. Gilligan, and Dr. J. W. Crump founded the St. Paul Urban League in 1923 to assist in finding jobs and housing for many blacks migrating to the area. An Honorary Board member of the St. Paul Urban League, he also helped to found the Hallie Q. Brown Community Center and the St. Paul NAACP. A member of the Pilgrim Baptist Church for 65 years, he was honored by the congregation on his 95th birthday. Mr. Hall was secretary-treasurer of the St. Paul Chapter of Associated Barbers and Beauticians for more than 27 years, assistant sergeant-at-arms, Minnesota State Senate for 12 years, and was four times Presidential Elector for the Republican Party. He was also appointed to the Mayor's Advisory Board in 1922. Born in Elgin, Illinois in 1878, he came to St. Paul in 1900. A leader in the fight for civil rights for blacks over 50 years ago until his retirement, he received many honors for his dedicated service before he died in 1975 at the age of 97. Mr. Hall is survived by the Theodore and Ermine Hall-Allen families.

RELIGION

Religion has always been the solid foundation in black communities, even at times when it was difficult for slaves to congregate and share their faith. Religion has provided strength and hope when all else failed black people in meeting the adversities of struggling to be free.

"Overlooking . . . the central teaching of Christianity," states Edwin Embree in *The Brown Americans,* "brotherly love was being preached by a people actively engaged in enslaving their fellow-men, the slaves found peace and joy in the Christian ideal of humility and the hope of a blessed life in another world after faith and suffering on earth. There was comfort also in the graphic accounts in the Old Testament of the trials of the children of Israel . . . which gave Negroes hope for their own freedom in America. Of the great world religions, none . . . could possibly fit a slave condition more happily than Christianity."[15]

The Black minister seems to automatically become a leader in the community as indicated by Robert

Zion American Baptist Church, Minneapolis.

Rev. Curtis A. Herron, Pastor at Zion Baptist Church, Minneapolis.

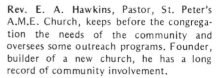

Rev. E. A. Hawkins, Pastor, St. Peter's A.M.E. Church, keeps before the congregation the needs of the community and oversees some outreach programs. Founder, builder of a new church, he has a long record of community involvement.

St. Peter's A.M.E. Church, Minneapolis.

Hickman's arrival in St. Paul as an ex-slave in 1863. Although considered "an outsider," a church that . . . he helped to establish . . . has always been a "pillar" of the community and Pilgrim Baptist Church still stands today as a monument to much progress for blacks. Innumerable public meetings were held at Pilgrim which made a long-lasting impact on the future of the black community in St. Paul.

Even today, Pilgrim's pastor, Rev. Amos Brown, is an active community leader who can oratorically be heard from the pulpit on Sunday mornings at Pilgrim, or before the St. Paul School Board as he protests against inequities of the education process in his fight for the black children of the community.

In Minneapolis, the St. James African Methodist Episcopal Church was formally organized in 1863, although members had been meeting in homes since 1860. In 1870 a new Methodist Episcopal church was erected across the river in St. Anthony. Through Reverend Hedgemann's leadership and hard work, it opened for services in November, 1870.

St. Peter Claver, a Catholic church whose congregation in St. Paul is predominantly black, was founded in 1892. One of its more prominent priests, Father

Rev. Ronald Terry, Jr., pastor, Greater Sabathani Baptist Church. Recently honored by his congregation, he is pres., Minn. Bapt. Convention, Metropolitan Bapt. Dist. Assoc.; He is Instrumentalist, Nat'l. Bapt. Convention. Mbr., Masonic Lodge; Amer., Soc. Clinical Pathologist; and Soc., Med. Technologist. Evangelist to Liberia; Many state and local Distinguished Serv. Awards; Doctor, Divinity, Trinity Hall. His wife teaches in Minneapolis.

Rev. Walter L. Battle, founder, exec. dir., Refuge Christian Youth Center for motivating boys and girls vocationally, academically, and religiously. It has inspired over 1500 young people since 1959. The facility is located on a 32-acre truck farm in Ball Club, Minn. Rev. Battle says, "Our heart and hand involved in community affairs offers much to the welfare of our social and spiritual motivation and stability."

Greater Sabathani Baptist Church, Minneapolis.

Stephen A. Theobold, was a St. Paul Seminary graduate and one of the first Negro priests in America.

After the 1940's some changes in racial prejudice began to take place through religion. In the past, Mankato, Minnesota was known for its anti-Negro feelings, but during the 1950's Negroes were asked to come and share services at several churches. Quite a change for a town whose local newspaper once publicly denounced Negroes. And in 1956, the Hennepin Avenue Methodist Church in Minneapolis merged with the all-Negro Border Methodist Church.

A year later, the Border Methodist pastor, Rev. Charles Sexton, became the pastor at an all-white church in Champlin, Minnesota.

Founded on a pioneering and religious spirit, religious discrimination in Minnesota has been minimal. Today, this is evident in one of the largest observances of Martin Luther King's birthday, held each year at the predominantly white Centennial United Methodist Church in Roseville, Minnesota. The Minneapolis, and the St. Paul Council of Churches and the groups of interdenominational alliances of ministers are striving and succeeding in

Mt. Olivet Baptist Church, St. Paul.

Rev. Willa L. Grant Battle, pastor, Mpls. Gospel Temple House of Refuge, founded Missions in Haiti with 50 churches and 10 schools there. A Cum Laude graduate of the U. of Minn. in Amer. Studies and Afro-Amer. Hist.; graduate of Northwestern Bible College; Doctor of Humanities, Trinity College. Member, Amer. Assoc., Univ. Women; Mpls. Ministerial Assoc.; National Council, Negro Women; Delta Sigma Theta; NAACP; and Christian Educators.

Rev. Stanley R. King, organizer and pastor in 1959, Sabathani Baptist Church; former pastor, Mt. Olivet Baptist Church, St. Paul. A certified HUD consultant, packaged 447 low and moderate housing units in seven yrs. Pres., Human Resources Consultants; vice pres., MIA properties; St. Cloud State U. communications and Human relations instr.; pastor, Twin City Open Door Fellowship. Former first exec. dir., TCOIC; OIC Denver; OIC Phoenix. Organizer, founder, Negro League of Voters and Mpls. Urban Coalition. Former member, many state and local commissions and organizations. From Oklahoma City, he has a M.A. Degree, St. Cloud State U.; B.A., U. of Minn.; doctoral candidate, U. of Mass.; joint degree in Law and City and Regional Planning; theological studies Grand Canyon College.

368

bring about "racial ecumenicalism."

Religion still plays a big role in the black community. The churches on Sunday mornings are filled with people who continue their heritage of worship and belief in the Christian ethic. The spitituals sung in many churches are just as soulful and moving as they were a hundred years ago. Since the early 1970's The Black Muslims have also become a part of the community and practice daily the teachings of Islam.

The black ministers are a dedicated group of individuals who strive to make life better in Minnesota. Many volunteer their time for things far-

removed from the pulpit. Rev. Samuel Robinson, for example, is on the Ramsey Action Programs Board. He spends time working in the criminal justice system, and recently managed the Intercollegiate Basketball Tournament at the Civic Center. Rev. Ronald Smith heads the S-U Neighborhood Planning Council. Rev. Ronald Terry, was recently dinner music guest pianist at the Minneapolis Urban League's 50th Anniversary Dinner Meeting. Rev. Thomas Sligh conducts human relations encounters. And Rev. William Young is Board presidents of the St. Paul Human Relations Council and the St. Paul Urban League. Rev. Linton Scott has a Sunday radio program and is a flight instructor during the week.

Dedicated, diversified, and determined are the ministers and key members of their congregation in Minnesota's Black Community.

Dr. C. Wesley Ellison, presiding elder, five-state area, and Mpls-St. Paul-Milwaukee Dist., Chicago Conf., African Methodist Episcopal Church. College board member and conference accountant, he has resided in Minneapolis for 16 years.

Rev. Maxie Turner is pastor of the Pilgrim Rest Baptist Church, 5100 James Ave. North in Minneapolis. From Chicago, Rev. Turner has pastored the 53-year-old church for six years.

Pastor of the Holsey Memorial C.M.E. Church, Rev. M.C. Conwell, Mpls., received early training in Ark. and Tenn. and seminary training at Heygood C.M.E. Institute in Pine Bluff. Assisted by the Parent and Child Cntr., his church was remodeled in '72. A brd. mbr, Hospitality House Clubs, his church members are in most community organizations.

Rev. Stanley N. Frazier, pastor, Emmanuel Tabernacle, Church of God In Christ, Minneapolis, was born in Fergus Falls. Early in life he was a boxer and Golden Gloves Champ. He attended Northwestern Bible College, was ordained and assn't. pastor at Emmanuel to the late Bishop W. B. Williams. He has purposed to "Trust in the Lord. . .and lean not unto thine own understanding." He lives in Mpls. with wife, Jeanette, and four children.

Rev. James C. Hodge Sr., founder and pastor of the Evangelist of The First Communion Christian Church. Graduated, U. of Minn., also attended Northwestern and Bethel Theological Seminary. Rev. Hodge and wife Mary Ann have six children.

Rev. Clyston Holman, Jr. of Richfield, Minnesota is a member of the Greater Mpls. Council of Churches. Also serves as a Youth Counselor and Street Minister.

St. James A.M.E., St. Paul.

St. Albans Church of God and Christ, St. Paul.

Camphor Memorial United Methodist, St. Paul.

Christ Temple, St. Paul.

Pilgrim Baptist Church, St. Paul

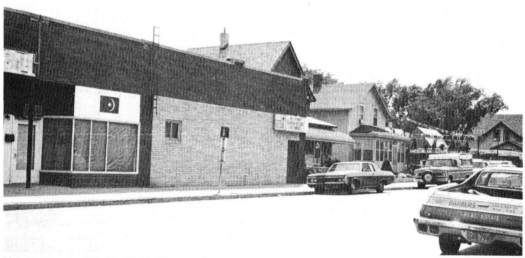

38th St. Church of God in Christ, Minneapolis.

St. James, African Methodist Episcopal Church, Minneapolis.

New Hope Baptist Church, St. Paul.

Shiloh Baptist Church, St. Paul.

Grace Temple, Minneapolis.

SOCIAL AGENCIES

SOCIAL AGENCIES

Minority-oriented social agencies in Minnesota today are basically outgrowths of "betterment" organizations originally formed to assist the influx of Negroes after the Civil War to the urban areas in the state. Other groups around at this time which added influence were the political clubs and the groups formed to share common interests.

Many ex-slaves who came were without money and without the know-how to be independent enough to begin to make it on their own. Thanks to the generosity and spirit of some of the already settled and established Minnesotans—black and white—the migrants were assisted in finding work, though often menial; a place to live; and a means for setting up some kind of community life by organizing religious worship groups, finding buildings to house the congregation and for getting schools started.

Thanks to the Christian missionary ethic, there were individuals who pressed for a better economic climate and for upgrading the plight of the new settlers, though their deeds were frowned upon by

William White, pres. and exec. dir., St. Paul Urban Coalition. He is a Juris Doctor, William Mitchell Law School, 1965; and a B.S. Degree, U. of Minn. An English and history teacher, St. Paul Schools ('59-'65), he was project director, Citizen's Community Center. Board, Amer. Baptist Churches; YMCA; United Way; KTCA-TV; Community Devlpmnt. Corp.

Human rights advocate, Gleason Glover, exec. dir., Minneapolis Urban League, city's oldest civil rights organization. Masters Degree, social admin., Case Western Reserve; B.A.; sociology, Virginia State. Active locally and nationally, he is second term pres., National Urban League Exec. Directors Council; Board, First Plymouth Bank; Minn. Group Health; Admissions Committee, Sch. of Social Work, U. of M.; Citizen's Committee; Voc. Educ., Mpls. Board of Educ.; Who's Who in Amer.; and Dictionary, International Bio. He and wife Josephine have three children.

Thomas Ellis, field repres., St. Paul Urban League. A native of St. Paul, he is a graduate of St. Paul Central High and Antioch College. Ellis is a member of the United Negro College Fund.

anti-Negro factions. But some noteworthy processes were in progress. The political parties in government were vying for control and the issues of the day were a free, versus a slave state; and Negro suffrage—the right to vote.

In 1860, the Negro population, according to the census, was only 259; by 1880 it was 1564. As the population increased and an active interest in the Negro's welfare increased, so did organizations appear for people to come together to better assist others in need. Probably the earliest group dedicated to helping those in need with food and shelter were the "mission society" groups of the religious congregations in the black communities. Yet jobs were still needed.

The Sons of Freedom, organized in 1868 after a six year anniversary Emancipation Proclamation meeting, seems to be one of the earliest forerunners of our present-day social agencies. Its membership was comprised of all Negroes in the state and no dues were necessary. A bit ahead of its time, the goals of the organization were to help fellow Negroes in any way (protect their homes and land, and personal possessions), and keep an accurate population count of those in and out of school.

Earl D. Craig, Jr., pres., Minneapolis Urban Coalition and past pres., Earl Craig Associates. He has taught at Southwestern Minn. State, Carleton and Mankato State. From St. Louis, he attended Kenyon College and Washington Univ. and has a graduate degree from the U. of Minn. A much listened to voice in the Democratic Party, he is former Chrmn., Demo. Black Caucus; member, Demo. Nat'l Committee; Minn. Press Council; Citywide Advisory Committee, and Chrmn., Minn. Human Rights Commission.

Marion McElroy, youth dir., Minneapolis Nat'l. Alliance of Businessmen. Loaned from Northwestern Bell and extended in 1976, she is nat'l dir., Youth Employment, Washington, D.C., developing summer and part-time jobs for disadvantaged youth. In Mpls., she initiated many unique and successful youth programs.

Spike Moss is executive director of The Way. He is very active in helping to bring about positive change and human rights for the Minneapolis black community.

As migration reached a peak around 1900 and the black population having tripled in 20 years to over 4,000, so did the living problems in the urban areas. Although the Negro had the right to vote in the state, and Minnesota was considered to be quite "progressive" even for a northern state, denying a person his civil rights had not yet been emphasized in legislation. It took the leadership of some of the professionals like Dr. Val Turner and newspaper editors J. Q. Adams and F. D. Parker to speak up for Negro rights and make sure their grievances were heard. Groups such as the Citizens Civil Rights Committee were formed to assist the work of the major organization, the Protective and Industrial League.

Segregation was becoming more of an issue locally and nationally—segregation in jobs, segregation in housing, segregation in education, segregation in equal justice under the law. The need for social reform was prevalent. Undoubtedly, the increase of more educated and professional groups of blacks across the country who began to take active interest in human affairs and economic uplift pointed the way toward a need for change.

"The Negro revolution cannot succeed without

Ernestine Belton, child development specialist, Mpls. Model City Day Care. 1968 recipient, Mpls. Urban League Family of the Year Award. Vice pres., Mpls. Urban Coalition; member, Mpls. Council; YMCA; Pillsbury-Waite; Nat'l Council, Negro Women; League, Women Voters; Sabathani Center; Planned Parenthood and Northwest Bank boards; and others.

Perry T. Shannon is a Probation Officer (Special Program Counselor) with Hennepin County Court Services. His responsibilities includes supervising clients on probation and preparing pre-hearing or pre-sentence investigation reports for the court. Mr. Shannon received his B.A. Degree in social work at Metropolitan State University.

Ruby Hughes is the director at the Messiah Willard Day Care Center opened in 1969 to serve families needing child care services in North Minneapolis. Seventy-two children — infants through grade three are cared for at 1530 Russell Ave. N.

378

dramatic, aggressive intervention by social workers at all levels. But if social work remains unidentified or just on the fringe, then it will have lost its reason for being and missed its greatest opportunity to establish, for all the world to see, its basic belief in the dignity of all mankind and man's ultimate right to realize freely his greatest potential."[17]

These words by Whitney Young were stated in 1964, but they were applicable 64 years earlier. In his book, *To Be Equal*, Young made some other remarks applicable to those times and struggles for civil rights.

"Employment opportunities play a major role in determining whether civil rights are meaningful. There is little value in a Negro's obtaining the right to be admitted to hotels and restaurants if he has no cash in his pocket and no job."

We must have jobs available to us that are commensurate with our education, ability, and interests. We must have the right to study, to worship, to travel, to live, and to work alongside our white countrymen. Then, and only then, can we walk with dignity as citizens of the modern world.

We must have all these things not just because it is right and just, but because every time they are denied us the whole American ideal is betrayed. One cannot

---

Theatrice Williams (T.), first state ombudsman in the U.S., has received wide acclaim in Corrections. M.S. in social work, U. of Penn.; born in Mississippi, grew up in Maine and Chicago; has a B.A., U. of Illinois with penology internship, Ill. State Prison. Exec. Dir., Phyllis Wheatley Comm. Ctr., he estab. Mpls. Urban Coalition to bring haves and have-nots together. He is pres., Minn. Nat. Assoc. Social Workers, and on other local and nat. boards.

Van E. Byers, Dir., Afro-American Cultural Arts Center, 24 E. 31st. Photo: Visit to West Africa to purchase artifacts for centers museum.

Museums Curator, Seitu, center of picture also made trip.

Born in Greenwood, Mississippi, on August 29, 1944, the present day chairwomanship of the National Association of Women Helping Offenders is Ida Mae Elam. Ms. Elam is the Secretary of the executive committee of the National Association of Blacks in Criminal Justice; and has membership in the American Correctional Association, National Association for the Advancement of Colored People, National Organization for Women, and National Council of Negro Women.

expect the world to accept America as a free land where all enjoy equal rights and equal opportunity when we deny both to every tenth American.

We all know this is easier said than done. To simplify matters, the core of the civil rights problem is the matter of achieving equal opportunity for Negroes in the labor market. For it stands to reason that all our other rights depend on that one for fullfillment. We cannot afford better education for our children, better housing, or medical care unless we have jobs.[18]

In the East, 1910 saw the formation of two black organizations formed to make change possible. Since the inception of the National Association for the Advancement of Colored People (NAACP) and the Urban League 66 years ago, they have done more for black people in six decades than any other groups. The NAACP was formed and dedicated to making the totality of civil rights for blacks a reality "no matter how long it took," while the Urban League became a crusader for better job opportunities, then branched into housing, health, education, social welfare service with equal rights and social justice included.

Minnesota's black leaders in the early 1900's were attuned to this national movement and were prepared to ask for national support. The leaders already had

Richard Jefferson is the board chairman for Minneapolis Housing and Redevelopment Authority (MHRA), and the first black to hold that position on the Board of Commissioners.

Earl Pettiford, is MHRA manager for the Williard-Homewood Project. A Minneapolis native, he is a nine year MHRA employee.

Prentice T. Gary, Sr., was the first black counselor hired by MHRA in 1964. Now special assn't. to the executive director, he was a relocation counselor supervisor and for three years, the Northside Mpls. area relocation director.

the advantage of working with their own similar groups here and also had the advantage of getting assistance among their ranks from many professionals who had moved to Minnesota from elsewhere and involved themselves in social issues.

Out of a concerns meeting of black leaders in 1912 grew the Twin City Protective League which became the St. Paul Branch of the NAACP. Two years later, a branch was established in Minneapolis. These two national branches were formed through the efforts of Dr. Turner, Frederick McGhee, W.T. Francis, J. Q. Adams, and Colonel J. H. Davidson.

And in 1923, in the Pilgrim Baptist Church, an idea became a reality. The idea had spread from S. E. Hall's downtown barbershop as a result of concerns by by Hall, Dr. J. W. Crump, and Father F. J. Gilligan for jobs and housing for the Negroes that were arriving daily. These founders and 41 other members gathered together and pledged $575.00 to form an Urban League affiliate in St. Paul. Once established, they went to the Community Chest who agreed to lend financial support. Elmer Carter was brought in from Louisville, Kentucky to become the first executive secretary. Among the officers and Board members

Carnell Hall, personnel director for MHRA, was hired as an employee for the agency in 1975. A University of Minnesota graduate, he formerly worked as a personnel officer for the Ford Motor Co.

Mabel Spaulding is MHRA assn't. project manager for North Washington Industrial Park-Industry Square. She is a native of Washington, D.C.

Ted Davenport, MHRA Equal Employment Opportunity officer, has been with the agency for eight years.

were Roy Wilkins, presently the national executive secretary of the NAACP, and W. T. Francis, who later became Ambassador to Liberia.[19]

Two years later, an Urban League branch was established in Minneapolis through Raymond W. Cannon, with Dr. Abram L. Harris as its first executive secretary. The St. Paul and Minneapolis League affilitates just celebrated their 52nd and 50th anniversaries respectively. The majority of the blacks in Minnesota today owe their livelihood, directly or indirectly to these two viable Urban League affiliates, for without them the progress blacks have made in

job opportunities, housing, social welfare, civil justice, and education would not have been possible through their dedicated efforts to promoting the quality of life for blacks in Minnesota.

Once much of the groundwork was laid toward equality of opportunity, other agencies began to organize with the NAACP and the Urban League affiliates lending their wholehearted support. Hallie Q. Brown Community Center was the outgrowth of a St. Paul Urban League project in 1929. Phyllis Wheatley Settlement House had already begun in 1924. Today the numbers of agencies in business to

Johnny Walker, purchasing agent for MHRA, is one of the earliest black employees hired. He handles all purchasing and bidding for the Authority.

Walter Jones is executive director for the St. Paul Drug Rehabilitation Program.

Kay Farris Williams. Attended A & I State University, Nashville, Tennessee in the field of Organization and Administration. He was in the U.S. Army from 1944 to 1947. Has Army credits from Cook & Bakery School and U.S. Medical Corps as medical technician and dental technician. His professional training includes community organization training, Protestant Ministry to Poverty — 1959-1961; Industrial Areas Foundation (Saul Alinski), St. Paul School of Theology, Kansas City, Kansas, 1962. He also worked in Industrial Areas Foundation and The Woodlawn Organization — 1962-1964. He has belonged to several organizations including: Elks Lodge; F. and A.M. Masonic Order; NAACP; Urban League; Southside Community Enterprises, Inc.; Board of Directors, Findley Place Housing Corporation; Board of Directors and Reachout Today, Inc., Board of Directors.

382

help blacks, minorities and disadvantaged people are endless. Certainly, no other groups of people as those who work for and are committed to social reform, have contributed so much through their individual groups.

The people depicted here are only a very small amount of the dedicated black workers who have aided countless numbers of people in community services, day care, health clinics, senior citizen's needs, job placement, educational services, family services, housing problems, vocational training, and many more activities. Their total achievements will be

Alberta N. Murray, campaign division director, United Way of Minneapolis Area, is responsible for the organization and operations of three campaign divisions.

Floyd R. Davis, is assoc. agency relations director, United Way of the Minneapolis Area. He assists member agencies in improving their fiscal management.

Michael Jordan, exec. dir., North Community YMCA. A Minneapolis native, he graduated in political science and physics, U. of Minn. He is a former Honeywell senior training supervisor.

Milton Harrison, vice pres., management services, Minneapolis YMCA. A NYC native, he is a Wayne State grad, excelling in track and pres., student body. He serves as vice chrmn., Hennepin County Social Services Board, and U. of Minn. Architect Selection Committee.

difficult to record but their efforts are obvious in Minnesota's Black Community.

The late Whitney Young, Jr. once lived in the Twin Cities and did much work in the social services field through his compilation of the *Negro Workers Progress in Minnesota*, a 1949 update of the original Governor's Report on Interracial Relations, his work at the University of Minnesota, and his work at the St. Paul Urban League. It is appropriate that we close this section on blacks in the social services with a quote from him. In part of his checklist for citizens and communities who are involved to bring about change, he states, "... Finally and most important, work for the adoption of a domestic *special effort* program in all areas of our society ... so that along with equal opportunity will go the opportunity to be equal."[20]

Anthony Scott, Div., Vocational Rehabilitation field office, St. Paul, is a counselor there. Born in Chicago, and son of the publisher, Walter Scott. He has a B.A. Degree, Mankato State.

Mark McCrea, DVR counselor, Pilot City Health Center. He holds the M.S. and B.S. Degrees from Mankato State.

Carl Davis, came from Reading, Pa. to Minn. in 1970. Entered the DVR Entry Level Prog.; now has the A.A. Degree, Metro State. He is a part-time student, Metro State.

Obie F. Kipper, Jr., Mpls. born and outstanding Washburn High athlete. He holds the M.S. and B.S. Degrees, Mankato State. On five championship teams there, he won the '69 fencing title. A career rehab. counselor, Div. Vocational Rehab.; pres., Counselor Advisory Action Committee; member, other prof. orgs.; active in the community.

Ronnie Lloyd, Entry-Level Paraprofessional Training Program, DVR, he is taking courses at the U. of Minn. and Metro State. From Oklahoma City, he came to Minn. at the age of ten. He is married with three children.

Maurice Jones has a Master's Degree, rehabilitation, Mankato State. From Lake Charles, Louisiana, he is now a case-load counselor, DVR, St. Paul office.

Edgar Smith, Chicago born, came to Minn. in 1951. Now taking DVR In-Service training, in St. Paul, he also takes courses at Metro State.

Maurice Keaton, born in Macon, Ga., 1915, came to Minn. in 1933. A dining car waiter, Pullman porter and construction laborer, he is now on the administrative staff, St. Paul Div. Vocational Rehab.; member, community faculty, Metro State; Board of Educ. Affirm. Action Committee; Police Advisory Committee, So. Mpls.; Board, H.I.R.E.

DVR Counselor, Mel Coleman, M.S. and B.S. Degrees from the U. of Wisconsin. At the Nicollet So. office, he worked in disability determination section, prior to his transfer.

385

Eleanor Jenkins is assistant director, Metropolitan Institute on Black Chemical Abuse. She started in the field as a volunteer at Southside Community Clinic's Chemical Dependency Program. She is the daughter of Mr. and Mrs. H.D. Witherspoon, and was born and raised in Minneapolis. Ms. Jenkins is now an extension student at the University of Minnesota.

Peter Bell is director, Metropolitan Institute on Black Chemical Abusers. He got involved in working with drug addicts and alcoholics as a result of his own recovery from chemical dependency. He is a graduate of Pharm House Treatment Center. Bell is the son of Mr. and Mrs. Earlin Bell and was born and raised in St. Paul. He attended St. Cloud State College and Mankato State College and is now a student at Metro State University.

Peter Bell and Eleanor Jenkins have been working together for a number of years. In their capacity as director and assistant director, MIBCA, they are responsible for conducting the training program in social service agencies that deal in large part with the Black community. In addition to that, Ms. Jenkins and Mr. Bell also have responsibility for a Multi-Cultural Training Program. That program is primarily conducted at the Johnson Institute, St. Mary's Junior College, and Metropolitan Community College. Much of their time and energy is spent in making the community aware of all of the services that Metropolitan Institute On Black Chemical Abuse offers and in seeking funds to continue this program.

Charles W. McCoy has been named assistant district director for minority small business by the Small Business Administration, it has been announced by Paul W. Jansen, director of the Minneapolis district office. McCoy joined the SBA in 1965 and held several positions involving SBA programs to help minority small businessmen. In his new role he will provide management and financial counseling to minority persons who are interested in starting new businesses, and will help existing businesses looking for ways to improve their operations. He will also set up business management educational programs.

McCoy was the first black to open an employment agency in the Twin Cities, 27 years ago. While with SBA he has received several citations, the last of which was in 1975 at which time he received a Civil Servant of the Year Award for his work at the Small Business Administration.

Magdalene H. Sing. Miscellaneous Documents Examiner, Loan Closing Small Business Administration.

Jerry Beal of St. Paul is in charge of all duplicating and stock control in the Minneapolis Regional Office of the Small Business Administration.

Leola Jackson, lifelong resident of Minneapolis, conducts the initial interview and evaluation at Concentrated Employment Program of clients to determine their eligibility. Leola also assists in the coordination of publicity for the C.E.P. program.

Robert L. Cox, Jr., an employee of the State of Minnesota. He is a Community Laision Representative. Robert works on a sub-contract basis for the Mpls. C.E.P. Program as Job Development Placement Specialist. Bob is responsible for development of employment and placement into jobs for program enrollees. Duties include intake selection orientation instruction enrollee assessment, job referral, placement, and post employment followup. Robert is a native of St. Paul. He pastored from 1956-1966 in the A.M.E. Church. Bob was successful as a Human Relations Consultant with Urban Crises Inc., Dayton, Ohio from 1968-74.

Ronald Bellfield, is one of the persons responsible for recruitment of potential clients to the CEP Program. He also conducts the initial interview and helps participate in the assesment of each client.

LaVerne Moore, an intake/outreach person, seeks out potential participants for the CEP program by recruitment, interviews, and assessment keeping. As laision person for the community, business and welfare is informed of CEP existence and function in the society. She also serves as supportive service staff person who gives support to help other staff persons, and helps to alleviate and resolve barriers that may interfere with upgrading skills or employment.

387

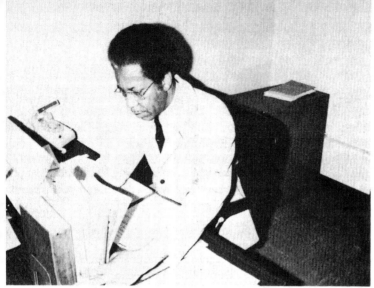

Samuel Mosley. Employed by the State of Minnesota Department of Employment Services for seven years. The agency through which I work, which is the concentrated employment program, provides me with an opportunity as a vocational counselor, to help minority members of our community, along with other economically disadvantaged persons find meaningful employment through assessing their concurrent skills level and thus guiding them to realistic job opportunities. This gives me a feeling of belonging to a community that has a viable concern about its citizenry. B.S. Degree plus graduate at U of M and graduate work at St. Cloud U.

Cozelle Breedlove is executive director of the Phyllis Wheatley Community Center on the Minneapolis northside. The Center has served the black community since the early 1900's.

Mrs. Judy D. Walker. Native of St. Paul, Minnesota. Attended University of California, Los Angeles and the University of Minnesota. Employed by the Minnesota Department of Employment Services for 21+ years. Worked in Unemployment Claims in Minneapolis for many years. Started with CEP when it was reorganized in 1971. First position at CEP was that of Orientation Supervisor. Now works as Training Coordinator.

Philosophy is: "Give me a fish and I eat for a day"
                 "Teach me to fish and I'll eat for a lifetime".

Hobbies are playing the piano and guitar for pleasure and writing lyrics and music. Husband is Harvey J. Walker, native of Hattiesburg, Mississippi and owner of Walker's Grocery, St. Paul, Minnesota.

388

PHYLLIS WHEATLEY

Community Center

A UNITED WAY AGENCY

50 YEARS OF SERVICE TO THE NORTH SIDE

October, 1974

Dear Friends:

Phyllis Wheatley was a slave with no formal education, whose natural wisdom, put into poetry, has influenced millions of lives throughout this country. In Minneapolis fifty years ago an institution was organized in her name to serve as a resting place for traveling blacks, a home away from home for black University of Minnesota students and athletes, a meeting place for black organizations, a school for learning black history, culture and pride, a house of worship for blacks, an athletic club and a place to organize and communicate with local black communities.

Fifty years ago life in Minneapolis for black people was a life of separation and a life of survival. Little did Minneapolis know that Phyllis Wheatley products would have a great influence on a better quality of life for citizens throughout the country. National figures such as Whitney Young, Carl Stokes and Roy Wilkins gave the Phyllis Wheatley concept to the country and local leaders such as Cecil Newman, Mary Kyle, Cozy Breedlove, Earl Miller, Larry Brown, Richard Green, Jim Jackson, Earl Bowman and many others have carried the Phyllis Wheatley concept throughout the state. The Wheatley gathered people of great love and compassion together. People such as Mary T. Welcome, Charles Fisk, Katherine Parson, Mamie D. Himmelman, Irving Nemero, Wendell Jones and all of those who served throughout those fifty years as Board members and staff. But most of all Phyllis Wheatley was a family, whose children were loved, respected and disciplined by Miss Gertrude Brown, who they considered their second mother. Miss Brown was the first head resident of the Wheatley, followed by Miss Magnolia Latimer (the late Mrs. James Coleman), Henry Thomas, T. Williams and Cozy Breedlove. Supportive staff who helped motivate and direct the family were Leo Bohanan, John Thomas, Mrs. Alice (Sims) Onqué, Mrs. Blanche Mason, Mrs. Marguerete Combs and of course Mae and Ray Hatcher.

As for me, thank God for the Phyllis Wheatley, for her many blessings, loving parents and family, true friends and the opportunity of living and growing near and with all of you. This is a great occasion, dear ones, for we are celebrating fifty years of love. Thank you for sharing this wonderful event together.

Sincerely,

W. Harry Davis
Chairman of the Board

WHD:rbs

Willie Mae Wilson
Executive Director

William Newsom
OJT Director

ST. PAUL URBAN LEAGUE staff members

(Total Staff: 48 members)

Katie McWatt
Director, Community Services

Talmer Curry
Director, Economic Development

Patricia Arrington
Health Specialist

Grant West (r.) and Cydney Williams
Housing Director and Housing Counselor

Jan Morris
OJT Office Manager

Ronald Scott
LEAP Director

Mary Price
Early Childhood Education
Director

Antoine Garibaldi
Street Academy Director

390

ST. PAUL URBAN LEAGUE
Fifty-Three Years Old ". . . A bright future."

Back in the early 1920's, some friends would gather in S.E. Hall's barber shop downtown and talk about some of the problems of the day. One main concern was what could be done for the increasing number of black people migrating to St. Paul from the South. More and more, the new residents were coming into the shop to find employment and housing, so, in 1923, Mr. Hall, Father F. J. Gilligan, the late Dr. J. W. Crump, and some other black leaders went to the Community Chest to secure funds for setting up an office to help them.

They approached the National Urban League in New York with the idea of establishing an affiliate in Minnesota. The leaders raised $545.00, established the St. Paul Urban League on July 5, 1923, and became a Community Chest recipient five months later.

Progressing since its inception, the St. Paul Urban League concentrated its efforts on improving the living conditions and opportunities specifically for black and other minorities, but also for the disadvantaged and anyone in the St. Paul community with a need for its services. Branching out more into the community, the St. Paul Urban League, in 1929, organized and directed the Hallie Q. Brown Community Center for educational, cultural, and recreational activities.

The League continued to maintain its employment corps as one of its priorities.

Through the forties and fifties the social agency continued to progress and strive for better housing, higher paying jobs, community organization, and special educational programs for training in the technical fields.

As the 1960's brought on racial unrest, the St. Paul Urban League was present to speak for the people being unjustly treated and to act as a catalyst for opposing factions. Out of this arose the League's assistance in establishing and organizing the Black Legal Defense Fund.

Today, the St. Paul Urban League continues to be funded by the United Way and by memberships, and contributions. Priorities extend into education, community services, health, welfare, employment, housing, economic development, community organizations, and financial counseling.

While servicing over 300 clients, the community department monitored fair treatment of inmates in the state penal institutions, referred needy clients for emergency assistance, assisted the University of Minnesota black medical students and other interested parties in resolving financial aid problems; conducted a community education seminar to raise some questions to the St. Paul Board of Education; conducted a national Basic Education Grants workshop; conducted a health workshop on high blood pressure; and continues to be of ready assistance for any other social needs that arise.

The economic development department works with the state and local government to ensure legislative action for

Thomas Ellis and Ronald Whitaker
OJT Field Representatives

Josephine Luna
Financial Counselor

Gloria Massey
LEAP Women's Component
Director

Marva Duke
LEAP Office Manager

Bonnie Raleigh
Program Assistant

minority economic development, and works with employers in developing equal opportunity and affirmative action programs, such as the new 1976 program with the Metropolitan Transit Corporation and United Hospitals.

Last year, in spite of the deepening recession, the employment section was able to counsel and be of assistance to over 305 persons seeking assistance.

The Labor Education Advancement Project (LEAP), which aids in placing persons in construction and trades categories, has for the last three years been number one in the country among 45 other LEAP programs in major U.S. cities. In 1976, its trainee apprentice applicant, Johnny Cotton, won the National Urban League LEAP Award. Of 875 clients interviewed in 1974, over 250 apprentices and trainees and over 50 journeymen were placed in the construction industry. It now has a women's component to find employment for women in nontraditional roles.

The On-The-Job Training program, is now funded under the Comprehensive Employment and Training Act (CETA) and continues to provide jobs for the disadvantaged while also providing its services for the City of St. Paul's program for the unemployed and underemployed. In 1975, OJT exceeded its quota of 300.

The Housing Department which oversees an emergency house for people without shelter, counseled and assisted over 1200 persons, and provides local input to other community groups involved in housing development.

The Early Childhood Program for the Developmentally Disabled, ages 3 to 6 years with learning difficulties, enhances the children's experiences through academic input according to their needs to prepare them for first grade.

The College of Education Street Academy provides an alternative school setting for senior high school students who are dropouts or disenchanted with the public school setup. The 40 students at the school are able to graduate with a high school diploma or G.E.D. and hopefully go on to further study.

Encompassing much input in the local community, the St. Paul Urban League, under the guidance of the 29-member Board of Directors with Rev. William Young as president. As of June, 1976, new Board president is LeRoy L. Martin. The 46-member staff is supervised by the Executive Director, Mrs. Willie Mae Wilson. To sum up 53 years of dedicated service to the St. Paul community in the words of its founder and honorary Board member, S.E. Hall, who died in 1975 at the age of 97, "The St. Paul Urban League was what new people to the city needed in 1923. People came then for help and are still coming. The St. Paul Urban League has a bright future."**

Marie Durham
Secretary

Betty Kyle
OJT Secretary

Johnnie Barnett
Receptionist and Clerk

Jessie Overton
Trainee Advisor

Grace Jaggers
Trainee Advisor

Jayne Gray
Employment Specialist

391

LABOR

LABOR

To quote directly from Governor Luther Young-dahl's 1949 Report of The Interracial Commission,

"Prior to 1932, relatively few white workers were members of labor unions. They were, nevertheless, prejudiced and often refused to work with Negroes. Gradually, as the white workers were organized, they carried into the unions their former prejudices.

". . . Few employers will go contrary to what they believe to be the union's position in this respect.

Craft unions organized about the various trades have also increased. Since they control the flow of skilled workers into many fields they are important to the Negro worker.

As an economic organization, the trade union seeks the improvement of the standard of living of its members through collective bargaining. In varying ways it attempts degrees of control over such practices as hiring, training, promotion, lay-offs, wages, etc. It follows then that the union has tremendous influence, within its bargaining rights, on the availability of job opportunities for minorities.

Anna M. Lewis, here with a labor repres., is chairperson, Human Rights Comm., Mpls. Central Labor Union Council, AFL-CIO. In Community services, AFL-CIO and Mpls. United Way, she was with the Hotel and Restaurant Workers Union for 36 yrs.

Leola C. McGraw, office secretary, Local Union No. 974, takes notes from Howard Fortier, secretary treasurer. The Union is garage machine warehousemen, repairmen, insidemen, helpers, and plastice employees.

Consequently, its policies, practices, and attitudes toward such minorities are crucial in determining the positions of minorities in plants and trades and will influence their ability to make a living commensurate with their qualifications. Anything less than full membership in unions in Minnesota with its attendant privileges and responsibilities tends to prevent Negroes from obtaining employment."[21]

Although much has been done to improve job opportunities for blacks in the trades industry, there is still work to be done. Getting more youth into vocational schools and trainees into such programs as the Minneapolis and the St. Paul Urban League Labor Education Advancement Program (LEAP), whereby blacks are assisted in getting apprenticeships and work to complete their journeyman status, are two means of economic improvement.

Much of the progress today was paved by such notables as Frank Alsup and the late Frank Boyd, who fought hard in the 1940's and 1950's for higher wages for black workers and for unity to achieve their goals. Alsup recently spoke at a ceremony honoring Boyd for his work with the Labor Council and for dedicating Boyd Park in the St. Paul Inner City.

Robert M. Patterson, gen. chairman, Local 516, Dining Car Employees Union, St. Paul. The union has reputation for providing economic benefits and better working conditions for its members; community service; and human rights causes for all.

Al Maddox, member, local Union 974, lives in Minneapolis. He is a machine operator and steward at the Juno Tool Plastic Co.

395

INDUSTRY

INDUSTRY

As depicted here, blacks can be found in every level of the work force in Minnesota. Yet, the unemployment factor, which encompasses a critical percentage of the black population (13 percent) has always been an economic problem for blacks. The move from "slave status" to "free status" for many Afro-American Negroes in early Minnesota was not an easy adjustment — especially for the migrants who came to Minnesota immediately after the Civil War.

In seeking a way to support themselves, they were resented by the European laborers already settled here because the Negro migrants were a new and competitive work force. Recorded in the newspapers of the time are incidents where the white immigrant workers stormed the boats and barges to dissuade the new arrivals or "contrabands" on board from disembarking. Another adjustment for them to make was some transition into the established and different white and even black communities.[22]

Seeds of discrimination were planted, the roots deepened and for many years to come, it would be

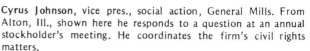

Cyrus Johnson, vice pres., social action, General Mills. From Alton, Ill., shown here he responds to a question at an annual stockholder's meeting. He coordinates the firm's civil rights matters.

John M. Warder is the busy President of the First Plymouth National Bank, Plymouth and Newton Avenue North. Founded in February, 1969, the bank has had a major role in the redevelopment of the North Side as a residential and commercial community. First Plymouth has some $15 million in assets; is affiliated with First Bank System, Inc.

Randolph W. Staten (right) Director, Corporate Department of Equal Opportunity, Cargill, is shown here with Robert Deercks (left), Vice Chairman, Cargill Board of Directors and Whitney McMillian, President, Cargill, Inc. Staten is a graduate (B.A. Degree), University of Minn.; graduate studies, New York University; N.Y. Dramatic Academy; and St. Thomas College of Management. He is a member of many national and local organizations. Some include the Minn. Affirmative Action Assoc.; National Mental Health Council; New Way, Inc.; National Alliance of Businessmen (co-founder, and Brd. of Directors); United Community Agency for Progress (pres. and co-founder); Minn. Assoc.; United Nation Affairs; Afro-American Pride (pres.); Chairman, Fireman's Employment Committee; State DFL Delegate '68-'72; and Legislative Candidate, 1972. Staten is the recipient, N.Y. Giants Unsung Hero Award by the N.Y. Times; 1975 Miss Black Minnesota Appreciation Award; City of Mpls. Distinguished Service Award; and is in the North Carolina Hall of Fame. Published one of many articles including *Whatever Happened to Blacks in America?*

difficult to stop its growth and branching and reaching out to stifle equal opportunity for the newcomers. But such was not always the case, nor was it a mandate in the new state. Individuals owned land and small shops, but many of the Negroes in the last half of the 1800's found jobs at which they were experienced; maids, porters, and domestics. Others were deckhands on the steamboats that plowed the rivers, while others could only find menial work in hotels, restaurants, and industrial plants.

But the state was open for migration of blacks and the Union Army supplied work as teamsters, jobs to replace Army personnel who could be used in other capacities, and in civilian positions.

Positive racial attitudes did prevail. The plight of the Negro in post-Civil War Minnesota could have been one of having to face complete race denial or total prohibition of rights. Such was the case in the adjacent states to the East and South. One person of interest who came to Minnesota during this period and was later looked upon as a leader who promoted some racial harmony and also concern for employment of blacks was Robert Hickman.

Accounts of how Hickman came to Minnesota are

Ray Eiland, recently named, vice pres., affirmative action, joined Pillsbury in '73 as affirm. action dir. after serving as local chief, U.S. office, contracts compliance. Known in the Twin Cities for his human rights efforts, he is a Drake U. graduate and is married with five children.

Robert Lee Morgan, architect, exec. vice pres., Adkins-Jackels Assoc. Arch. Degree, Kansas State. Involved in St. Philip's Gardens and Lonnie Adkins Crts., St. Paul; Hamilton School, Mpls.; and Good Shepard Lutheran Church, Orono.

Richard Barrett, Honeywell engineer, is supervisor of evaluation and test lab for aircraft flight systems such as the DC-10 pictured here. From Nassau, he lives in Maplewood with his family.

mixed but not necessarily contradictory. One report states that many Negroes in Boone County [Missouri] planned to escape, received protection by Union forces, and were promised aid by the Underground Railway. This account asserts that around three hundred were smuggled aboard the "War Eagle" and taken north. Not knowing for sure where they were going, these Negroes referred to themselves as "pilgrims." Hickman probably was a member of the group brought to St. Paul. ₂₃

The founder of Pilgrim Baptist Church in St. Paul, Hickman was a forerunner in the struggle for equal opportunity in Minnesota. His predecessors today (see Religion) are viable leaders in Minnesota's Black Community who as part of their imparting religious doctrine commit themselves to positive change in the black community. Born a slave in Boone County, Missouri, on January 1, 1831, he died in St. Paul in 1900. As a slave he was taught to read and he had permission from his master to teach and preach to other slaves — a not uncommon method for establishing some unity among slaves.

Regardless of the exact ship or date on which Hickman arrived, the essential fact was that he and others soon established a Baptist church. Since Hickman was licensed only to preach, he assisted a white minister at the Pilgrim Church until his ordination in 1877. When

Vera Sutton's job at the Greater Minneapolis Chamber of Commerce is to answer many information requests about the city in her role as assistant to the director of research.

Warren E. Simpson, Chicago born 26 yrs. ago, is presently employed by Cargill Inc. as an attorney in their Law Dept. A graduate of Carleton and Northwestern U. School of Law. A resident of the northside for 2 yrs., Mr. Simpson is married to Patricia, a graduate student of Broadcast Journalism at the U. of M. They have one 13-month-old daughter, Maiysha.

Julia Byrd, accounting teller, Twin City Federal, is shown making changes for savings and mortgage account holders. She is also responsible for a cash drawer and training in her department.

the church was first organized in 1863, its congregation included whites as well as Negroes, and until a building could be obtained, services were held in the homes of various members. The whites gradually withdrew, a building was finally found on Cedar Street, and an all-Negro church was actually incorporated in 1870.[24]

Hickman was obviously aware of the Negro's plight, having lived it. As a Minnesota citizen and as a minister and leader, he did much to raise the economic levels of his fellow brothers.

Toward the end of the 19th Century, industry had greatly increased. Meat packing companies, flour mills, ironworks, lumbering, and stone masonry were a few of the industries to be found there.

Certain jobs were available for skilled workers, but most blacks were still pursuing the endeavors of being cooks and porters on the railroads, and janitors, matrons and handymen in manufacturing. Meaningful jobs on a higher level and wage scale were slow in coming.

This was expressed years later by the Governor's Interracial Commission in 1945. They stated that, "Job discrimination can be a lethal type of restriction for the members of any minority group in the United States. There are communities in the United

Mrs. Erma L. Mazingo, underwriter, Northern States Insur. Co. Minn. Underwriters Assoc. Board, the only woman, and first invited to join the 150-member org. WCCO "Good Neighbor" Award; past pres., St. Paul NAACP; Minn. Orchestra Women's Assoc.; Pragmateia; '72 Woman of the Year, Amer. Bus. Women's Assoc.; appointed to St. Paul Human Rights Council.

Jeffrey L. Bartlett is manager, Michigan Insurance Services, Div., in Prudential Insurance, Mpls. He supervises a 70-person administrative staff. B.A. Degree from West Virginia State, he is a Board member, Outreach Community Center and precinct chairman, Independent-Republican Party. Bartlett lives in Edina with his wife Joy and two sons.

Customer accounting repres., Greg Asia, Twin City Federal. In a management training position, he is learning work in the dept., and answers customer questions on savings and explains internal control.

401

States where inert custom or studied policy limited Negroes to domestic service and porter jobs. In those places, they can vision no dream of advancement. Often even those service jobs do not give full employment and in times of depressions the white group absorbs those.

"As a consequence, the educated youth who would be the future leaders either migrate from the community or, if they remain, they become cynical and receptive to revolutionary philosophies. The older members inevitably lose initiative and many become charges upon public agencies."[25]

As more social and political groups began to organize for the Negro community, opposition toward discrimination also became more of an issue rather than isolated incidents. For example, arrangements were made to organize a free labor bureau after an Afro-American Labor League was formed to protest the replacement of some Negro laborers on an asphalt pouring job with workers brought in from Indianapolis. The black workers were not rehired, but some gains had been made ". . . people were coming together, sometimes through legal action and sometimes through discussion, pressure, and simple perse-

Cecil Dewey Nelson, Jr., artist and art director for a local major art studio specializing in corporate design. Nelson has had a long and varied career in creative art. From Champaign, Illinois, he has received many awards, including national painting prizes and recognition as a Negro painter in the 1940's and 1950's. Nelson is a commissioner for the City of Bloomington (advertising BP&D Commission); Afro-American Cultural Center Brd. of Directors (chrmn, New Building Design and Site Committee); currently planning an art exhibit on Black American History. He lives in Bloomington; is active in civic affairs there and in the Twin Cities. Nelson was co-editor and designer, *Negro Minneapolis Profile*.

Checking a layout, Donjia Taylor supervises printed matter and promotion literature for H.B. Fuller Co. Born in Mpls. and now lives in St. Paul, she worked for Ramsey County Citizen's Committee and St. Paul Council, she is studying social sciences, U. of Minn. and has two girls.

verance" to do something about unfair practices toward blacks.

Certainly some milestones were gained when previously mentioned John W. Cheatham, a former slave, became a Minneapolis fireman, then appointed to Captain in 1899; and when "St. Paul appointed a Negro policeman in 1881 and Minneapolis the next year." Another inroad was Frederick L. McGhee's arrival in Minnesota in 1889. Born of slave parents, and attended Knoxville College, he studied law in Chicago and was admitted to the bar. He was the first black to be admitted to the bar and practice law

in Minnesota. McGhee helped lay the groundwork for a 1912 branch of the NAACP to be located in St. Paul.[26]

By the time war broke out in Europe in 1914, over 50 years had passed since the Civil War, but for the most part, blacks were still being treated as second class citizens in the United States. Some 5,000 blacks had fought in the American Revolution with courage and dignity; 200,000 black Americans served in the Union Army with an equal amount working as laborers. In three wars, including the Spanish-American War, blacks had proved their loyalty, but

---

Walter Reece Jones, Edina, Minnesota. Graduate of Lake Forest College, Lake Forest, Illinois. Member of St. Peter AME Church. Is presently a Graphic Arts Coordinator for Creative Merchandising and Publishing, Inc. in Hopkins, Minnesota. Chicago born, he and his wife Marie have one daughter, Marissa.

Wilbur S. Rogan, training assn't., Burlington Northern mechanical division. He produces color instructional videotapes. Here, he operates the camera and master console used for editing. His talents were used for the St. Paul Area United Way Campaign, '75.

Commercial artist, Ashby D. Reed, Jr., earned his B.A. and Certificates from Burnley Professional School of Art in Seattle, Wash., where he worked extensively with black newspapers. N.Y.C. born he effected an Advertising Dept. for JAFCO, Inc. in Seattle, Wash., and transferred to Minneapolis three yrs. ago as layout and keyline artist for Creative Merchandising, Inc. He now heads layout and production at National Catalog Productions. Married to Antionette Moore Reed, a Northwest Airlines Stewardess, they have one son. Is also co-editor and designer of this book, *Minnesota Black Community*.

America was still reluctant to give them full status in the military services.

As Negroes passed into the World War I period, more democratic demands were being made for equality in employment and for rights as equal citizens. During the war, one of the voices for the blacks was the Minnesota Negro newspaper, the *Western Appeal.* It stated that every American should be treated as an American. All citizens should be prepared to fight for his country, but the nation should also reciprocate.

Some branches of the military services did not accept Negroes at all. Those who did serve, including black Minnesotans, were placed in all-Negro units. Although none were in the higher eschelons as advisory or commanding officers, some black Minnesotans such as Lieutenant Paul Wigington and Captain J. R. French attained the rank of commissioned officers. Others became noncommissioned officers. These officers and enlisted men returned to Minnesota from Europe with citations for valor in defense of their country. (At home, some outstanding blacks served in the Minnesota Home Guard. One for example was Captain Clarence W. Wigington, an

Ward T. Bell, Jr., Product Manager at Medtronic for implantable leads and accessories. They design, manufacture and market devices of a cardiovascular, neurological and rehabilitative nature. The world's largest manufacturer of pacemakers and pacemaker support systems.

Walter Lee Pone is a personal banker trainee at Farmers & Mechanics Bank. He is studying for a B.A. Degree, U. of Minn. and industrial relations certificate. He is married and has two children.

Dr. Marvin Trammel, director of personnel development for the Pillsbury Company. Dr. Trammel formerly taught English and debate at Edison High School. He was assistant principal at North High, principal at Minneapolis Central High, and West Area superintendent for Minneapolis Public Schools. He is on the Board of Directors for the United Way and the Northside YMCA.

architect who designed the water tower at Highland Park in St. Paul. A plaque was recently placed there in honor of "Cap" as he was affectionately called.)

While in France during World War I, blacks were treated as equals, and they got a taste of what human relations should be like. Back home, Marcus Garvey, W. E. B. Dubois and others were calling for self-determination, freedom, and opportunity. Soldiers returned to America with much self-esteem, only to be faced with regressive discrimination they had left on America's shores. Although they returned to discrimination in employment, discrimination in housing, discrimination in use of public facilities, and discrimination against their own person, the black Americans who had fought for their country in World War I were not to accept this readily.

A time for social change was already in the works, because black leaders were preparing to do something about it and black-oriented groups were becoming more organized to take a stronger stance against human injustices. Two men who were to become national figures and were already giving some impetus in Minnesota were Roy Wilkins, National NAACP executive secretary, who grew up in St. Paul and

Jack LeFlore, vice pres., sales, School Div., Josten's; the first black salesman hired there in 1954. Serving the nation's schools for 29 years, he now leads the largest and most profitable sales force in the industry.

Audiovisual specialist, Andre Florenz, coordinates all presentations at the Federal Reserve Bank Mpls. Also responsible for operation and maintenance of all equipment, he lives in Burnsville with his wife, Gloria, and three children.

Alvin Riley, Sr., Oklahoma born, came to Minnesota in 1959. He joined Litho Technical Services, Inc. in 1961 as an offset pressman and is now one of its top salesmen. He is production coordinator for *Minnesota's Black Community*.

attended the University of Minnesota, and W. T. Francis, a lawyer, who later became Ambassador to Liberia.

Black leadership had to decide how to right the wrongs of discrimination and prejudice, for these were the deterrent factors for employment, better housing, and social equality. Minnesota as a state had made a progressive start in providing for the rights of an individual at statehood in 1858, but by World War I, much of what many of the founding fathers had done for integrating blacks moreso into society, had been undone by socially unhealthy mores and precepts in the minds of some Americans and put into practice by others who were determined to keep blacks in the "second class citizen" role. As the social revolution progressed in the early 1900's, inroads were being made by the newly formed action groups such as the NAACP, the Urban League, the earlier Sons of Freedom, and the Citizen's Civil-Rights Committee in attempting to promote more racial opportunity. More doors began to open but unemployment was critical for blacks across the country and in Minnesota as well. The majority of blacks in the South worked in agriculture. When the

Gene Washington, formerly with Dayton's Department Store Affirmative Action Program, is now personnel manager of Dayton's Distribution Center.

Judith Peterson is a Dayton's assistant department manager with women's and misses' coats.

Department manager, George Blackwell, works with Dayton's 700 Shop, men's shirts and neckwear, and men's accessories and gifts.

Robert King is a Dayton's Department Store area store manager.

406

cotton crops were rendered useless by the boll weevil, many blacks moved North to attempt to find work with the big industries where a labor shortage had been caused by the decline in European immigration when World War I began. And in the words of Dr. L. D. Reddick, Temple University history professor and author of the National Urban League's *Blacks and U.S. Wars*, "Pastures always seem greener in prospect than in retrospect. But to a black man, who was a farm laborer or an unskilled worker in a southern town, New York, Philadelphia, Pittsburgh, Chicago and especially Detroit during World War I,

did indeed seem like the 'promised land'."[30]

To summarize, the 1920's for black Minnesotans was a period of widespread unemployment. This in turn created some needs other than jobs for the increasing Negro population. Decent housing was a critical issue and so was feeding the family, thus the St. Paul Urban League was founded in 1923 and the Minneapolis Urban League in 1926 to help meet these three crises affecting the black community. As the Urban Leagues, the NAACP, and the Negro Citizen's Defense Committee fought for better living conditions, Negro migrations also began to dwindle.

Alonzo Evans is a fashion illustrator for Dayton's Department store.

Beverly Franklin interviews prospective employees at Dayton's.

James R. Lawrence, American General Diversified, Inc. Executive Vice President, Chief Operations Officer. A multi-faceted construction, development, and consulting firm, A.G.D. has received national recognition in the fields of cyrogenic insulation, solar heating, and acoustical design. Under the guidance of Lawrence and partners, Noel Totten, Jr. and Lowell Nelson, A.G.D. is now one of the larger minority owned construction companies West of Chicago. Lawrence, a 1962 graduate of Central High School, Mpls., received a B.A., economics, and B.A. and M.A. in English from the University of Minnesota. He lives in Eden Prairie, with his wife Margaret, and son Jason.

During a 20-year span from 1920 to 1940, the Negro population increased only by 1,119, probably because high anti-Negro feelings were at a peak, people felt somewhat more secure in their familiar surroundings, and because major industry was not on the increase in Minnesota.

Even though industrial complexes were not as concentrated in Minnesota's urban areas as in other major cities, and the population did not increase as rapidly, many blacks in Minnesota were forced to live on insufficient incomes. But as the labor shortage became more demanding for industry, more people found their way into the work force. Then came the "Great Depression" and the doors to decent employment were shut again for blacks, and again, due in part to discrimination. As stated by the 1945 Interracial Commission Report, "The explanation for the phenomenal unemployment during that great depression is twofold: First, that a considerable number of Negroes were already unemployed prior to the stock market crash. Second, that when they worked they were limited largely to personal service occupations which are the first to contract in the face of a threatened depression." According to an Urban

Photographer, **Kenneth Coleman**, applies technical skill and creative talent to his daily work at 3M Co. Here he makes camera adjustments prior to shooting for a trade journal.

Graphic Arts designer, **Marv McClure**, started out as a crater for Pako's Engineering Division in 1965. He applied for a drafting position and got it. Since then he excelled as a detail draftsman, then moved up to his present position. His work and dedication at Pako have benefited the company's award-winning engineering staff and himself. He exemplifies the attitudes and skills that earned Pako the distinction of being named one of Minnesota's Engineering Wonders for 1976.

Theodore F. Allen, is a certified life insurance underwriter (CLU) with North American Life in St. Paul for 37 years. In his second six-year term as a member, St. Paul Charter Commission, Allen has been pres. and vice pres. of city and state health underwriters assns.; and was the first black to be awarded a CLU Degree. His wife is the contralto, Ermine Hall Allen.

Cleve Staley, Napco chief manufacturing engineer. He is in charge of design, developing and processing tool equipment. Originally from Detroit, and once moved to Mass. for the company, he now lives in Crystal with his wife, Mary and son, Jim.

League study "... in Minneapolis in 1930 ... two-thirds of the colored workers were employed in three hotels as waiters, maids or housemen. Seventy-five per cent of all Negroes in that city were in domestic work.

When the depression came, white workers occupied some of those domestic jobs. For example, in several hotels white girls were substituted for Negro men as waiters—partly because of a change in dining customs and partly because it was assumed that the customers would prefer white girls."[31]

According to Father John LaFarge, a race relations scholar, "As usual, in some instances, no one group, whether management, foreman, workers, or other elements could be definitely labeled as the principal source of discrimination. It became apparent that in many instances it was due to a complex of apathy or misunderstandings and in some instances would yield to a program of interracial education...."[32]

Across the United States, at the beginning of World War II, many Negroes were out of work.

... while building contractors were ordered to construct defense plants at top speed and shouted for skilled labor of various kinds, 75,000 Negroes experienced as carpen-

Coleridge T. Hendon, personal banking officer, Northwestern Nat'l. Bank, Mpls. In graduate work at the U. of Minn., he has a B.S. Deg., Wilberforce. He is dir., Children's Home Society of Minn.; member, Amicus; Monitors; Boule; Alpha Phi Alpha; YMCA; and Zion Baptist Church.

Junior analyst, Evelyn Bell, U. of Iowa grad.; assists the IDS dir., marktng. Research in defining advertising, pub. relns., and direct mail, then reports to the home office and sales force.

James Mitchell, IDS college relations supervisor, based in Mpls., he recruits at colleges; fills managerial positions; and is IDS liasion with Junior Achievers. He is a St. Cloud U. graduate.

ters, bricklayers, painters, etc., had difficulty finding defense jobs. Aircraft industries announced that 250,000 workers were needed, but no Negroes, regardless of training, could get jobs. Similar discrimination was reported in defense plants all over the country.

Negroes were incensed. Resentment boiled over in the threat that thousands of them, led by A. Philip Randolph, would march in a mass picket line in Washington on July 2, 1941. Recognizing the justice of the demands, President Roosevelt called a conference of Negro and white leaders, which resulted in Executive Order #8802, banning discrimination in defense industries and appointing a committee to make the order effective.[33]

As stated by Spangler in *The Negro in Minnesota*, "During World War II, Minnesota Negroes did the jobs that were given them, felt the same pain, slept in the same mud, loaded the same ships, built the same roads, and died the same deaths as did their fellow soldiers all over the world. Those who returned were glad to be home, but they came back determined that there must be no such regression as there had been after World War I.[34]

Those who helped at home were people like the late Cecil Newman who insisted on jobs for Negroes in the defense plants. As a result, some 1,200 were

Marlene Allen Bryant is personnel staffing specialist for the VA Hospital. She is responsible for administering an active placement program covering all Civil Service grades. She was Cantinos Choir director, 1963-1972; St. Peter's A.M.E. Church. Married to Carl Bryant, Pillsbury; member, salesman, they have one child.

Yvonne Gray is a financial analyst at International Multifoods. Originally from West Va., she is a business admn. graduate, U. of Wisconsin.

Louis Moore, EEO mgr., International Multifoods, from St. Paul, he is an economist and marketing specialist; member, Mpls. Chamber of Commerce; exec. council, Minn. Historical Society; TCOIC board; and Nat'l. Minority Bus. Campaign Brd.

Ken Warden, Transportation Dept., Abbott-Northwestern Hospitals, Minneapolis, drives the hospital van to transport patients, mail, and other items for the hospital complex.

employed and graded on the basis of skill and performance—a sign of better things to come in Minnesota, in employment, for blacks.[35]

In many respects, World War II was a turning point for the American Negro. Even in Minnesota he came home from the Battle of the Bulge, the bombing of Munich, and the Sands of Iwo Jima as an American hero who fought for freedom. With the aid of those fighting on the homefront for first-class citizenship, black Minnesotans were virtually ahead of much of the nation. In one of the major urban areas in the state, for example, where over 68 percent of

the Negroes were on relief before World War II, 1947 saw less than one percent of the Negro population at that level. The determination at the end of the war that there would be no regression saw many blacks striving to achieve full equality of opportunity. They realized that although gains had been made during the war and in employment for more blacks, much still had to be done to accomplish the status of becoming "first class citizens."

The question had already arisen though: "How many Negroes will be laid off as the war industry dwindles and more white employees return to other

Control Data's **William English** (r.), gen. mgr., Corporate EEO, with (l.) **Gerry Hollingsworth**, prog. dev. specialist; **Linda Patterson**, pers. administrator; and **Herb Pearl**, senior pers. administrator, are some CDC representatives of the Black community.

Sales Repres., **John Young**, American Dixie Sales, Div., American Can Co., reviews correspondence with secretary, **Lucille Williams**. He heads home paper prod. sales in North Minneapolis and northern Minnesota.

Danny Davis is a compliance specialist for the Minneapolis Board of Education.

411

jobs?" Thanks to the drive for meaningful employment by such leaders as Newman and the Urban Leagues of the Twin Cities, some industries recognized that Negroes needed jobs too. Another project which gave great assistance was the foresight of Minnesota's Governor Edward J. Thye who believed that preventive action is always preferable to remedial measures, so he set up his Governor's Interracial Commission. The Commission acted as an advisory body and studied significant conditions and social disorders then reported to him in the document, *The Negro Worker in Minnesota.* Governor Thye stated in the Forward of the report that: "The vital point in this report is the finding of the Commission that while during wartime all Negroes in Minnesota can obtain both full employment and a fair opportunity for upgrading, yet in peacetimes a much larger proportion of Negroes than white persons cannot secure any employment; and of the Negroes employed few enjoy opportunities for being upgraded. In addition to this information, the Commission has tried to explore the mind of industrial Minnesota to determine why the Negro is denied employment."

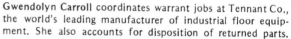

Walter Collymore, vice pres., commercial data services, Control Data and gen. mgr., transportation industry mgmnt., talks with (l.) John Jantzen, mgr., tech. support, and Duane Andrews (center) senior CDC publicist.

Marie Hammonds, data entry supervisor, keypunch, American Linen Supply Co., Mpls. She was trained in U. of Minn. and Hennepin Cty. offices before joining the American Linen national office in '72.

Gwendolyn Carroll coordinates warrant jobs at Tennant Co., the world's leading manufacturer of industrial floor equipment. She also accounts for disposition of returned parts.

The Commission found some interesting insights. For example,

Most members of the white group believe that they are entirely free from racial prejudice. Yet when they are confronted with some concrete situation, they so act that often their practical attitude towards the Negro is different from what their attitude would have been towards a white person. Those situations suggest that latent in many white persons is the virus of racial prejudice. To this tendency the people in the Twin Cities and Duluth are no exceptions. When they act as employers or employees or customers, they reflect that tendency and also the community pattern. And in most cases they are entirely unaware of the consequences of their own actions. Most white persons in those communities never suspect how difficult it is for the Negro to secure work. And they will never become conscious of it from reading general statements about unemployment among Negroes. The human mind does not function in that manner. The citizens will become concerned only when they are presented with a list of industries where Negroes do not work or are not upgraded.[37]

The Governor's report was updated in 1949. The new Governor Luther W. Youngdahl in the Forward to *The Negro Worker's Progress in Minnesota* stated:

Ronald L. Johnson, 29, works in the voucher and dental section at the Fort Snelling Veterans Administration Out-Patient Clinic, St. Paul. He also teaches marshal arts (Karate) at the Martin Luther King Center, St. Paul. Johnson lives in South Minneapolis with his wife, Janet, and two children. Janet is a Northwest Orient Airlines stewardess.

Mrs. Thelma Smith, responsible for maintaining a permanent file on all Munsingwear patterns, also keeps tape files for a computerized cutting machine. She raised three children alone these past seven years; is an active member, Twin City Golf Aux. and two year Championship Golfer.

Ernestine Dukes, programmer, Federal Reserve Bank, Mpls., solves business problems and transfers clerical information to computers. From Waterloo, Iowa, she attended the U. of Minn. School of Business.

"If we are to build this needed understanding and trust among the nations of the world, the place to begin must be right here at home. In America, in Minnesota, in every community, in every family, church and school, we must fight prejudice and discrimination in all its varied forms.

It is to this grim task that the Governor's Interracial Commission seeks to give guidance. It fulfills this mission by providing for our citizens the true facts that will overcome the ignorance which breeds bigotry and intolerance."

An indication of progress, this advisory commission is now the full-time State Human Rights Department headed by a black, Commissioner William L. Wilson (see LAW AND GOVERNMENT).

These reports in the 1940's added a totally new dimension to the aspect of discrimination in employment. They supplied some long needed answers to human situations that previously had been either ignored or totally misunderstood.

"No society can tolerate the denial of equal opportunity to a segment of its population and hope to prosper. To deny Negroes equal access to education and employment is morally indefensible, eco-

John Mason, a native of Minneapolis, is emplymnt. coordinator, Federal Reserve Bank. A poli. sci. graduate, U. of Minn., he directs selection and placement of personnel and implements affirm. action.

Employee benefits administrator, Lynn Wilson, Bemis Co., now saves time by using a sheet of microfiche film. She gets the same information she once got from books of computer print-outs on each employee.

Marietta Jones Person is a stock inventory clerk at Midland Cooperatives. B.S. Degree in education from Eastern Ill. U., her activities include the Phi Beta Sigma Silhouette, freelance modeling, sewing, and tennis.

nomically unprofitable and politically unwise." So stated Lawrence Borom, the St. Paul Urban League Executive Director in 1966.

Today, employment in industry has made a big change. Not only can blacks be found on every level of work, but they are recruited to come to live and work in Minnesota. Yet, all is not complete, for many blacks find discrimination through subtle racism in employment from individuals they work with, nor are Affirmative Action laws always abided by. We live today in a world, in a nation, in Minnesota, to be more specific, where people of all ethnic backgrounds live and work together. The hope is that very soon all and not just some can reach a harmony and understanding that helped to found Minnesota through its pioneering spirit and progressiveness.

Lillian F. Warren is EEOC and counselor coordinator, First National Bank of Minneapolis. A weekly columnist for the *Twin Cities Courier*, she is a life member, NAACP; Brd. Member, TCOIC, Mpls. American Red Cross; Aquatennial; Women's Assoc., Minn. Orchestra; and EEO Council; and others. Appointed to many local and national councils, she is the recipient of numerous honors and awards, including Who's Who In Amer. Politics, 1973-1974; 1975-1976. Originally from St. Louis, she lives in Minneapolis.

Wesley Simmons, Controller, North Memorial Medical Center, Minneapolis, joined the staff as an accountant in 1972. A graduate of St. Thomas College, St. Paul, with a degree in economics and accounting, Mr. Simmons was formerly assistant controller at Lutheran Deaconess Hospital. A resident of South Minneapolis, Mr. Simmons is married and is the father of five children.

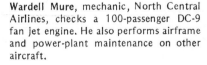

Wardell Mure, mechanic, North Central Airlines, checks a 100-passenger DC-9 fan jet engine. He also performs airframe and power-plant maintenance on other aircraft.

415

Edward Greene, in his 25th year with Thermo King, serves as a quality assurance inspector in the refrigeration Coil Department. Before becoming the inspector, Ed held several positions in the Coil Department, including assembler, tube solderer, and the precise silver solderer position. Ed takes particular pride in his work to make sure quality is built into every part made in his department. Pictured left, Ed inspects a refrigeration coil in an early stage of production.

L.B. Gray has been employed by Smith System Mfg. Co. for 24 years. He began there as a teenager and his many years with Smith make him an invaluable asset. Today he is molder-craftsman and night crew supt. L.B. is married and has three children.

Walter Groce for the past 24 years has worked at Smith System Mfg. Co. His position with the company is molder-craftsman.

PROFESSIONS

PROFESSIONS

Unlike most of the Negroes who migrated to Minnesota shortly after the Civil War with little education and few skills, a few with previous training elsewhere came and established themselves in business, as lawyers, as ministers, physicians, funeral directors and newspaper editors, but the numbers were few. Today, many of the blacks that arrive are young professionals recruited from colleges or other jobs across the country. It is also evident that other blacks (nonprofessionals) are also arriving because the black population has increased by 55 percent since 1960 in the Metropolitan Area. Even so, the black population among professionals is still low in comparison to the white counterparts working in similar positions and so are their salaries. These statements were made by State Human Rights Department Commissioner William Wilson at a "State of the

---

Cornell L. Moore is an attorney with the Minneapolis Law Firm of Robins, Davis & Lyons. He has been affiliated with the firm since July of 1974.

A native of Statesboro, Georgia, Mr. Moore received his Bachelor of Arts degree at Virginia Union University (Richmond, Virginia) in 1961. He graduated from the Howard University Law School (Washington, D.C.) in 1964.

Upon graduation from law school, he moved to San Francisco where he worked in the Trust Department of the Crocker Citizens National Bank. In 1966, he returned to Washington as a Senior Staff Attorney for the United States Treasury Department in the Office of the Comptroller of the Currency. Mr. Moore came to Minneapolis in 1966 when he assumed a position as the Regional Counsel for the National Bank Examiner's Office. In 1968, he was appointed as Assistant Vice-President and Legal Officer at Northwestern National Bank of Minneapolis. He later was elected Executive Vice-President of the Shelter Mortgage Corporation. In 1973, he became President of Leverette, Weekes & Co. Financiers, a nation-wide real estate finance company.

He is or has been a member of the Kiwanis Club, the National, Federal, Minnesota and Hennepin County Bar Associations, the Minneapolis Aquatennial Committee, the M.O.E.R. Board, the Board of the Minneapolis Chamber of Commerce, the Housing Advisory Committee for the Metropolitan Council, the Housing Sub-Committee of the Minnesota Bar Association, the Minnesota Mortgage Bankers' Association, the State of Minnesota Personnel Board and the Civil Service Board.

He and his wife, Wenda, have a daughter, Lynne.

Archie Givens, Jr. became Chief Executive Officer of Willows Convalescent Centers, Inc. and Rainbow Development Company, Inc., upon the death of his father in 1974. Willows Convalescent Center is listed in Black Enterprise Top 100 Black Business in America. Givens is also a partner in the Rainbow Development Company and manages Greenvale Place in Northfield. Further projects include Camilia Rose Nursing Home in Coon Rapids and the Fairway Woods Apartments in Winona, Minnesota, which are nearing construction. He is active in civic and charitable affairs presently serving on the board of the National Association for Mental Health. He is President, Mental Health Association of Minnesota; Board, First Plymouth National Bank of Minneapolis, Health Task Force, Minneapolis Urban League, and is a past member of the Executive Committee of the Governor's Conference on Aging and the University of Minnsota "M" Club. He is Adjunct Professor, Program in Long Term Health Care, at the University of Minnesota. Archie attended Central High School in Minneapolis and the University of Minnesota from which he earned a master's degree in Hospital Administration. He took his internship at Bethesda Hospital, St. Paul, and subsequently served as Assistant Administrator at Hennepin County General Hospital. He is married to the former Jeanne Collins and they have two daughters, April and Sunny.

Economy" workshop sponsored by the Urban League and the University of Minnesota CURA Intercultural Programs in early 1975.

By all indications of the influx of more blacks to the state, the black population should increase from 31,000 to 51,000 by 1980. But according to the economic trend in 1975, according to Commissioner Wilson, it was indicated that the job market would become very tight and already are blacks being indiscriminately fired. Something to be seriously considered.

Nevertheless, the professionals come because interesting positions are offered to them, the business institutions that recruit sound progressive enough for them to make the change or to seek their vocational aspirations here. Much of this until recently, was due to firms having to comply with Affirmative Action regulations. The other is the attitude that Minnesota is healthy, a good place to raise a family, and a good place to succeed and grow with the overall 0.9

Cassius Ellis, III, the only black surgeon in Minn., is chief of surgery, Mt. Sinai Hosp., Mpls. From Frankfort, Kentucky, his M.D. is from Meharry, his B.S., Kentucky State, and general surgery, U. of Minn. Fellow, Amer. College of Surgeons; Nat'l. Med. Assoc. Region VI vice-chairman; Board, Mpls. Children's Hosp.; Antioch College. He has a private practice in Mpls., is married to former Phyllis Hannah; they have four children.

Henry L. Smith, MD, Univ. of Rochester; B.S. Degree and Magna Cum Laude, Howard Univ.; a native of Portsmouth, Va. Now at St. Louis Park Med. Center, he is assoc. prof., U. of Minn. Medical School; consultant, internal medicine, *Modern Medicine*; board, Minn. Heart Assoc.; Amer. Rehab. Fndtn.; Upper Midwest Kidney Fndtn.; Phi Beta Kappa. Diplomate, Amer. Board, Med. Examiners. Married to Diane Jones, one child.

Rodney W. England, MD, a graduate of the U. of Illinois College of Medicine; interned at Mpls. Gen. Hosp. A U.S. Air Force flight surgeon, he started practice in St. Paul in 1962. He is a diplomate, American Board of Internal Medicine, active in the Ramsey County Med. Society, and teaches at Miller Hosp. He is member, St. Philip's Episcopal Church.

percent black population.

Many of the minorities in the St. Paul School System, for example, were recruited by Mabel Evans Cason, a very dedicated black woman in the Twin Cities. She has been very instrumental in getting some good black professionals to come and help educate our youth. Other professionals have come to Minnesota on their own because they have heard they can get a chance to see some immediate fruits of their labor.

Back in 1866, one hundred years ago, black professionals like the teacher, Moses Dixon, and the clothier, J. K. Hilyard who helped to establish the *Western Appeal* black newspaper, were already living here. Frederick McGhee arrived in the 1880's. McGhee was the first black lawyer west of Illinois and the first to be admitted to the bar and practice law in Minnesota. A civil rights advocate, he helped to lay the groundwork for the first Minnesota NAACP Branch in St. Paul. Other Negro lawyers came, but

Charlotte Lee, MD, a staff physician, Family Practice, Hennepin Cty. Med. Center, views the oscilloscope of a machine that aids diagnoses. She also works in the U. of Minn. Med. School, she attended Fisk, and Stephens College; internal medicine, Indiana U. Lives in Plymouth with husband, Richard F. Sentz, one child.

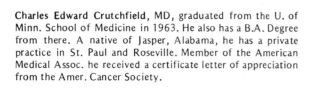

Charles Edward Crutchfield, MD, graduated from the U. of Minn. School of Medicine in 1963. He also has a B.A. Degree from there. A native of Jasper, Alabama, he has a private practice in St. Paul and Roseville. Member of the American Medical Assoc. he received a certificate letter of appreciation from the Amer. Cancer Society.

they will be mentioned in another section.

Frederick McCracken was a successful real estate and insurance man in the urban areas. Another real estate broker was T. H. Lyles. He also helped to found the *Western Appeal*. The first licensed Negro physician to practice medicine in the state was Dr. Robert S. Brown, who came in 1898. Dr. T. S. Cook was the first Negro to receive his license here and Dr. J. E. Porter was number two. Dr. Val Turner was on the staff at St. John's Hospital, while the prominent Dr. Hector J. Bell practiced dentistry. Another well-known person was Dr. J. W. Crump. Very active in public life, he was first Negro to become a member of the American Medical Association. In 1925, the Minneapolis Urban League reported that the Negro professionals in that city entailed seven attorneys, two dentists, eleven ministers, two pharmicists, and two physicians.

Many women who worked at home may also be considered "professionals." The upkeep of their

Dr. Curtis E. Davis, A.B. from Temple University, 1958, M.D. from Howard University, 1962. Residency; University of Minnesota, 1965-1969. Became a Diplomate of the American Board of Internal Medicine in 1970. Thereafter, spent the next two years in the Renal Service of the VA Hospital. Has been in private practice approximately five years. His specialty is Internal Medicine, and his sub-specialty area is Renal Disease.

Supervisory microbiologist, **Oscar Jones**, is clinical instructor, Veteran's Hosp. and in the Dept. Lab Medicine and Pathology at the U. of Minn. From Tampa, Fla., he attended Talladega College, Alabama and the University of Oklahoma. He is a member, Minn. Interlaboratory Microbiology Assoc.

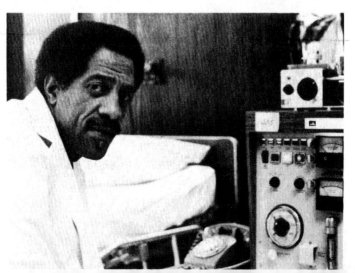

Tom X. Weaver, hemodialysis technician, Regional Kidney Disease Program, Mpls. Medical Research Foundation. He works at the Hennepin County Med. Center with acutely ill patients suffering from kidney failure who dialyze on artificial kidney machines. His responsibility is to prepare, maintain and repair the machines, and he has worked there for eight of the ten years the project has been in existence.

homes and the pride they took in doing so indicated this. They were excellent cooks, and as seamstresses, they often made all the clothes for their family. Still they found time to entertain the family with a few renditions on the piano as was the case of "Grandma Brady," the grandmother of St. Paul's Katie McWatt and mother of the late Helen Brady Curry. Mrs. Curry, incidentally, was employed by the post office and worked until she was 70.

Although many of the young Negroes from Minne-sota went to college in other states, others who were graduating from the southern Negro colleges found their way to Minnesota to build a livelihood for themselves. Some notable graduates from colleges here were John Hickman, Minnesota born, and the first Negro to earn his degree in law from the St. Paul College of Law. The first Negro graduate at the University of Minnesota in 1887 was Andrew Hilyer. Catherine Lealted was the first to graduate in 1915 from Macalester College with the highest senior class

Edward W. Posey, MD, chief of psychiatry, Veterans Hosp., attended Ohio State (B.S.); Meharry (M.D.); and U. of Minn. (residency, psychiatry). From Youngstown, Ohio, he is a Fellow, Amer. Psychiatric Assoc., member, Nat'l. Med. Assoc.; Minn. Psychiatric Society; and Diplomate, Board of Psychiatry and Neurology.

Psychiatric social worker, Jo Anna Williams-Brown, is employed by the Veteran's Admn. From Los Angeles; has a M.S. Degree, Boston U. Sch. Social Work; B.S. Degree Mt. St. Mary College (Cal.). With the V.A. since '71, she has worked in Mass., Mo., Md., and Pa. She is married to William L. Brown.

scholastic achievement. Many who came to Minnesota to attend college chose to stay. This assisted greatly in raising the educational level among the black community. The cultural level increased, more Negroes owned their homes, and the illiteracy was the lowest in the country among other Negroes as a direct result of the increase in professionals who came in the early 1900's.[38]

No longer confined to specific vocations, many blacks, as depicted throughout this book, have been able to branch into all fields of endeavour. In Minnesota today, one can find blacks such as Felton Dean, John Landry and Linda White represented in banking, public relations, government—municipal and state, private business, law firms, personnel, medicine, environmental research, and many other categories. But there was a time in Minnesota, 35 years ago to be exact, when it was very difficult for blacks who came out of the colleges with reputable degrees in their hands, found the doors to job opportunity would not

Dr. Herman Saul of Fairview Hospital

Cheryle Dawn Southern, M.D., born Nov. 12, 1944, Cincinnati, Ohio. Parents are Mr. and Mrs. Charles Southern of Cincinnati, Ohio. Graduate of U. of Cincinnati College of Arts & Sciences. B.S. Biology, 1966. Graduate: U. of Cincinnati College of Medicine, 1970. Internship, Hennepin County Medical Center 1971, Residency, U. of Michigan Hospitals, Ann Arbor, Mich. 1972-1975. Presently associate physician Pilot City Health Center and attending physician Hennepin County Medical Center.

Leo Bond, Jr., is a recreation therapist at the VA Hospital. From St. Louis, he was in the USAF for seven years, and became a Staff Sgt. He completed the U. of Minn. Drug Counselor Prog., and is married with five children.

open when they knocked. They had to look elsewhere to make a living, usually as waiters, or porters, or other jobs. But thanks to some fellow professionals already at work for equal opportunity through the black newspapers, social agencies, or who raised a loud voice to law-making bodies, much change has taken place.

Discrimination in employment is against the law, and therefore very difficult to pinpoint, particularly now that many Affirmative Action records have become confidential, but is also manifested in subtle racism, which sometimes can be more devastating. Once all of this is erased—particularly for all people to live "the good life in Minnesota," then can more minorities look forward to better jobs in the professions, especially in management levels of the larger institutions that represent millions of dollars on the national stock exchange, or all levels in the job force for that matter. Black tokenism, needless to say, is good only for the one or two black persons who hold

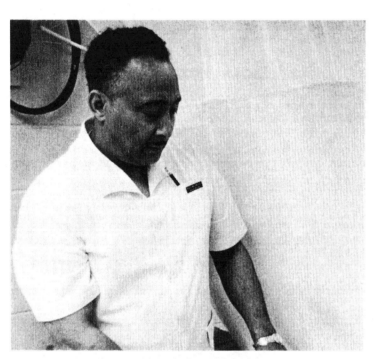

Erle Le' Williams, R.P.T., M.S., U. of Penn.; B.S.; Hampton Inst.; further grad. study, U. of Florence, Italy. He does physical therapy at two offices in Edina and lives in St. Louis Park.

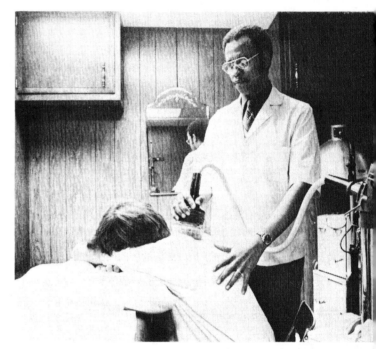

Physical therapist, Rozmond Kennon, has 17 yrs. experience in his field. A Talladega and U. of Colo. Sch. of Phys. Therapy grad, he is consultant to four nursing homes in Mpls. He is a brd. member, Southdale YMCA; and Edina Human Rights.

Dr. J. Cleveland Cradle, chiropractor; born in South Carolina, 1908; moved to Philadelphia after W.W.I. Attended Indiana Coll., Physiotherapy, a WW II volun., he was in the Army Med. Corps overseas. A Northwestern Coll., Chiropractic grad; he entered the U. of Minn. for two years. He and his wife (married in Italy, '46) remained in Minn. His practice has been in St. Paul for 20 years.

426

high-ranking positions. At least they are making a decent salary. But the fact that only one or two black faces are daily seen in the executive dining room or toilet as one who uses the service is not the answer to equal opportunity for all Americans.

But by all indications here, blacks in Minnesota's professions are well-represented. Many are dedicated servants in the medical profession and others are depicted throughout in other categories. The future of young blacks in Minnesota lies in the responsi-

bilities and commitments these members make to society.

Head nurse, **Gerry Tate** (left), special care unit, Methodist Hosp., St. Louis Park; looks over patient charts with Chaplain Alverna O'Laughlin.

Harold McClung, MD, anesthesiologist, U.S. Veteran's Hosp. He has specialty training in anesthesiology, U. of Minn. Hosp.; M.D., Meharry Med. College; Internship, Miami Valley Hosp. (Ohio); B.S. Degree, biol., Detroit Inst. Technology; B.S., pharm. Wayne State U. from Hamtramck, Mich., he is married to RN LaRue McClung; two children, they live in Mpls.

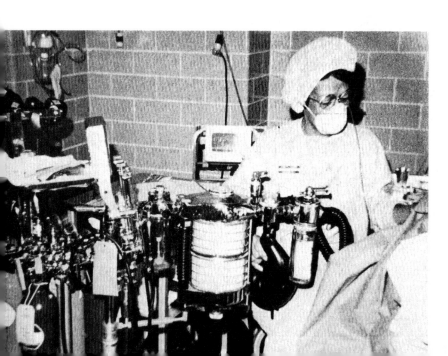

Anesthetist, **Thelma E. Oldham**, C.R.N.A., at Methodist Hospital, St. Louis Park, and clinical teacher, Hennepin Cty., Sch. of Anesthesia. From Dayton, Ohio, she became an R.N. in Kansas City, Mo. and graduate and certification in Anesthesia, U. of Minn. Hosp. Member, Amer. Assoc., Nurse Anesthetists and lives in St. Louis Park.

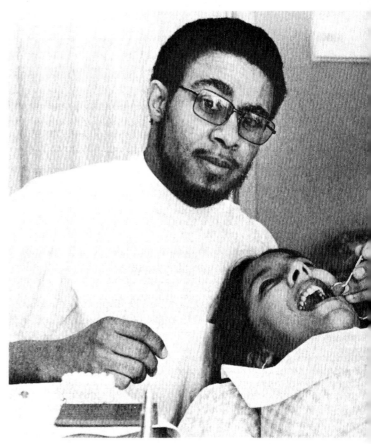

Dr. Collis Johnson, Jr. received his dental degree from Meharry and postgrad training at Martin Luther King Genr'l Hosp., Los Angeles. He is also a graduate of Langston U. and from Okmulgee, both in Oklahoma. Married to Marsha Johnson, he is a member of Alpha Phi Alpha.

Freeman L. Waynewood, D.D.S., came from Seattle to settle in St. Paul and combine a wholesome community for living and wholesome growth and economically stable livelihood with the citizens who needed his services in '74. He and wife Beverly Jean have a daughter and son.

Mrs. Mildred L. Cox, assn't. professor, nursing, College of St. Catherine. A specialist in community nursing, she chats here with St. Paul seniors Peggy Jones (left) and Jeanne Hauenstein. She is chairperson, Professional Practices Committee; member, Minn. Nurses Assoc.; Twin City Med. Profsnls. She and husband Walter A. Cox have three children.

L.A. Otieno, D.D.S., has a dental clinic in Mpls., and a sizeable dental practice in the city. Born and raised in Kenya, he is a graduate of the U. of Wisconsin, Meharry Med. College, and the U. of Minn. His dental assn't. is Alfreda Turner from Kentucky. He and wife Agnes have three sons.

Dr. Elliott L. Munalula, born in Rhodesia. Studied at the University of Oregon, Eugene. Graduated 1971 with B. Sc. attended Dental School at Meharry Medical College, School of Dentistry and graduated in 1975 with a D.D.S. degree. Currently in private practice on 2136 Lowry Av. N.

Graduate nurse, Erma Knighten, at Abbott-Northwestern Hospitals, Minneapolis, was a nursing student when this photo was taken with one of her colleagues.

Podiatrist, **Dr. Frank L. Smith**, practiced in Saskatchewan before he came to Mpls. 16 yrs. ago. From Portsmouth, Va., he is a mbr., State Brd., Podiatry Examiners; State Allied Health Credentialing Advisory Committee.

Veterinarian, **Harry E. Chiles**, D.V.M., heads the 20 year old Chiles Pet Hosp. in St. Paul the 1st black to pass the State Veterinary Brd. as a practitioner, he worked for the U.S.D.A. for 13 years before opening his small animal clinic. From Topeka, his professional training was completed at Kansas State U, School Veterinary Medicine.

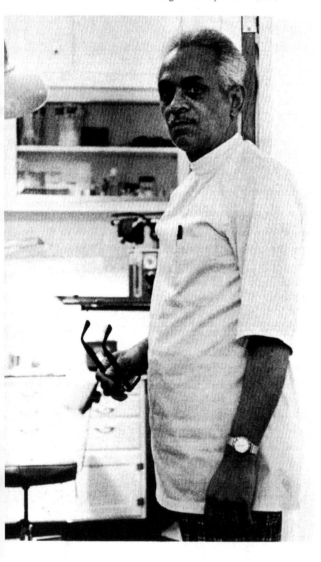

Veterinarian, **Dr. Henry Philmon**, graduate of Iowa State in 1958. Practiced in Davenport, then moved to Minn. in '69 and constructed his small animal hosp. in '72. He is program coordinator, Veterinarian Medical Technician Program, Medical Institute, Minn. A Captain in the U.S. Army Vet. Corps, he is married to Grace B.; two children.

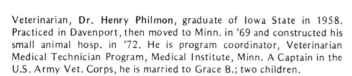

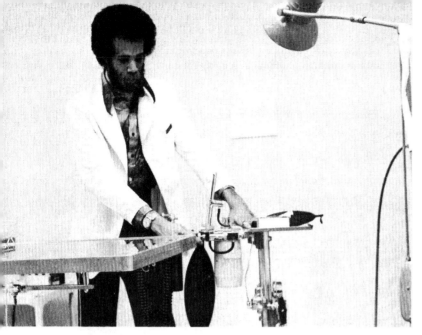

Dr. Milton P. Crenshaw, veterinarian; born Tuskegee Inst., Ala; B.S. and D.V.M. Degrees there. His practice restricted to medicine, surgery, dentistry, pet animals and caged birds; co-owner three clinics in Twin Cities. Member, Amer. Veterinary Med. Assoc.; Minn. VMA; Minn. Acad., Vet. Practitioners; Metropolitan VMA; Amer. Vet. Radiologists.

Thomas H. Johnson, M.D. Born in Crockett, Texas, husband of Henrietta Flagg Johnson and father of six children. Received B.S. from Wiley College in Marshall, Texas. Taught school in Kennard, Texas before coming to Minneapolis. Entered U of M and attended Graduate School in Zoology from 1940-42, graduated from U of M Med School and began practicing in 1954. Served in the U.S. Army 1942-1945. Served in the U.S. Public Health Service 1945-1949. Member of the Omega PSI PHI Fraternity. A 32nd Degree Mason. A member of the Shriners.

Dr. John M. Warren, is a Podiatrist, 23 years in practice. Member of Minnesota Podiatry Association, American Podiatry Association. Member of State Board of Podiatry Examiners from 1965-1970. Member of Academy of Ambulatory Foot Surgeons. Podiatry is the specializing in medical, surgical, and orthopedic problems of the feet.

W.D. Brown, Jr., M.D. Born in Mpls., Minnesota. Graduate of Howard University of Medical School 1956. Internship and Residency at Freedmen's Hospital Washington, D.C. Member Fairview Hospital Medical Staff and various civic organizations. Son of the late W.D. Brown, Sr., M.D. Grandson of the late R.S. Brown, M.D. both practicing physicians and surgeons in Minneapolis, Minnesota.

Bernese Hendon, cleric nurse, Pilot City Hlth Center, works with pregnancy, counseling and family planning. A U. of Minn. Sch. of Nursing grad, she is now enrolled in the nurse practice course.

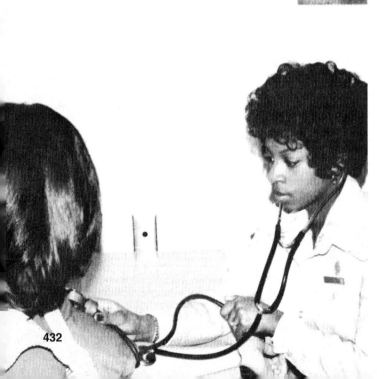

432

Shirley Fenrick Bowens, a Duluth native, B.S. Degree, Nursing, U. of Minn. and studying for a M.S. in public health nursing. Employed by the Mpls. Health Dept., she provides nursing services and counsels in child growth and development, nutrition and family planning. Studied ballet in Minn. NY, and Germany. She is married to Michael Bowens, a U. of Minn. child psychology major. Daughter of Dottie and Albert Fenrick, Mpls.

Arva Jones, R.N., is a nurse practitioner, Mpls. Pilot City Hlth. Center. Married with three children, she graduated from Gen. Hosp. School, Nursing, Kansas City, Mo. and the U. of Minn.

April Estes, RN works with a patient at the triage desk, Hennepin Cnty. Med. Center, emergency room. Triage is a system used to separate emergency from nonemergency cases and refer patients to the appropriate treatment area.

Patient advocate, Nate Williams, Hennepin Cnty. Med. Center emergency room, works directly with patients or concerned persons to assist them in any problems, or questions they may have in the emergency room.

FASHION MODELS

FASHIONS

As more and more blacks go into the fashion and modeling field, many find it difficult to be able to work at this profession full-time. Therefore, most of them are in other fields to at least be able to work free-lance.

Fashion shows are popular in Minnesota as indicated by the recent United Negro College Fund sponsored Ebony Fashion Fair in the Twin Cities. As part of their evening's entertainment, many social club dances or other functions such as the Miss Black Minnesota Pageant present the latest fashions by local models in the business.

There were times in this country, and only too recently, when it was rare to see a person of color in a commercial advertisement. But with the struggle for equal recognition among minorities—and particularly blacks—to be a part of the mainstream of social consciousness, more blacks are now seen in newspaper and magazine ads, and on television repre-

Cassandra Ellis, born in Columbus, Ohio, attended the U. of Minn., has modeled for five years. Runway, photographic and filming for T.V. commercials are to her credit. Dayton's and Donaldson's are two of her major accounts. Cassandra has done promotional work for Northwest Orient where she is an airline stewardess. She is the Vice-President of the Modeling Guild, an organization booking mainly black models in the Twin Cities.

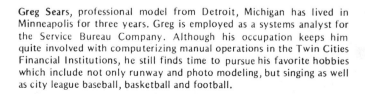

Greg Sears, professional model from Detroit, Michigan has lived in Minneapolis for three years. Greg is employed as a systems analyst for the Service Bureau Company. Although his occupation keeps him quite involved with computerizing manual operations in the Twin Cities Financial Institutions, he still finds time to pursue his favorite hobbies which include not only runway and photo modeling, but singing as well as city league baseball, basketball and football.

436

senting the use of products from major companies. At first, the trend was for advertisers to use black models in the black media for selling such products as whiskey and cosmetics and on billboards in the black community. These were obviously directed to black consumership.

But through the slow process of change, and in the belief that blacks are "fellow Americans" too, and through indications that sales have not gone down because a dark-skinned person has appeared next to or was seen holding a can of deodorant, eating cereal, or using some detergent to wash clothes, more blacks are finding work in the modeling field.

This is socially significant! As indicated by many white people who grew up in rural Minnesota towns, the first blacks seen were indirectly through television commercials or modeling clothes in a Montgomery Ward catalog! Understandable. Although the black population has increased, total black population in the state is only 0.9 percent — 95 percent of which live in the three major urban areas (Duluth, Minneapolis, St. Paul).

Inez Graves is a free lance model and works exclusively for Dayton's and the Up-2-Date Shop in LaSalle Court. Her other career is that of an AllState Insurance Agent. In photo and advertising modeling, she has made national TV ads for Pepsi Cola and Norge washing machines. A University of Minnesota graduate with a degree in business administration, she was a recent Model of the Year 1st Runnerup in Minnesota. From the Twin Cities, she has two children, Philip and Molly.

Margaret Lawrence, daughter of Elizabeth Brewin and wife of Jimmy Lawrence has lived in Minnesota for 22 yrs. Besides being a housewife and mother, Margaret has two careers as a Cabin Attendant with Northwest Airlines and as a professional model. As a model her credits are runway modeling; educational and corporate films; and modeling still photos; videotape; voice on camera; and national commercials for Arrid Extra Dry and Mardi Gras paper towels. As a Northwest Cabin Attendant of 10 yrs. her credits are: minority rep. for Affirmative Action Program; career day speaker for high schools and seminars on college campuses; personal representative for thirty cabin attendants; company model for stewardess uniforms and Northwest Airlines national advertising.
Photo above: Modeling assignment with John Gilliam corner wide receiver for the Vikings.

Black models are a small group in Minnesota, but they are distinctive, talented, and expressive. Diversified, their pictures can be found on the pages of newspapers advertising a local product; many are seen on television spots; while others get some national magazine coverage. They have contributed much to the black community. Their presence indicates to others that "We Do Exist. We Too Are Somebody."

Model and fashion designer, **Loretta Breckenridge** of Mpls., attended Ophelia DeVore Modeling School, Fashion Institute, Design and Meyers School, Design, New York. Has worked with agencies in NYC and L.A.; Eleanor Moore and Creative Casting, Twin Cities. An AFTRA member, some of her credits are Pepsi, Taryeton's, Feed-a-mends, and others.

Stacey Varnell, St. Paul Urban League Street Academy student, models some new casual wear at the 1975 NAACP Youth Council Fashion show.

Twin Cities high fashion runway and photo model, Cathy Hill, can credit many magazine and newspaper ads to her career. Namely, one is for Bemis Bag Co. in New York's *Women's Wear Daily*. From Meridian, Miss., she works with The Agency, coordinates fashion shows, and is a senior in business administration at the U. of Minn.

Alice Johnson, professional model, does free lance fashion modeling and photo modeling for Eleanor Moore Agency. From Minneapolis, she holds a B.A. Degree in English with a minor in history. She began her present career in her Junior year at Augsburg College and studied with Estelle Compton. Locally, Alice has modeled for the Mpls. Downtown Council, Buttrey's, Anthony's, Donaldson's, MTC, Midwest Federal, and Perkins, with some national work for General Electric. She holds the 1972 Minneapolis Universe title and was 3rd Runnerup for the 1972 Miss Minnesota Pageant.

Joyce Lewis, model; stewardess, Northwest Airlines; winner, four beauty contests. She came from Mississippi to attend Concordia College, St. Paul. She has begun theatrical and vocal training, and will shortly audition in N.Y. for a role in "Call Me April."

Lively professional model, Juanita Powell, St. Paul born, is a Northwest Airlines stewardess. When not traveling she involves herself with reading or tennis and skiing during the winter months.

Tiffany and Tristan Slemmons, model Kid Duds sleepwear pajamas at a recent fashion show in Minneapolis. They live in St. Paul with their parents.

Deanna Franklin, photo and runway model for Eleanor Moore, Talent Agency, Dayton's, and others. She has won several modeling awards, with many commercials, magazine and newspaper ads to her credit. A computation operator in Roseville, she is in sales-marketing at the U. of Minn.

Nicole Edelston, a television and educational commercial model, spends some leisure time listening to music or in gymnastics and dancing.

Jimmy Edelston, Jr., has made television commercials, modeled at educational conventions, and enjoys do-it-yourself building projects in his spare time.

442

Cathy Hill, local professional model, and nephew, young O.V. Lewis. He has modeled professionally for children's magazines.

Anthony "Sugar Bear" Cryer, tests out his prowess for future Minnesota Twins games as he models a Wonderalls tumble suit. Anthony lives in St. Paul with his parents.

ENTERTAINMENT

ENTERTAINMENT

Entertainment has always been an integral part of the black community. After the Civil War until a bit after World War II in most entertainment facilities across the country, blacks had to go to segregated clubs for diversion. This did not hinder but helped to create an atmosphere and phenomenon unsurpassed in any other culture. At first one or two people would get together with musical instruments or use their voices just to entertain themselves, then their friends, and finally they expanded into a group or were backed by a group to entertain audiences. They also found a new way to meet living expenses.

The music grew, and before long, its popularity was not just confined to the black community; it could be heard on steamboats up and down the Mississippi River, at afternoon picnics, funeral processions, and in "for white only" ballrooms. Soon it was in popular entertainment spots in St. Louis, Kansas City, Chicago, Detroit, and New York. Jazz took over as "King" from Blues and before long all American people were dancing to the same music, and in much

Nettie Hayes Sherman, long-time singer and dancer from St. Paul. She has performed with some of the world's top artists,—Louis Armstrong, Billie Holiday, Duke Ellington, Cole Porter, Fats Waller and Nat King Cole—at clubs like The Cotton Club in Harlem, Colony Club in Chicago, and did Connie's Hot Chocolate Revue on Broadway. Still today at 75, Ms. Sherman performs for benefit concerts in the Upper Midwest.

the same way as blacks creatively did for freedom and relaxation in their segregated clubs. In his book, *Brown Americans*, written in 1944, Edwin Embree states that jazz "... expresses so perfectly the bafflement of human beings at the feverish tempo of industrial and urban life, that jazz and the jazz age are marks not so much of the Negro as of America generally and the whole world of Western industrialism. Jazz is modern American life caricatured by the expressive new race.

The beginnings of jazz were the ragtime songs called the blues. They reflect a groping for worldly satisfactions quite contrary to the heavenly hopes of the spirituals."[39]

Embree further stated in 1944 that black "... musicians have strongly and subtly influenced modern music. Orchestra leaders and their all-Negro bands, such as Duke Ellington, Cab Calloway, Count Basie, Louis Armstrong, Jimmie Lunceford, and others are known throughout the land. Negro arrangers are used by practically every big-name band in the field of swing."[40]

He also noted that "The Negro's life has flowed full and strong. In spite of toil and torment he has

Buddy Davis, one of the busiest musicians in the Twin Cities area. At times Buddy has worked as a single, playing some of the Metro and out state areas. Buddy is a native of Chicago. Son of a piano player, he is the father of six children. His youngest son, Randy, is an aspiring pianist.

Female vocalist, Mattee Robinson, has performed in many churches, social functions and supper clubs in the Twin Cities. She lives in Mpls. and works for the Minn. Dept., Public Welfare. She has a B.A. Degree, Antioch, and is seeking a Masters.

not wasted away nor become exhausted. Always there has been abundant energy, flowing over in spirituals and field songs, in laughter and dance, in sharp furious hates and loves, even in loud rhythmic moaning in sorrow. This exuberance . . . has flowed so richly into folk art. . . .".41

Thoroughly assimilated into American life, historical jazz, blues, and black musical rhythm and dance can be seen expressed today anywhere, including Minnesota. Take dance for instance. The basic principles of Afro-American expression through movement can be seen in any two partners on a dance floor at Othello's, the Flame, or Uncle Sam's in Minneapolis. On any given night you will find persons of different ethnic groups executing now modified dance steps that originally came out of the early black dance halls of America. Also true with music. The most music heard—whether at a discotheque, jazz or rock concert at the Civic Center, or on a local radio station—it mostly stems from the basic blues and jazz ties of the haunting strains of Negroes singing as slaves, or the early instrumentals of Scott Joplin's era and the soulful sounds of the black trios that played in the New Orleans music halls a hundred years ago.

Sounds of Blackness

Aquarians and Zodiacs of St. Paul

448

Entertainment is alive in Minnesota, so expressed by the blacks devoted to the field. By far, the best music for entertainment during a "night out on the town" can be heard in places like Central Park, a new black-owned Minneapolis night club; the long-standing Nacirema Club in the black community in South Minneapolis; in the American Legion and Elks Clubs in St. Paul; and at The Establishment in the heart of downtown Minneapolis. One has really succeeded in making a great evening for himself if the entertainment found is being provided by such excellent local talent as "The Mystics," "Haze," "Philadelphia Story," "The Prophets of Peace," "Midwest Express," "Good Vibrations," "Flyte Time," "Wee Willie" Walker, Grant West, and Irv Williams. Minnesotans are really in for a treat if they can locate Kim Livingston or Mystics lead singer "Rocky" belting out a song in some small night club in the Twin Cities.

These Minnesota entertainers represent only a few of the serious and talented musicians, singers, magicians, dancers, instrumentalists, and other artists who very adequately express their trade and professional talent to the public. Entertainment by blacks in Minnesota is alive and growing.

MUTIMA Black Theatre Group Photo courtesy of Don Morstad

The late Frank Edwoods

B.T. James

Bobby Lyle

Prophets of Peace

Rocky and the Mystics

Sweet Taste of Sin

Midwest Express

Bill Jefferson

David Ruffin with Philadelphia Story

The Family

FLYTE TIME

Wee Willie Walker

THE NEW WAY

SPORTS

SPORTS

Blacks made inroads in sports around the turn of the century when the St. Paul Amateur Baseball Association was formed. The St. Paul [Colored] Gophers baseball team won the 1909 Negro World's Championship. Obviously, blacks had to play on segregated teams. An Afro-American Athletic Association was formed to be the Negro's "... own salvation," and a means for Negroes to participate in athletic events denied them. Even the State Boxing Commission in 1915 prohibited boxing matches with black and white opponents. But mixed bouts became legal in 1923 through an injunction brought against the Commission and was ruled favorably in court.

As popularly known, blacks have excelled in sports in America for many decades. Jesse Owens, who recently came to Minnesota on a speaking engagement, has already gone down in history for his

---

Former Minnesota Gopher player **Maurice (Mo) Forte**, now coaches the Gopher running backs at the University. From Hannibal, Mo., Mo joined the staff as assistant coach in 1970 after earning a Bachelor of Science Degree.

Richard Robinson is a native of Minneapolis. He played football, basketball, and track at Central High. Attended Michigan State, he graduated from Augsburg and made All-Conference in football; was captain, basketball team. Head football coach at Central High, and outstanding coach in '72. He is married with four children.

Donald W. McMoore. He was a black kid on welfare, a ward of the county for two years when his parents were hospitalized. He had some modest dreams, some worthwhile ambitions. But those did not include what happened Dec. 23, 1975 when he was named athletic director of the largest school systems in Minnesota.

458

achievements. He was the black person who caused Adolph Hitler much consternation at the 1936 Olympics in Munich. He won three gold medals before thousands of cheering and applauding Germans. Of course, this did not lend much support to Hitler's "Superior Race" theory.

All sports in Minnesota are widely received by the people of all races. So are most of the blacks who play on the professional teams, on college teams, and other amateur groups. Some of the black profes-

sionals have made their homes here and their civic-mindedness and national recognition are assets to the community.

Too often black athletic youth do not get the recognition they deserve. More recognition needs to be given to school teams such as Washburn, Minneapolis Central High, Mechanic Arts High, and the St. Paul Central High School girl's basketball team who were the 1975 State Champions. The young aspiring athletes at Phyllis Wheatley and Hallie Q. Brown

Frank Gilliam is director of player personnel for the Minnesota Vikings.

Richard Robinson, football coach of Minneapolis Central High School.

Community Centers, Oxford Playground, Sabathani, and others merit attention. This section on Sports is thereby dedicated to them. . .To the black youth of Minnesota for their athletic achievements and for continuance to play the game with good sportsmanship. Hopefully, a new Pelé will soon emerge on the Minnesota Kicks Soccer Team.

Depicted here are only a few of Minnesota's blacks that participate in sports. Blacks represent some of the best athletes on the high school and college track teams, basketball teams, and swimming and baseball teams. Although few blacks play hockey on the school level, none are found on the pro team in Minnesota.

As leisure sports, blacks play softball, they bowl, ski, play tennis, play handball, basketball and many other competitive games. One of the most exciting pastimes in the summer for the blacks who are spectators is to watch a Little League game played by the predominantly black "Little Roads" team, or a

Dexter Pride, majors in Afro-American studies and rushing for the U of M's Gopher squad. The senior running back hails from Southern Pines, North Carolina.

Keith Simons, the Gophers 1975 captain, from Belleville, Michigan is the U of M's leading candidate for post season honors. The defensive tackle has started every game since joining the team in '72.

Michael Thompson, of Nausau Bahamas, is a junior at the U. of Minn., plays center for the Gophers. Mike will graduate in '76.

Osborne Lockhart

softball game played by the Crispus Attucks team. Another interesting tournament to watch is the Minnesota Blind Sports Club at their blind bowlers tourneys.

Many blacks go boating and fishing and take advantage of Minnesota's 10,000 lakes in the summer. Others get away from urban living and spend their weekends at cabins or resorts far North and away from the busy cities.

But nothing is more exciting for all Minnesotans than to "tailgate" at Met Stadium to watch a Minnesota Vikings football game or invite friends over to watch the sport at home on television. The game is special because the well-represented blacks on the team are well-known to many in Minnesota's Black Community.

Tony Dungy, an economics major at the U. of M. Is from Jackson, Michigan. Tony, at age 20, is the captain of the '76 football team. The All-American candidate for '76 was last year's leading passes in the Big Ten.

Milfred "Bubby" Holmes, a 21 year old, senior running back from Monessen, Pennsylvania was the U. of M. leading ground gainer last year. Bubby majors in Business Administration at the U.

John Briggs

Rod Carew, from Gatum, Panama Canal Zone, lives in Golden Valley. A winner of the esteemed American League batting title five times. The Twins' second baseman will play his tenth season in '76 all with the Twins.

Dan Ford, Los Angeles, California product plays outfield well enough and bats better, to be the Twin Cities "Baseball Writer Chapters" pick as the clubs "Rookie of the Year". '75 his first of many seasons with Twins.

Larry Hisle, Ohio born and with the Twins since '72 is a ball player the Twins feel can be their All Star contribution this year. At one time lead the team in homeruns, total bases, RBI and stolen bases.

Lyman Bostock, from Birmingham, Alabama, enjoyed a fine rookie season in '75 with the Twins. Lyman goes by his baseball talent naturally, as his father was a star player in the old Negro leagues. He and father, Lyman, Sr. were recently honored by the Downtown St. Paul Council at a banquet premiere of the movie, "Bingo Long and His Traveling All-Stars and Motor Kings."

Tony Oliva, from Pinar del Rio, Cuba, enjoys his 12th season with the Twins. A player coach for the 1st time in '76, Tony is possibly the most experienced and respected exponent of the art of hitting in the game today. Living in Bloomington, Minnesota, Mr. and Mrs. Oliva have three children.

Matt Blair, linebacker; football captain at Iowa State. An effective special team member, he was born in Honolulu and now lives in Dayton, Ohio. He has a degree in education.

Steve Craig, tight end, native of Akron. Went to Northwestern and high school and college with Jim Lash. A Master's Degree, Radio-TV journalism.

Charles Goodrum, tackle; Florida A. & M. All-American from Deland, Fla. He was a sociology major.

Chuck Foreman, running back; a key rusher and receiver. From Frederick, Md. and U. of Miami graduate, attended graduate school during off-season.

464

Autry Beamon, safety. New to the team in 1975, he played college football for East Texas State.

Minnesota Vikings Nate Wright centerback; football and basketball, San Diego State. Native of Madison, Fla.; taught in a convalescent home off-season and coached an all-girls track team.

Jim Marshall, defensive end. Unit Captain and longest playing streak in the NFL. All-American, All-Big-Ten Ohio State. From Danville, Ky.; lives in Bloomington.

Alan Page, defensive tackle. All-American at Notre Dame; a political science degree. Started law school at Texas, transferred to U. of Minn. A native of Canton, Ohio, he now lives in Mpls. He was the 1975 UNCF fund raising chairman.

465

Fred McNeill, linebacker. Majored in economics at UCLA and three-year defensive end. Born in Durham, North Carolina, now lives in Baldwin Park, Calif.

Jim Lash, wide receiver. All-Big Ten at Northwestern; a history and sociology major. From Akron, he and Steve Craig played for the same high school and college football teams.

Steve Lawson, guard. A Kansas U. All-American; degree in education. From Atlanta and now lives in Cincinnati.

Carl Eller, defensive end. All-American, U. of Minn. Native of Winston-Salem; lives in Mpls. He has acted in movies, produced a pilot educ. football film; narrated with the Minn. Orchestra in February, "Happy Birthday, America."

Brent McClanahan, running back. All-Conference, Arizona State; an agri-business major. He attends the U. of Minn. off-season. From Bakersfield, Calif.

Robert Miller, running back; new to the team in 1975. Attended Kansas U. and majored in business, he is a native of Houston, Texas.

David Winfield, professional baseball player, San Diego Padres. Signed as pro baseball player after being drafted in football by the Vikings. From St. Paul, he attended the U. of Minn., majored in Poli. Sci. and member, basketball (Big Ten Champs '71-'72) and Baseball (Big Ten Champs '72-'73) teams. One of few to have never played the minor leagues and the only black person to accomplish this.

Donald E. Hudson is assoc. professor, phys. ed. and head football coach at Macalester College. He is shown here with basketball star Wilt Chamberlin.

467

GOVERNMENT AND LAW ENFORCEMENT

GOVERNMENT AND LAW ENFORCEMENT

As depicted here, blacks are represented in all echelons of government in Minnesota, from the state level to the municipalities in rural towns. Many of these positions have been held since the 1800's by blacks. John Francis Wheaton, for example, was the first black elected to the Minnesota Legislature back in 1898. He won his legislative seat as a Republican in a district with less than 100 Negroes, and in a year when the Republicans lost the governorship. Two years after graduating from the U. of Minnesota Law School in 1894, Wheaton was a member of the

Minnesota Delegation to the Republican National Convention.

Another black person of note in government during this time was "Billy" Williams. Williams was appointed executive office aide in 1905 and served in that position under 14 governors until 1957 when he retired.

But blacks had already played a role in Minnesota's governmental process. During statehood preliminaries in the 1850's the constitutional convention was markedly split over whether the territory should come into the Union as a free or a slave state, and if

Assn't attorney general, James Bradford, sectry., Brd. of Pardons. St. Paul College of Law, '50; Minn. Bar, '51. Atty genrl. staff in '55, and he is first pres.; Maplewood Human Relations; pres., Retreat House; Neighborhood Justice; NAACP; in the Masons and Shrine.

Judge William S. Posten, trial lwyr., ten yrs.; Hennepin Cty's 17th Municipal Judge. Posten was sworn in as district court judge by Supreme Court Justice George M. Scott, for whom Judge Posten worked when Scott was a Hennepin County attorney. Judge Posten, a municipal court judge when appointed to the district court took the place vacated by former Judge Andrew W. Danielson. He is a Brd. mbr., Turning Point; Genesis II; NAACP; Salavation Army. Past brd., Community Health and Welfare; March of Dimes. Member, American Bar Association.

Negroes should have the right to vote. As Minnesota's history goes, it became a free state in 1858 and Negroes gained suffrage in 1868.

Since this time many blacks have run for state and local public office, but few have succeeded. Some of those who enrolled to run are still responsive citizens in the community. They are Harry Davis, Deputy Chief James Griffin, Kathleen McWatt, Bobby Hickman, Chris Durand, and others.

Probably the most well-known black Minnesotan, locally and nationally in the 1920's, and involved in government was the lawyer, W.T. Francis.

From Indiana and educated in Minnesota, Francis was St. Paul's leading black lawyer after World War I. He was appointed to many state and local positions, and was on the St. Paul Urban League Board when it was founded in 1923. Francis was named United States Minister to Liberia in 1927. He died there two years later of yellow fever.[42]

The early black newspapers were instrumental in making some strides in law enforcement and other municipal positions. As the migrations of Negroes increased, more were needed on the police force. One each were found in Minneapolis and St. Paul, but the

Judge Stephen Maxwell, Juris Dtr., '53; Morehouse, '42. Minn. Dist. Crt. Judge since '68. Municipal Crt., St. Paul, '67-68; Repub. Congr. candidate, '66. Brd, Amer. Red Cross; Boy Scouts; St. Paul Winter Carnival; Amer. Arbitr. Nat. Bar Ass.; Midwstrn Sch., Law; St. Philip's Episcopal Church.

B. Robert Lewis, State Senator, 41st Dist., St. Louis Park. He is Dem. chairman, subcomm., Adult Corrections; Health and Welfare Corrections; Committee; Education Committee; and Metropolitan and Urban Affairs Committee.

State Repres., **Ray Pleasant**, Bloomington; Bloomington City Council, three yrs. before election to the State House in '72. The only black Representative, he is on the House City Gov't. Committee; Genrl. Legislation and Vet. Affairs Committee; and as governmental operations sector coordinator, he guides policy devlpmnt. from a Republican point of view.

papers called for more representation. Actually, this took some years to become a reality. One of the first black policemen was George Brady, the great grandfather of Katie McWatt who just a few years ago herself, was active in politics and ran for City Council.

Within the last year, 11 firemen and 10 police recruits in 1975 were added in St. Paul through the diligent efforts of some black leaders. Among the group is Debbie Montgomery, an active community worker and the only black woman to pass the exams. She also made the highest score.

Perhaps one of the most widely effective projects that assisted Negroes in the 1940's in Minnesota was Governor Edward J. Thye's appointment of an interracial commission to study Negro problems. The author, H. Spangler mentions in *The Negro in Minnesota*, "This was set up because of a concern for the future of race relations, and as a result of the recent disastrous race riots in Detroit. Talmadge B. Carey, Major Sam Ransom, and S. Vincent Owens were among the original Negro appointees. The work done by this council, and by the Governor's Inter-

---

Richard Rolle is Deputy Commissioner, State Department of Human Rights. Formerly a financial officer with the State Crime Commission, has a B.A. Degree in Business Administration from Florida Atlantic University, Boca Raton, and is a Masters candidate in Urban Studies at Mankato State Univ. He and his wife have one child and live in St. Paul.

Richard Session, Commissioner, Personnel, State of Minnesota; formerly with Minn. Public Service Commission; Mpls. born; Central High grad; holds a U. of Minn. certificate, indus. relations; B.A. public admn., Metro State. First regional postal EEO counselor, '69; appointed by Gov. Wendell Anderson, Dir., State EEO, '71. Exec. sectry., State Commerce Commission, '73. NAACP Mpls. exec. board; Amer. Soc., Public Administration board.

William L. Wilson, State Human Rights Commissioner; M.Ed. Degree, U. of Mass., and doctoral candidate. B.S. Knoxville College. From Evansville, Ind., and active in sports. Former coordinator, Intercultural progs. CURA, U. of Minn., he implemented the continuing educ. prog. and other progs. in Univ. Ethnic Studies Depts. Convener, St. Paul Citizen's Participation; founder and exec. dir., St. Paul Inner City Youth League; coordinated youth progs. in Mpls. His wife, Willie Mae, is exec. dir., St. Paul Urban League. They have two children.

racial Commission, as it was later called, remains one of the outstanding contributions to improved race relations in Minnesota or any other state."[43]

The Governor's Interracial Commission continued under the new Governor Luther W. Youngdahl who stated in his Forward to an updated report on *The Negro Workers Progress in Minnesota*, "In the world of today, it becomes more and more apparent that there will be a tomorrow for civilization only if men learn and learn quickly to live together in peace and unity."[44]

This Commission was the forerunner of today's State Department of Human Rights, headed by the young black, Commissioner William L. Wilson, who appears in this section. Wilson heads a staff of over 40 people dedicated to investigating and ruling on all discrimination complaints submitted by anyone throughout the state who feel that their equal rights have in some way been violated.

Other blacks represented in government and law enforcement are shown here. Their influence and responsibilities positively reflect the black community throughout the state and nation as well.

R. Nathaniel Scott is Assistant Commissioner, Administration State of Minnesota.

Robert P. Elcan is Assistant Commissioner, Civil Service, State of Minnesota.

Ronald O'Neal is Assistant Commissioner, Employment Services, State of Minnesota.

Fire Captain, **LeRoy Coleman**, St. Paulite; attended West Va. State, two yrs.; graduate, Dunwoody Inst., 1949; joined the St. Paul Fire Dept. in 1943. Fire Engineer, '49; Fire Capt., '52; was cited in Ebony Magazine.

Andrew W. Haines III, assn't. prof. of law at William Mitchell College of Law. Born in New Orleans he has a B.A. Degree from the Univ. of Minn. and Juris Doctorate, Univ. of Michigan. Haines has a business directorate with M.E.D.A. As a volunteer, he is on the Mpls. Commission of Human Relations, Ramsey County Legal Assistance Board, Twin Cities Fed. Exec. Brd., Minority Business Development Committee, and was a member, State Brd., Human Rights to '75. Haines and wife, Judith Ann, have two children, and live in Minneapolis.

Gene A. Shokency with former Governor Rolvaag and Commissioner Marshall. Shokency was the first Negro to receive an appointment to the Highway Patrol.

Howard L. Johnson, health care administrator, Minn. State Dept., Corrections. Consults, plans and implements departmental health care programs.

Cook County Sheriff, **John R. Lyght**; 1st black elected sheriff in Minn. by 93% of the vote in '74. Rec'vd. a letter of recog. from Pres. Nixon, when appointed in '72. He has lived in Lutsen Township all his life. A veteran, he was in the Air Force. Mbr., ARDC Criminal Justice Committee and Human Resources Coord. Committee; Natl. Police and Fire Fghtrs. Assoc.; Natl. Police, Peace Officers Assoc. Married to Anne M., they have three children.

John D. Hartsfield is a Detective in the Criminal Division for the Hennepin County Sheriff's Department, Minneapolis.

Reginald Commodore is a General Deputy Sheriff working as a Bailiff in the Service Division for the Hennepin County Sheriff's Department, Minneapolis.

William Wade is a Senior Deputy Sheriff in charge of the District Court Bailiffs in the Service Division for the Hennepin County Sheriff's Department, Minneapolis.

475

Otto Burroughs, Ramsey County Sheriff Dept.

James Corr, Ramsey County Sheriff Dept.

Arthur Blakey, Ramsey County Sheriff Dept.

Delroy Hawkins, Ramsey County Sheriff Dept.

Frank Brown, Ramsey County Sheriff Dept.

Harry M. Ballard, Jr., Ramsey County Sheriff Dept.

Purcell Jackson, Deputy Sheriff of Hennepin County.

Eugene Robinson, Deputy Sheriff of Hennepin County.

Reuben Arrington, Deputy Clerk, Hennepin Cty. Municipal Court, 28 yrs., he is one of two blacks there. Very active, he directs Bethesda Baptist Church Senior Choir; pub. relns., Minn. Gospel Music Wrkshp. Enrolled in U. of Minn. Exten. Div.

James Griffin, St. Paul, Deputy Chief, Police. A St. Paulite and Central High outstng. athlete; attended school in West Va., U. of Minn.; graduated Metro State U. First black promoted to Sgt., '55; Capt., '70; and Deputy Chief, '72. St. Paul Sch. Brd; married, three daughters, one deceased.

WENDELL R. ANDERSON
GOVERNOR

STATE OF MINNESOTA
OFFICE OF THE GOVERNOR
ST. PAUL 55155

Mr. Walter R. Scott
Mr. Anthony R. Scott

The publication of your new volume, "Minnesota's Black Community", is particularly timely during this year of our Bicentennial when we are attempting to give greater recognition to America's diverse heritage as a nation.

It should help to focus public awareness on the highly significant role that Black people have played throughout our growth and development as a state and nation.

From such greater understanding can come new respect for human dignity and much needed encouragement for all of our citizens to work more harmoniously together to achieve our mutual goals and aspirations.

With my warmest personal regards,

Sincerely,

Wendell R. Anderson

Wendell R. Anderson

WRA:jah

478

MAYOR CHARLES STENVIG

April 30, 1976

Mr. Walter R. Scott, Sr., Publisher
"Minnesota's Black Community"
5801 Duluth Street
Suite 216
Minneapolis, Minnesota 55422

Dear Mr. Scott:

Please accept my congratulations on behalf of the citizens of Minneapolis on your forthcoming publication of "Minnesota's Black Community."

Endeavors such as your will help give residents of our City and State a fuller appreciation of achievements of members of the Black community, and an understanding of new opportunities that are being developed. Such efforts are to be commended.

Sincerely,

Charles Stenvig
Charles Stenvig
M A Y O R

LAWRENCE D. COHEN
MAYOR

May 20, 1976

Mr. Walter R. Scott
Mr. Anthony R. Scott

        I am very happy to know that a
pictorial book is being published on Minnesota's
Black Community and that it depicts the heritage
and progress of black people in the state, the
urban areas, and specifically in Saint Paul,
where historically they first concentrated.

        I am sure the publication will give
everyone greater insight on the black community,
the progress individuals have made, and the role
blacks play in our striving to achieve a better
life for all Minnesotans. I hope everyone will
read it.

                                Sincerely,

                                LAWRENCE D. COHEN
                                Mayor

LDC/lm

CITY OF SAINT PAUL

OFFICE OF THE MAYOR

GEORGE LATIMER
MAYOR

October 14, 1976

Mr. Walter R. Scott, Sr.
Mr. Anthony R. Scott
Litho Technical Services
1600 West 92nd Street
Minneapolis, Minnesota   55431

Dear Messrs. Scott:

Please allow me to take this opportunity to commend you on the publication of Lee Lambert's new book, <u>Minnesota's Black Community</u>.

Chronicles of the heritage, progress and achievements of blacks in Minnesota are beneficial in that they serve to heighten public awareness and appreciation of the role of blacks in our state's history. Saint Paul was the site of early black settlement in Minnesota and the accomplishments of the black community since those early years are especially noteworthy and sources of pride to our citizens.

On behalf of the people of Saint Paul, I congratulate you on the forthcoming volume which will illuminate for us all the history of a significant segment of Minnesota's marvelously diverse, yet harmonious, population.

Sincerely,

GEORGE LATIMER
Mayor

GL/lm

STAFF of MINNESOTA'S
BLACK COMMUNITY

Walter R. Scott, Sr., Publisher

Anthony R. Scott, Co-Publisher

Ashby D. Reed, Jr., Graphics Coordinating Director

LeClair Lambert, Executive Editor and Writer

Chaunda L. Scott, Marketing Director

Ronnie Lloyd, Photographer

Charles Chamblis, Photographer

Jim Lindguist, Photographer

Lisa Davison, Assistant Marketing Director

Leo E. Browne, Public Relations Director

PRODUCTION DIRECTOR . . . . Alvin W. Riley, Sr.
PRINTING . . . . .Litho Technical Services
BINDING . . . . .Litho Technical Services
MARKETING DIRECTOR . . . . .Chaunda L. Scott

MINNESOTA'S BLACK COMMUNITY
Published by W. R. Scott Publishing Co., Inc.
Minneapolis, Minnesota

NOTES

Ed. note: The following information gives acknowledgement to specific quoted materials.

1. George W. Williams, *A History of the Negro Race in America* (New York: G. P. Putnam's Sons, 1883), II, p. 300.

2. Earl Spangler, *The Negro in Minnesota* (Minneapolis: T. S. Denison & Co., 1961), p. 46.

3. Edwin R. Embree, *American Negroes: A Handbook* (New York: John Day Co., 1942) pp. 62-63.

4. Spangler, *The Negro in Minnesota*, p. 13.

5. Embree, *Brown Americans: The Story of a Tenth of the Nation* (New York: The Viking Press, 1944), p. 132.

6. Dr. Herrington Bryce, *Economic Progress of Blacks After 200 Years*, Black Perspectives on the Bicentennial, 2nd Series (New York: National Urban League, Inc., 1976), p. 18.

7. Ibid.

8. Lawrence Fortenberry, "Freedom's Journal: The First Black Medium," *The Black Scholar*, Vol. 6, No. 3 (November, 1974), p. 34.

9. Robert E. Staples, *"The Lower Income Negro Family in St. Paul*, St. Paul Urban League Report (St. Paul: The St. Paul Urban League, 1967), p. 12.

*   James D. Williams, *The Black Press and the First Amendment*, Black Perspectives on the Bicentennial, 3rd Series (New York: National Urban League, Inc., 1976), p. 21.

10. Spangler, p. 77.

11. Eleanor Holmes Norton, (Closing Speech, 65th Annual Conference, National Urban League, Atlanta, Georgia, July 30, 1975.)

12. *St. Paul Daily Pioneer*, August 9, 1865, "Minnesota Annals" (Minnesota Historical Society-Manuscripts Division), Newspaper Extracts.

13. *St. Paul Daily Pioneer*, April 13, 1869, from "Minnesota Annals."

14. *The Negro and His Home in Minnesota*, The Governor's Interracial Commission, 3rd Report (St. Paul: June, 1947), pp. 9-10.

15. Embree, *Brown Americans*, pp. 10-11.

16. Spangler, p. 147.

** LeClair G. Lambert, "A Brief History of the St. Paul Urban League," for the Urban League 1975 Board-Staff Institute.

17. Whitney M. Young, Jr., *To Be Equal* (New York: McGraw-Hill (Paperback Edition, 1966), p. 167.

18. Ibid., p. 54. (The first paragraph of the quote is taken from a statement made by the late President John F. Kennedy, duly noted by author Young.)

19. *51st Annual Report (1974)*, St. Paul Urban League (St. Paul: 1975), p. 4; St. Paul Urban League Historical Records.

20. Young, op. cit., p. 253.

21. *The Negro Worker's Progress in Minnesota*, The Governor's Interracial Commission, 5th Report (St. Paul: June, 1949), pp. 39-40.

22. *St. Paul Daily Press*, May 15, 1863; May 16, 1863, from "Minnesota Annals."

23. *Minneapolis Spokesman*, May 27, 1949; Spangler, p. 52.

24. Edward D. Neill, *History of Ramsey County and the City of St. Paul* (Minneapolis: North Star Publishing, 1881), pp. 388-389; Spangler, p. 54.

25. *The Negro Worker in Minnesota*, The Governor's Interracial Commission, 1st Report (St. Paul: March, 1945), p. 6.

26. *Minneapolis Spokesman*, May 27, 1949; Spangler, pp. 60, 68.

27. Dr. L. D. Reddick, *Blacks and U. S. Wars*, Black Perspectives on the Bicentennial, 4th Series (New York: National Urban League, Inc., 1976), pp. 5, 10.

28. *Western Appeal*, June 30, 1917.

29. St. Paul Urban League Historical Records; Spangler, p. 90; *Twin Cities Courier*, July 15, 1976.

30. Reddick, op. cit., p. 18.

31. *The Negro Worker in Minnesota*, p. 16.

32. John LaFarge, *The Race Question and the Negro* (New York: Longmans, Green and Co., 1943), pp. 139-140.

33. Embree, *Brown Americans*, p. 118; Reddick, p. 19.

34. Spangler, p. 124.

35. Ibid., p. 125; *Minneapolis Star*, October 17, 1945; Cecil Newman, "An Experiment in Industrial Democracy," *Opportunity*, XXII (April, 1944), pp. 52-55.

36. *The Negro Worker in Minnesota*, Forward.

37. Ibid., pp. 16-17.

38. Spangler, pp. 78, 94; *Western Appeal*, August 24, 1901.

39. Embree, *Brown Americans*, pp. 192-193.

40. Ibid., pp. 193-194.

41. Ibid.

42. Saint Paul Urban League Historical Records; Spangler, p. 70.

43. Spangler, p. 126.

44. *The Negro Worker's Progress in Minnesota*, Forward.

SUMMARY

The editors and publishers of this book wish to thank the countless numbers of people, firms, municipal and state facilities, and associates who helped to make this vast undertaking possible. We specially wish to thank the Minnesota Historical Society for use of photographs and written materials, Earl Spangler and his staff who compiled *The Negro In Minnesota*, thus providing very useful information, and the St. Paul Urban League for use of its historical records.

We hope you find this book to be a lasting memento of Black Minnesota's hopes and struggles of the past and strengths and hopes of the present and future. The Walter Scott Publishing Company is in the process of extending this worthwhile effort through future publications to Iowa, Wisconsin, Kansas and Missouri.

Time is a relative thing! To most of us, two hundred years is a long time — greater than man's average life span — but to the historians, a Bicentennial is about a split second since the dawn of mankind. To give in detail the growth and development of Minnesota's Black community into a part of a thriving modern state within two hundred years or even fifty years, is not the purpose of this book. Rather, here is a unique segment of this populated state of nearly three million people in a pictorial resume of what is today and regretfully, not what was yesterday . . . . here are highlights of significance . . . . here is a bird's eye view at some of the Black people in Minnesota today and some of the reasons for Minnesota's greatness.

This then . . . . is Minnesota's black community where the river and natural resources provide power and industry for the initial step of progress . . . . where pioneer spirit, enterprising leadership, financial resources and education have gotten in step with progress and in turn, stepped up the tempo of progress . . . . where intense interest in religion has matured the spiritual side of man and where modern scientific developments in medicine safeguard his physical side . . . . where natural beauty has been preserved and dedicated to health and recreation . . . . where Black awareness, artistic, and cultural achievement come naturally as a result of this perfect formula for a great state — Minnesota.

Index